DAVID**GINOLA**

le magnifique

DAVID**GINOLA**

le magnifique

the autobiography

DAVID GINOLA
with NEIL SILVER

Collins Willow

An Imprint of HarperCollins*Publishers*

First published in 2000 by
CollinsWillow
an imprint of HarperCollins*Publishers*
London

© David Ginola 2000

1 3 5 7 9 8 6 4 2

A CIP catalogue record for this book is
available from the British Library

ISBN 0 00 710099 X

Typeset by Rowland Phototypesetting Ltd,
Bury St Edmunds, Suffolk

Printed and bound in Great Britain by
Clays Ltd, St Ives plc

The HarperCollins website address is
www.**fire**and**water**.com

Photographic acknowledgements

All photographs supplied by the author with the exception of the following:
Action Images (p 15 top), (p 22 top, bottom); **Agence Angeli** (p 5 top right, bottom),
(p 6 top, bottom left & bottom right, p7 © Dominique Jacobivès), (p 8 bottom © Daniel
Angeli, Frédéric Garcia & Bertrand Rindoff Petroff), (p 9 by Max Colin), (p 10 bottom
right), (p12 © Dave Bennett), (p 14 top, p 15 centre right, p 16 © Patrick Siccoli),
(p 17 top, bottom, p 18, p 19 top, bottom, p 20 top, centre, bottom left © Frédéric
Garcia); **Allsport** (p 13 bottom © Vandystadt / Allsport), (p 23 bottom), (p 24 bottom
© David Rogers); **Chaumet** (p 10 top); **Empics** (p 15 bottom © Tony Marshall),
(p 22 middle © Michael Steele); **Christian Gavelle** (p 3 top, p 3 centre right); **PA Photos**
(p 2 bottom), (p 8 left by Michael Crabtree) (p 23 top), (p 24 top © Phil Noble),
(p 24 middle © Tom Hevezi); **Pictor** (p 24 bottom); **Press-Sports** (p 2 top); **Reuters**
(p 11 top right by Eric Gaillard); **Studio F.E.P.** (p 13 top by Jean Bibard).

This book is dedicated to all the fans who have supported me all through the years — through good times and bad. You are all part of my success.

CONTENTS

ACKNOWLEDGEMENTS

I would like to thank my friend and adviser Chantal Stanley for her encouragement throughout the writing of this book. Of course, none of this would have been possible without the love and support of my parents Rene and Mireille, and grand-parents Desire and Julliette, through both the good times and bad. My wife Coraline, and children Andrea and Carla, have always been there when I've needed them, and this book is a tribute to their patience and understanding.

Finally, thanks to my publishers, HarperCollins and to the man who helped me put my thoughts down on paper, Neil Silver. It has been a privilege working with such professionals.

CHAPTER ONE

Heroes and Villans

'He [George Graham] is the reason I am
not at Spurs today. He pushed me out'

I never wanted to leave Tottenham. I always thought White
Hart Lane would be the place where I ended my playing career,
and I am upset that I could not see out the full five years of my
contract with the club, taking me up to the end of the 2001/02
season.

But I was pushed out of White Hart Lane, forced to leave by
manager George Graham.

Having said that, I am lucky to have found a club in Aston
Villa who truly wanted me, and a manager and chairman in
John Gregory and Doug Ellis who have made me feel wanted
and appreciated. I know I shall be happy spending the rest of
my footballing days at Villa Park.

The story of my departure from Tottenham Hotspur and
subsequent arrival at Aston Villa began in May 2000, and once

again I was to find that my summer holidays – the time when I so look forward to switching off from football and getting away with my family – were to be spoiled by the worries and upheaval of another transfer saga.

I returned from my Red Cross trip to Cambodia and within a couple of days I was heading off to Mauritius with Coraline, Andrea and Carla. My agent Chantal Stanley had arranged a dream holiday for us at the stunning Beau Rivage resort, which is one of those idyllic destinations you fantasize about in travel magazines. Everything was perfect, from our luxury suite, to the food, the people and the surroundings. Then, one day, I happened to be chatting to the manager of the hotel, Phillippe Requin.

'Monsieur Ginola, I have a request for you from a guest at a neighbouring hotel. Doug Ellis, the chairman of Aston Villa, would like to meet you and so he has invited you to join him and his wife for dinner.'

I did not read anything into this invitation from the chairman of Aston Villa. Everyone in Mauritius had heard of my arrival on the island – people were waving at me in the street – and as far as I was concerned, we were just two people from the world of football who were enjoying a holiday in the same exotic location, and I thought he was just being sociable. Football is hugely popular in Mauritius, especially the English Premier League, because our games and all the goals are screened there every week. I had met Doug Ellis once before, at Langans Brasserie in London. I was having dinner there with Chantal who was meeting with representatives from L'Oreal and finalising my contract with them. Doug Ellis, who was sitting at another table with his wife, came over to us in the restaurant and introduced himself, telling me he was a big admirer of mine, which was very flattering. I finished my meal first that night, so before leaving Langans I went to say good-bye to him and his wife and told him to enjoy the rest of the night.

Anyway, I was very relaxed in my peaceful surroundings at the Beau Rivage and did not want to leave there, so I asked Mr Requin to invite Mr and Mrs Ellis to have dinner with me there instead – an invitation which they accepted. We had a very pleasant meal together on the terrace of my suite and talked about many things. Doug Ellis is a very interesting figure who sits on FA and FIFA committees, so it was nice for me to talk to him about issues in the game, such as the need for footballers in England to have a winter break. Then, towards the end of the meal, he put an intriguing thought in my head.

He said: 'I am playing tennis next week with Alan Sugar. I would love to have you at Aston Villa and I shall ask him if I can buy you.'

I paused momentarily.

'Mr Ellis, first of all I am on holiday with my wife and my children and it is important for me to spend time with them. I have had so many bad holidays in the past because I have been forced to think about my future, so I would rather not talk about this now.'

I never imagined for one second that Alan Sugar would allow me to leave White Hart Lane. The last time I had spoken to my chairman was the previous winter, when he told me not to think about leaving Spurs, because I had two more years on my contract.

A few weeks later I was playing golf in the Algarve with some friends and when I spoke to Chantal she told me that there were a few stories in the newspapers in England linking me with Aston Villa, and that something was going on. It was serious, because Sugar and Ellis had agreed a £3 million fee for me, and Tottenham had given Villa permission to talk to me and try to negotiate personal terms.

All of a sudden everything was changing. I knew it couldn't be Alan Sugar who wanted to sell me – it must be George Graham. Alan Sugar was the chairman of Tottenham and he was carrying out the demands of his manager, who wanted to get rid of me as soon as possible, preferably before the start of the season. I know that when all the negotiations were going on, Graham came out publicly and said that he did not want me to leave the club. But that was nonsense. He was the manager of Tottenham and he decided which players he wanted to keep and which ones he wanted to discard. It was simple: if he really did not want me to leave, then all he had to do was tell the chairman to reject Villa's approach for me.

But he never did. I wasn't surprised that George Graham wanted me out. Ever since he arrived at White Hart Lane I was under pressure to play out of my skin for him to put me in his team. But even with me playing well, he substituted me in 36 of the 79 matches I started for him. I could never understand why he did that, especially in the games when we were playing at home, in front of our own fans, and which we were winning well, yet he was taking me off with five or ten minutes to go. When you have a key player who is entertaining the crowd, then surely he deserves to stay on for the last few minutes of the game and demonstrate his full repertoire of skills – what more could you ask for than a good result and entertaining football at the same time?

I know I will never get the answer to this question, although I also know that maybe I was too much for him to cope with in terms of my personality, image and popularity with the fans. I don't want to accuse George Graham of jealousy because I cannot see the purpose of him being jealous. When you are a person of a certain age, with a certain intelligence, like he is, then why, if you are the manager, would you be jealous of someone who is playing well and who is loved by the fans? Surely that adulation is a positive reflection of you as manager? So I think Graham was naïve, because he should have used me for his own image, claiming that as manager he got the best out of David Ginola. Then the crowd would think: 'Well done George Graham!' But whenever journalists spoke to him after a game and said: 'Didn't Ginola play well today!' he would always say yes, *but* he didn't do this or he didn't do that. He would always look for the negative things to say about me, trying to put me under pressure.

I tried my hardest to be the best player on the pitch and to play well, to satisfy the manager and the crowd, but Graham would always give me hassle. I knew he wasn't a big fan of mine, and he wanted to be the tough guy, but he should have respected what I could do. He would always try to put me down in front of the other players, especially at team meetings. He would single me out and criticise something in my game, so that I lost the respect of my team-mates. Even if I had been the best player on the pitch, he would point to me in the team meeting and say: 'I expect more from you, it was not good enough.' Yet he never did that to anyone else, he only picked on me. Because I respected the team, I didn't want to take a confrontational stance with the manager – but I didn't deserve such treatment.

My move to Aston Villa took time to finalize, as Chantal skilfully continued negotiations with Doug Ellis, securing the right contract for me. I didn't want to leave Tottenham, but if I was going to be pushed out I wanted to go on my terms, not theirs. I was not going to let them dictate to me what I should do, especially for what might be the last contract of my career.

Tottenham Hotspur Football Club was my entire life and what George Graham was doing to me was tearing me apart inside. However, whereas a weaker person may have cracked under the strain, I found strength, thanks to the support of my agent Chantal, with whom I was in contact daily to discuss everything that was going on. It just goes to show how important it is for footballers to surround themselves with the right people.

After the summer break, I reported back to Tottenham for pre-season training. The atmosphere was okay though, because I don't think Graham wanted to risk upsetting me in case I spoke to the newspapers and criticised him in public. Many Spurs fans will never accept Graham, because they will always see him as a former manager of Arsenal, their arch rivals, and that is the worst thing that could happen to their club. So he didn't need negative publicity, especially concerning the player who the fans liked the most. Instead, he hardly spoke to me. On the one hand, he never called me in and said he wanted me out of the club; but on the other, at no point did he tell me that he wanted me to stay at Spurs. I would have preferred him to be man enough to call me into his office and tell me that he wanted me out, that he wasn't planning to play me. I am 33 years old and an experienced player, so we could have spoken openly and honestly and found an amicable solution.

George Graham wanted to get rid of me but he had to be careful not to upset the fans, so he tried to put all the pressure on Alan Sugar by saying in the press that he didn't want me to leave, but that the chairman had accepted a good offer for me from Villa. Yet the bottom line is that Graham had the responsibility for choosing who played in his team, not Alan Sugar.

As I hadn't yet resolved my future, I think Graham felt

obliged to take me on the club's pre-season tour to Scandinavia. He even started me in all three friendlies – presumably to show the fans that George Graham was a nice man because he was playing David Ginola! But he took me off after 45 minutes in every match. It was hard to motivate myself to play good football when the manager was playing games with me, but I kept smiling. It was during this tour that we saw a different side to George Graham – one that I, and I think the rest of the players, didn't like. His attitude was that football gives so much to the players, and the wages are so fantastic, that the club wanted to get its money's worth. When we arrived in Sweden, the hotel we were based at wasn't very comfortable. For a start, the rooms were a bit shabby and the beds were very small, so the taller ones like me had our feet sticking out the end. Some of the players complained and so Graham called a meeting.

'Your five-star luxury has finished,' said Graham bluntly. 'It's good for bonding to be in less fancy accommodation.'

I believe he was wrong. Just because you are in a poor hotel, it won't make you work harder, or bond more as players. In fact, it works the other way because if you know you have a nice hotel to go back to after a hard day's training, then you are grateful to the club and the management for looking after you, and it has a more positive effect.

Shortly after we returned from Sweden, David Pleat called me into his office on the pretence of wanting a chat because he had not spoken to me for a while. It turned out he was really just trying to find out what offers I had received from other clubs.

'Nothing is happening at the moment,' I said. 'I am still a Spurs player and if I have to remain a Spurs player then that will be fantastic for me, because that is what I want.'

A short time later, the chairman telephoned me.

'What's going on?' Sugar asked.

'It is simple,' I told him. 'If I do not get a suitable offer, then I will be staying at Tottenham – and I shall be very happy to do so.'

'But George Graham will not play you, and you'll sit on the bench.'

'That is my decision.'

'Yes, but he will make you play at St Albans every week in the reserves, and make you train with the reserves.'

I was very sure of myself here and I said: 'Do you really think George Graham would be able to play me in the reserves?'

At this point Sugar backtracked a bit and just stumbled: 'Er…well, well…I am sorry David, I know what you mean. It is not my choice. It is George's and I cannot interfere with the running of the team.'

I knew that Graham wouldn't play me in the reserves, as it would have shown the fans that he wanted to get rid of me, and he didn't want to admit this and incur their wrath. I got the impression he wanted me out during the previous season but felt it would be easier to stage-manage my departure if he waited until the closed season.

Everything came to a head on Saturday 29 July when we went to play a friendly at Birmingham City. Graham knew my agent was talking to Aston Villa and so the day before we left for the Midlands he called me into his office.

'Would you prefer to stay in London, in case you are not right mentally?' he asked.

'I am absolutely fine,' I told him. 'Until anything is sorted out with Aston Villa or anyone else, I am still a Tottenham player and there is a game at Birmingham City tomorrow in which I am happy to play my part.'

'That's fine then,' he replied. 'You'll come with us tomorrow.'

On the day of the match we arrived at St Andrews and got changed in the dressing room. Graham said I wasn't in the team, but I assumed I'd be one of the substitutes, like the rest of the players who had travelled with the squad, and I went on to the pitch to warm up with the other lads. When it was time to go back to the dressing room, a steward stopped me in the tunnel and asked for my autograph. He handed me a team sheet and I looked down it to find my name, so that I could sign my autograph beside it. However, I had to look twice because I couldn't find my name. It was then I realised that I wasn't even one of the substitutes, even though it was a friendly, and as a result my name was not on the team sheet. I had changed into my kit and I had done the warm-up, but I wasn't even in the squad, and the manager never told me.

I sat on the bench anyway, and the fans were chanting my name, but the other players just looked at me and we laughed. Surely Graham could have told me that he had no intention of playing me when we spoke in his office? But he didn't seem to have any respect for his players. He wanted to upset me to make me hurry up and leave the club. The icing on the cake came at the end of the game, when Graham made me train on the pitch with the rest of the players who never got on against Birmingham. Stewart Houston took the training session and I was looking at him with a smile on my face.

'Why are you smiling?' he asked.

'Because you are so pathetic,' I replied. 'It is unbelievable how you are treating me, and it makes me laugh.'

It again made me take stock of the whole situation. I had given so much to the club for three years: I had won two Footballer of the Year awards; I was the lifebelt of the club, keeping it afloat during the times it was in deep water; I entertained the fans during the relegation struggle, then I gave them more and helped the team to win a trophy. I was looking forward to playing for another two years; then all of a sudden this manager – who hasn't really proven himself at the club – takes it all away from me. I was so dedicated yet I was treated so badly. I don't want to judge people, and that includes George Graham, because I am stronger than that. But I do not think he was straight with me. He was never man enough to tell me face-to-face that he didn't want me at the club any more. This is the way things are at Tottenham now. It is like the army, with Graham as the General. Some of the staff used to talk openly to me at the training ground and say very nice things about me. But as soon as Graham came into the room they had to be careful what they said, because they knew he didn't like me. I find that sad.

All I can say is that he is the reason I am not at Spurs today. He pushed me out. I am fighter, but I didn't play football for 15 years to get to the age of 33 and have to battle every day with a person I don't even know, a person I don't have any feelings for. If you are fighting with someone you love and trying to achieve something, then that is the kind of battle I will pursue until I die, but what is the point of waking up every morning and driving to training knowing that I will be involved in yet another bust-up with the manager. I'll fight for my place in the team, I'll fight for the ball on the pitch, and I'll fight to be the best. But I won't fight with a person who doesn't want me, no matter what I do.

Graham also hurt my family, because my children did not want to leave London, where they had all their friends and they were happy at school. It is hard when you are faced with the upheaval of having to start all over again somewhere new, and you see it affect the people you love.

My transfer to Aston Villa was sealed the day after the

Birmingham game. Villa had pursued Chantal all summer, trying to get me to sign for them, and I finally went to meet John Gregory. Chantal had already built up a good rapport with Gregory and she felt he was someone who I could really work well alongside. There had been interest in me from clubs abroad, including France, Turkey and America, but my heart still belonged in the Premiership. Gregory was instantly likeable and he spoke with a passion for the game and for his team which I admired. I liked the look of the squad he was building: Paul Merson, Dion Dublin, Alan Thompson, Steve Stone, David James, Luc Nilis, Alpay, the list goes on. He wanted me to be part of that, and I relished the challenge of becoming a Villan. It was nice to have a manager again who was prepared to welcome me with open arms. I had also spoken to my close friend at Tottenham, Jose Dominguez, who had played for Birmingham and enjoyed living in the city, so I knew it would be a good place to go. So once I said I wanted to join Villa, Chantal continued thorough negotiations with Doug Ellis until she got the contract just right. Once everything was agreed, Chantal performed a bit of a scoop. She arranged for the transfer to be announced on my personal website, *www.ginola14.com*, and we had all the national press chasing the story from there. Because I was able to write the story myself, I knew that every dot and comma was exactly how I wanted it, and it was nice to feel in control of my press for a change! It was the truth, the official news about David Ginola, and I definitely see this as the way of doing things in the future.

Two days later I was unveiled at a press conference at Villa Park, and hundreds of Villa fans were allowed into the stadium to give me a tremendous welcome – many already wearing Ginola and number 14 on the back of their shirts. I was amazed by the attention surrounding my signing. It was also quite funny to see that people who had been whistling at me every season since I arrived in England and played for an opposing team, were now showing so much enthusiasm for my arrival at their own club.

Fortunately, this transfer will not be similar to when I left Newcastle to join Tottenham. Many Geordie fans resented me for leaving and treated me very badly. But at least this time, the Tottenham fans understand the situation and they know that I did not want to leave the club. Even as I was signing for Villa, there were letters arriving at Villa Park from Spurs fans, telling me how sad they were to see me go, and wishing me all the best for the future. I have a lot of fans who have followed my whole career, such as a man in Newcastle named John White, who somehow seems to know my movements before I do. I feel sorry for the Tottenham fans – but they know how much I valued their support, and I look forward to seeing them when Spurs play Villa in 2000/01.

I already feel my decision to sign for Villa has been justified. The nice thing about John Gregory is that I feel he understands me more as a player than maybe George Graham ever did. I am grateful to Graham for boosting my fitness levels during my pre-season at Spurs, thanks to all the hills we ran up and down in Epping Forest. But at 33 my body has different needs and limits to when I was 20. So, for example, after three days of hard training at Villa I asked the boss for a rest, and he was more than happy for me to just do a 30-minute jogging session and then have a massage. The staff at Villa ask me what I want to do, because they know that I know my own body, which is a welcome change to the way Graham used to work me. It is just a matter of common sense. I know that by treating me like this, John Gregory will get the best out of me. Sometimes it was like Graham was put on this earth to give me a hard time, and that was frustrating. Yet if he had handled me differently, he would have seen even better things from me. If I become a manager, I will know how to respect people and how to treat them. Everyone must be treated like a human being, not just a piece of meat which you squeeze until there is no more juice. As a manager I would be a dream for the players, but a nightmare for my family because I would be so dedicated!

I gave my best for Tottenham and don't think I could have done anything different. Of course you can always do better, but then you can also do worse. I think the fans forgave me for a few average performances, because the great ones more than compensated. Before I left White Hart Lane, I saw that my name was on a board in the executive box-holders' lounge three times in a row, as their player of the season for each of my three years at Tottenham. I looked at that wall and saw some great names, such as Glenn Hoddle, Gary Mabbutt, Paul Gascoigne and Jurgen Klinsmann, but the only name that appeared three successive times was David Ginola: in 1997/98, 1998/89 and 1999/2000.

I have settled in well at Villa Park, and my new team-mates have been very supportive. I was made to feel welcome on one of the first days I went training. Paul Merson arrived at the training ground with his children – and every one of them wore a Villa shirt with my name and number on the back. Fantastic!

My thoughts now are for Aston Villa, and I have new dreams and ambitions to win things for this club. I hope we can be successful because I think it is a club that deserves to be. The chairman is very enthusiastic and John Gregory and his staff are all pulling in the same direction. It is up to us players to fulfil all the expectation.

I also genuinely hope that Spurs can go on and be successful. I love the club and I like the people who work there. Just because the manager didn't want me any more, it doesn't mean I wish anything less for the club. I wish Alan Sugar all the best, because he is ambitious for success and I think he was caught up in something he had little control over. But George Graham is now living on the edge. He has to provide something big for Spurs this year – otherwise he is finished.

CHAPTER TWO

Sleeping with the enemy's wife

*'I knew my days were numbered the very first time
I met him [Dalglish] and I looked into his eyes'*

Kevin Keegan was the main reason I signed for Newcastle – if it
had not been for him I never would have come to England in
the summer of 1995. I remember in my days as a youngster
watching Liverpool, with Keegan in the team, playing against
St Etienne in the European Cup quarter-finals in 1977, and I
became a big fan of the guy. When I found out he was manager
of Newcastle, I felt it must be worth joining the club; and when
they realised they could get me for just £2.5 million, they knew
they had to have me.

I flew into Newcastle with my wife Coraline and we were
taken to a hotel in the city centre to meet the directors. Once
the formalities were completed, we were driven to St James'
Park for a press conference. As soon as I walked into the
ground I was greeted by the statue of former striker Malcolm

Macdonald, a legendary figure at the club, and pictures on the walls of the great players to have pulled on the famous black and white striped shirt, such as Keegan and Peter Beardsley. When I walked out on to the pitch I immediately felt at home, and I knew this was a place where I could enjoy playing my football. The fans were lining up to meet me and that gave me an immediate insight into how passionate the supporters are up on Tyneside, because football and Newcastle United mean so much to the area. I was amazed that there were a couple of thousand spectators who turned up to every training session we had. People would sit around the edge of the pitch having a picnic, watching us train, then ask for autographs afterwards. I thought it was nice that Keegan's policy was to allow the fans to get really close to the players and the club – he never turned them away. I felt very much at home straight away, but it wasn't so easy for Coraline to settle at first. I recall one day she was driven around by the chairman's chauffeur to look at potential houses for us, and when she came back she was crying, because it was such a contrast to Paris. But she is a very strong person, and I reassured her that things would be okay.

Newcastle wanted a striker and while they were signing me, they were also trying to buy George Weah, such was Keegan's ambition for the club. They knew we had linked up well together at PSG, with me supplying his goals, and they wanted to bring that successful partnership to the Toon army. But George also had an offer to play for Milan, which he accepted, so Newcastle instead bought Les Ferdinand from QPR for £6 million. At least I justified the club's judgement early on in the season when I was named Carling Player of the Month for August, the first time a foreign player had come straight into the Premiership and won the award.

Every day, training was enjoyable. The relationship with the fans was brilliant, the players all did a lot for charity, and we really were the pride of the north east. Even through the winter months when we were training in the snow on the pitches at the University of Durham it was enjoyable, because we were successful, and everyone was waking up with a smile on their face.

However, after my first season at St James' Park my manager Kevin Keegan really disappointed me. I told him in the summer that I had been contacted by Bobby Robson at Barcelona. I was relaxing in the south of France when I received a phone call from my agent in Paris who said: 'Listen David, I don't know how to present this to you, but I have been approached by Barcelona and they want to sign you.'

My agent told me Bobby Robson wanted to speak to me and so I told him to pass on my number in the south of France. Sure enough, a few minutes later, Bobby called me.

'Hello David, how are you? I want you in my squad.'

I couldn't believe it and told him I was under contract to Newcastle, and it would be difficult.

'I will leave that to my chairman Josep Nunez to sort out the deal,' said Robson, 'but this is just to let you know I want you to join Barcelona for next season.'

I thought this would be fantastic. I then spoke to Keegan.

'David,' he said, 'I know the story, and I know a move to Barcelona would be something fantastic for you – I know that. But you have to understand me. Last year I sold Andy Cole to Manchester United and I can't afford to sell one of my most popular players again, in case the fans turn on me. I can't let you go, the fans will not let you go, especially after the season you have just had.'

'Gaffer, this is the chance of my life,' I pleaded. 'I am 30 years of age and this may be my last opportunity to join such a big team. I am not saying we are not a big club here at

Newcastle, but Barcelona are one of the biggest in the world. To join a club like that would be fantastic for me, and you have to understand this.'

There was a moment's silence. 'I understand David, but you have to realise the position for me too, as manager of Newcastle United.'

I knew in my heart then that he would not let me go, and it was terrible, a really awful feeling. I knew Keegan was representing the club and he was showing compassion for the fans and for the people he represented by blocking my move. But six months later when he left the club, I realised he wasn't being fair, because if he did genuinely have compassion for the club and the fans he would not have left himself. When he departed, it was for personal reasons, he did not think about me and what he had said to me six months earlier.

It wasn't fair for someone to tell me why he couldn't let me go, then six months later walk away himself.

I do not regret my time in Newcastle, because I had some very happy moments there, especially under someone as special as Keegan, and it was an important part of my career, but things started to go sour for me after Keegan walked out of the club during my second season.

I didn't know who would arrive in his place, but when I found out it was Kenny Dalglish it was the worst possible thing for me. I had heard of Dalglish as a player and as manager of Blackburn, so I was prepared to wait before pre-judging him. But I knew my days were numbered the very first time I met him and I looked into his eyes. I knew straight away that he would give me a hard time. I know by experience when somebody likes me just by the way they look at me – the eyes reveal so much – and immediately I felt he didn't like me.

Dalglish never once made an effort to have a decent conversation with me. He was talking always to Alan Shearer or David Batty, the former Blackburn players, and for me and the other foreign players like Faustino Asprilla, Philippe Albert and Pavel Srnicek, it was terrible. Dalglish knew he was working with 'Kevin Keegan's foreigners', and I am sure that at the back of his mind he wanted to get us out and bring in his own players to stamp his authority and personality on the team.

Unfortunately for Dalglish, it was a fiasco. Keegan brought a spirit to the club. He brought a whole new football education to the team and the fans and earned respect throughout the game with his attractive style of football. But under Dalglish we didn't play at all.

It was Dalglish and Shearer all the time, and it was quite funny to observe the pair of them together, laughing at their own jokes. But for the rest of the players it was like being a foreigner – even for the British ones.

I knew straight away that I would have problems with Shearer, because he was the blue-eyed boy as far as Dalglish was concerned, talking to the manager all the time, and I knew that for some reason if I wasn't crossing enough balls for Shearer, or not passing to him enough, he would go running to Dalglish and tell him not to play me again. This was a great shame, because I can honestly say that I can think of no forward I would rather have in my team than Alan Shearer. If ever I became a manager I would break the bank to find a striker in the Shearer mould. I would have loved to have played off him at Newcastle, with him as the main striker and me as the link man, because I think it could have been an explosive partnership, but Dalglish was not prepared to give us that chance.

I got the impression that Shearer didn't like me from day one. When he arrived at St James' Park in the summer of 1996, he knew that mine was the best selling shirt at Newcastle at this time. The people there loved me, I was the 'French kiss' in the team and we'd had a wonderful season, almost winning the championship. He arrived when the team was on tour in Japan, and he saw the game in which I was man-of-the-match. I received a cheque and my picture was all over the place, and I bet he thought to himself: 'I will have to be careful with this guy.' I suppose I was a threat to his chances of being the fans' favourite, because his aim was to be number one, the prodigal son returning to his Geordie homeland. If he could keep me quiet, he knew he could be number one.

This was how he played on my situation with Dalglish and I remember in particular one of the early games of that 1996/97 season. We were on the attack and I had the ball and went past a couple of players, but instead of going outside to cross the ball I cut inside and had a shot. Shearer was shouting to me really angrily: 'Why didn't you cross the ball?' The next day I saw him speaking in hushed tones with Dalglish and I realised at this time that something was wrong. Then, for no apparent reason, I was dropped for the following game. I had to ask myself whether Shearer had been responsible for this. Anyway, I was really annoyed and I knew then I had no future at the club. If you have the captain of the team and the manager working together against you, then you have no chance.

I don't remember receiving any kindness or any attention from Dalglish. Shearer was the number one focus of the team, and Dalglish issued me with tactics to benefit only Shearer. He told me that when I got the ball on the wing, I was to go outside and cross for Shearer, rather than cut inside and curl in a shot. At this time it was only my second season in English football, and I wasn't as established as I am now, so I didn't feel able to challenge the manager, even though he was stifling my natural game and stopping me from scoring goals and doing the things I am good at. But I wouldn't let that happen today. Ironically, I feel that I would be able to play in the same team as Shearer today and still be myself as a player.

Alan Shearer is an institution. I don't have time for the man, but as a footballer I respect him a lot for the things he has done in the game. He has been fantastic for a long period of time, consistently scoring goals at the highest level. I feel that I too have established myself in English football and I am entitled to my freedom on the pitch. This is where Dalglish wasn't very astute, in my opinion. If you speak to George Graham or any people who work with me in training, they know my strengths. If you talk to defenders they will tell you that the main worry they have with David Ginola is that because I am two-footed they don't know which way I am going to go. So by Dalglish telling me only to go on the outside and cross the ball, the defender's job is made easier, because he knows what I am going to do every time. In one fell swoop, Dalglish had taken away half the things I was good at.

The way Dalglish treated me, he made me feel as if I'd had an affair with his wife. I actually said that to the press and the next day things became so bad that the two of us almost came to blows during training, and we had to be pulled apart by the rest of the players.

He had organised a meeting in the middle of the training pitch with all the players and addressed me in front of everyone.

'David, why did you say that about my wife?'

After a heated conversation we almost had a fight, but instead I walked away.

'I don't want to talk to you, you don't understand,' I said.

'You don't understand that for me, as a foreigner in the

21

north east of England who was having such a good time the season before but who now sees no future in a team that is playing crap . . . there is no interest here for me.'

I knew from that day on that I would not be able to stay at the club. I can't speak for the other foreign players at the club at that time, or even for the British ones, but you would have been crazy not to notice that Dalglish's relationship with his former Blackburn players was completely different to the rest of us.

By doing everything contrary to the way Keegan had run the club, Dalglish undid all the good work of the year before. It made it difficult for the players because we didn't play the same football. The fans noticed it, they saw that they had lost the enjoyment and attention that Keegan had provided for them. It was a big step in the opposite direction. Keegan was so much more open with his attitude whereas Dalglish was introverted. I don't think Dalglish is a bad fellow, and obviously his family and friends think he is very nice, but I am talking about him the way I saw him at this time, as David Ginola, a foreigner at Newcastle who was given a rough ride by the manager.

I wrote a letter asking for a transfer and explaining the reasons why I wanted to leave Newcastle. The club didn't understand and it didn't go down too well. But it is always the same: when everything is going well, everyone is happy and smiling; but when things go wrong and you ask for a transfer, everyone is miserable. They don't talk to you any more, even though you are the same person. You become alienated. It wasn't my fault that I didn't have a future at the club, and I didn't have time on my side to wait around. I couldn't afford to spend two years in Newcastle sitting on the bench, so I had to move on. It was a big decision because it also affected my family. I wasn't a single guy, going out on the town every night enjoying myself; I had a wife and two children, a career to manage and a passion to play football.

I am sorry for the fans that I could not stay on, but I think the majority will see my point of view and not hate me like some of them unfortunately do. The supporters were the first to say that Dalglish killed off all of Keegan's work, so they should know that Dalglish was the reason I asked to leave.

Some Newcastle fans who read this will say I never loved the north east. That's not true, but it was difficult for me to adapt because I am from the south of France. During that season, after I made it known I wanted to leave, I had a couple of elderly fans come up to me at the training ground one day.

'David, we understand you. We went to the south of France for a week and visited your home town, so we know what you are all about. We give you a lot of credit for coming to live in the north east because we saw where you were born, and where you have your roots, and it must be so hard to stay here all year long with your family, thinking of where you really belong.

'We love the north east because this is our homeland, but we want you to know we understand you. We cannot criticise you when you say you cannot live here, and we don't find it offensive; we know it is just because you don't belong to this part of the world. You have stayed here for a year and given us your best, and we are very proud of you for this. We understand if you have a problem with the manager and you want to go, because on top of your football you have a life of your own and we know it is tough for you.'

That meant a lot to me and it was touching to have them telling me something which I thought a proud Geordie would never say to me – even if he thought it.

I told the people who were working for me that I wanted a

quiet summer holiday, and I wanted them to sort me out with a new club before I went on holiday. We were contacted by Barcelona again but it was the same story. This time Bobby Robson was the director of football there, but he said he still wanted me. It even got to the stage where an agent telephoned Coraline in the middle of the night and told her to go to Barcelona to choose a house because the deal was done. But my wife is very sceptical where football is concerned and she was proved right because the move collapsed again. It turned out that the Barcelona manager, Louis Van Gaal, was keener to buy Dutch players, and so the deal just fell through.

I was then told that Tottenham wanted me, but I did not want to rush into anything, so I told my advisers to hold fire while I considered all my options. But I also knew that I did not want my summer to be wrecked by the uncertainty of not knowing where I would be playing football the following season. I don't think Newcastle made it too widely known that I was available, because I believe they were expecting me to return to St James' Park at the end of the summer and play another season there. But I had made up my mind that I didn't want to go back to Newcastle.

Time was moving on and we needed to find a solution, so Newcastle accepted Tottenham's £2 million offer for me. I was on the beach back in St Tropez with my family and friends when I received a phone call from my agent to say that Alan Sugar, the chairman of Tottenham, wanted to meet me to discuss personal terms. He was on his yacht in Ville-France-Sur-Mer, near Monaco, one of the most beautiful bays in the Mediterranean.

It was 14 July, Independence Day in France when everybody celebrates with parties and fireworks. All the people go down to the coast for the day and all the roads are very busy. I had rented for the day an off-shore boat with two 750 horsepower Lamborghini engines, capable of speeds of up to 70 knots, and I was just off the beach on the boat with all my friends and family. When the phone call came to say that Alan Sugar wanted me to join him for dinner on his yacht, I knew it would be pointless going by car, so I decided to extend the rental period for another day and go to meet him by boat.

The meeting was scheduled for 8 pm that evening. Sugar didn't know I would be coming by boat, so he had told my agent he would have his dinghy standing by to pick me up from the marina. I was wearing just a tee-shirt, shorts and cap and didn't have time to change. I kissed my wife and children and said goodbye to all my friends. By road the journey would have taken at least an hour and a half, but, in the company of another friend, we reached the bay in Monaco in exactly 56 minutes, racing along at 65 knots in the calm waters, passing St Raphael, Cannes and Nice.

When we sped into the bay at Ville-France-Sur-Mer it was initially very quiet, but the loud engines of my boat soon broke the silence. I remember I could see Alan Sugar in the distance, standing on his yacht, arms folded, looking out towards this noisy boat coming into the bay . . . and wondering who was shattering the peace! I could see he was furious – he never imagined it would be David Ginola as he expected me to arrive by land at the marina. I was waving at him, in my tee-shirt and cap, and he must have wondered who the hell this guy was! But as I got closer he recognised me and his mood changed visibly. He helped me moor my boat alongside his yacht and climb aboard.

'I was just asking myself, what the hell is going on with these guys coming into the bay in their noisy boat when I am trying to have a quiet time?' said Sugar.

25

We sat down to dinner on his magnificent yacht and discussed my move to Tottenham. Sugar is a man with great charisma and I had made up my mind before going to see him that I wanted to join Tottenham, so it was really just a formality to shake hands on a deal with him. During the discussions he phoned his manager, Gerry Francis, who spoke to me and told me how keen he was to have me in his team. Then Sugar had some pictures taken of the two of us on the deck of his yacht. He brought out a bottle of tonic water and held that in the picture, which he then sent straight off to the *Sun* newspaper. (The headline the next day above the picture read: 'Gin and tonic for Tottenham!')

After dinner I got ready to go home. But it was dark, and Sugar was worried about me finding my way back safely by boat.

'You can't go back like this – you are now a Spurs player and your welfare is important to me!'

'Please don't worry,' I said. 'I know the area very well and can find my way back without any problem, I know every single rock in the water.'

But he would not let me go, and he made me and my friend sleep on his yacht that night, so we could return home in the morning when it was light again.

I packed my bags the next morning, met Daniel Sugar – the chairman's son and the director of operations at the club – to officially sign my contract, and then flew straight out to Norway to join my new Spurs team-mates who had already begun a pre-season tour.

CHAPTER THREE

Kamikaze George

'What is going on here? Hey, Mr Graham,
can you tell me why you are doing this, please?'

The 1998/99 season ended on a high for Tottenham as we won
the Worthington Cup and so booked our place in the following season's UEFA Cup. But on a personal note, there was even
more glory when I was named Footballer of the Year by both
the Professional Footballers' Association and the Football
Writers' Association.

Some people have said that surely this means it must have
been the best season of my entire career. But I won the same
awards in France in 1993/94 and had four very good seasons at
Paris St Germain, so I would prefer to say it was the best season
of my career in England thus far. I felt I was very consistent
during the course of the season but nevertheless I was very
surprised to win these awards.

I arrived for the PFA dinner at the Grosvenor House Hotel

in London without any knowledge that I was going to be named as the winner of the PFA award. But soon after I arrived I was asked to pose for some photographs holding the trophy. The people around me thought that was a good indication of the result.

'David, it must be you, well done.'

'Come on, there is no chance,' I said. 'I don't play in a team good enough to have this trophy.'

I wasn't criticising Spurs by saying that, I just felt that the award usually went to a player from a team who were challenging for the title, such as Arsenal's Dennis Bergkamp, whereas we were having only an average season in the league. So when the photographers started taking pictures of me, although I wasn't admitting it, in my heart I was thinking: 'This is fantastic, after just four years in English football, one of the best football countries in the world, I have won this trophy, which is voted for by my fellow professionals – it is such an accomplishment.'

When Sir Geoff Hurst went on stage and announced I had won, the standing ovation I received from the audience must have lasted about three minutes. I didn't realise how much appreciation and respect there was for me from players in other divisions, and this touched me deeply. I realised all the work I had done, all the time I had spent on the training ground, had been worthwhile. I was so happy, I rushed straight out after the presentation and called my wife, my parents and my agent. For me to have won this award at 32 years of age proved a point to the people who said that I was incapable of playing any more top-flight football. I answered their criticisms in a positive way, no 'buts' about it. Tony Blair famously said: 'I am proud to be British.' Well, I am proud to be adopted as British.

When I looked at all the names that preceded mine on the trophy, such as Colin Todd, Pat Jennings, Kevin Keegan and Alan Shearer, it brought home to me just how big an achievement this was – I would go down in history with all the other special players. Sir Geoff made a point of thanking me for turning up in person to the dinner, as some of the other nominees had not bothered. I thought that was a bit of a snub on their part, because I have always attended this dinner because it is the PFA's night and the players should be there – whether or not they are winning an award – just to support their fellow players. It is a night for footballers, our one night of the year when we have the chance to get together and celebrate our beautiful game.

It was another big surprise when I received the trophy from the football writers. To be chosen by the players was one thing, but I thought the journalists would give the award to someone at Manchester United, who were on the verge of a unique treble. I hadn't played in the World Cup the previous year, 1998, which was a huge disappointment, so these two awards were like my own victory, showing my country that I too could still win trophies.

It was an amazing feeling when I went up to receive the Football Writers' trophy at the Royal Lancaster Hotel in London, two days before the FA Cup final. I was on a platform looking down at more than 800 journalists and guests from the football world. Looking along the top table, I could see famous faces like Sir Bobby Charlton, a former winner of the trophy, and again I felt proud to be in such distinguished company. I had not prepared a speech, I just said what came into my mind at the time. It was a thrilling experience.

Both awards that year were wonderful moments in my life – they would be in the life of any footballer playing in England.

The joy of winning, however, was tinged with disappointment. I was very hurt by the fact that nobody in charge of my own club Tottenham, not even chairman Alan Sugar, telephoned me to offer their congratulations or to say they were proud of my achievements – especially as this reflected very well on the club. I'm convinced that Sugar only made the call after being stung into action three or four days later. A journalist apparently called Sugar's secretary and asked to speak to him. The secretary would not put her through, but asked what it was about. The journalist said: 'I am just ringing to ask Mr Sugar what he said to David about the fact that he has scooped these two prestigious awards, and I was wondering if the club would be doing anything special to honour Ginola.' Coincidentally or not, within ten minutes of that phone call being made to Sugar, he was on the phone to me offering his congratulations. He apologised for being too busy to have called earlier.

'Don't worry Mr Chairman,' I said. 'It is never too late.'

I had every reason to return to Tottenham in the summer of 1999 full of hope for the season ahead. After the Worthington Cup final I said that I hoped Alan Sugar would now open his cheque book and that George Graham would bring in some top-quality players to strengthen our squad and boost our assault on Europe. We still desperately needed new talent because apart from winning the cup it had not been a great season in the league, as we finished only 11th and there was still a lot of work to do. I really thought the club would break the bank, especially now we were in Europe, but they didn't. They spent a total of just £8.5 million on three summer signings – Chris Perry from Wimbledon for £4 million, Willem Korsten from Vitesse Arnheim for £1.5 million, and Oyvind Leonhardsen from Liverpool for £3 million – and I think the fans and the players were expecting more. I still thought there would be some big names arriving before the season started, but they never came.

The problem today is that the transfer fees for the top players are astronomically high – just look at Luis Figo's move from Barcelona to Real Madrid in July for £37 million! But there is another, even bigger, problem for a club like Spurs: how can they attract big players if they are not an attractive club? If they are not in Europe or are not successful, then the really big names will not be keen to come to White Hart Lane. So even if Spurs had the money and were prepared to spend it, it still doesn't mean they would be able to get the best players. On the other hand, if the club wanted to buy someone in their early twenties with big expectations in their career, they will not want to come to Tottenham if they think the club are not investing money in players.

When players report back for pre-season, some of them like to look around and see fresh faces. Of course, some players may worry if one of the big new signings plays in their position, but I don't fear competition. When we reported back in the summer of 1999 there was no abundance of new talent to liven up the squad, and it was frustrating for me to see that we would be starting the new season with virtually the same team that finished the previous one, especially as we would be playing against teams who had really improved their squads.

However, after winning a trophy a few months earlier to get into Europe, there was still plenty of hope. For me, especially, I was determined to get off to a good start and avoid what had happened in the previous two seasons, so I worked really hard.

We started well, but then we had our first real test: how would we cope with losing key players through injury? The whole point of having strength in depth in your squad is that you can replace your top players with equally good ones if they get injured or suspended. Take our main rivals Arsenal, for example: last season Arsene Wenger could replace Dennis Bergkamp with Kanu or Davor Suker, and he could replace Thierry Henry with Marc Overmars – quality for quality. It is the same when you look at the bench of Chelsea or Manchester United, they do not have to worry so much. But in the first half of the season we had injuries to key players – Sol Campbell, Darren Anderton, Les Ferdinand and Steffen Iversen – but we didn't have players of equal ability who could come in and cover for them. I did not say anything but I was frustrated we had not gone out and signed some really world-class players. I expected more from the club.

We were among the early challengers in the league, so there was plenty of confidence at the club when it was time to begin what we hoped would be a long European adventure. We were drawn to face FC Zimbru, the champions of Moldova in the first round, and we made sure they did not become a banana skin for us by doing all the hard work in the first leg at White Hart Lane. They were an unknown quantity and George Graham had appealed to the fans to be patient, in case we didn't get an early goal, but he needn't have worried as Oyvind Leonhardsen scored inside the first ten minutes to set us on our way to a comfortable 3–0 victory. The job was done, which was impor-tant because you never know what to expect when you go to a country like that. The second leg in Chisinau was a formality and we drew 0–0, although I was rested because I had been carrying a slight knock and failed a late fitness test. I don't like sitting in the stand, watching the team play, but I had no choice on this occasion, and from the team's point of view it was a good trip.

Spurs were back in Europe and it was a nice feeling for me to also be back there. I knew it would be hard for us to go through all the rounds of the UEFA Cup and make it to the final, but I wanted it so much because I was thinking about all my past adventures in Europe with PSG, and they were happy memories. I was in Europe every year when I was with PSG and we played some of the great teams: Barcelona, AC Milan, Napoli, Real Madrid, Juventus, Arsenal, Bayern Munich, Dinamo Kiev and Spartak Moscow. This Tottenham team was inexperienced in European terms, with only myself and Steffen Freund having had any real experience under our belts, so I felt we were important to the team and could give it strength.

Our reward for getting past the Moldovans was a very hard tie with FC Kaiserslautern of Germany. I was disappointed that we were drawn to play the home leg first because it is always better to play the second leg in front of your own supporters, as they can be worth an extra goal to you, and, besides, you know what you have to do. We knew Kaiserslautern were a typically strong German team who would keep it tight, although they had the ability to play football and had some good foreigners in their team, such as their captain Ciriaco Sforza and my former French international colleague, Youri Djorkaeff.

I had a good game at White Hart Lane, and it was from one of my runs that we earned a penalty after the German goalkeeper tripped me in their box. That gave us a 1–0 first leg lead, but we missed a few chances and I was worried that a single goal might not be enough to see us through in the return game. You have to take your chances in front of goal if you want to be successful in Europe – you don't get a second chance in these knockout competitions.

I was all over the German newspapers after the first game. Steffen Freund brought them into training and translated the stories, one of which said: 'David Ginola showed once again that he is one of the best players in Europe.' So when I travelled out to Germany with the team for the second leg I never thought in my wildest dreams that I was going to be dropped for the game. I was in good spirits, I'd had a good first leg, and I knew they were scared of me, so why should I have any doubts about my selection?

The bombshell came a couple of hours before the game, when we had a team meeting at our hotel and George Graham read out the team for later that night. Usually, when Graham announces his team he reads the names out at a leisurely pace. But this time it was different. He raced through the 11 names, almost as if he was hoping it wouldn't sink in that my name was not among them. I think maybe he was a bit nervous about the reaction he might get, so he never left a gap between the names as he called them out.

'Walker, Carr, Edinburgh, Campbell, Perry, Leonhardsen, Sherwood, Freund, Clemence, Armstrong, Iversen,' He continued: '. . . and the substitutes are Baardsen, Vega, Dominguez, Young, Fox, Ginola and Gower.'

I wasn't in his team. But I would never react in a situation like that, in front of the rest of the lads. Of course I was surprised – I was not the only one – and most of the other players looked at me for some reaction. I didn't move. I didn't want to show any emotion, I just sat there and accepted it.

Deep down, however, I was not pleased at all because I really felt I could help the team in this game; I couldn't fathom why Graham was thinking the opposite. I had played something like 25 games in the European Cup during my time with PSG, so I had the experience, especially on foreign soil.

The other players may have been expecting me to react and to say something at the meeting, but my first thoughts were for the team, and I did not want to unsettle the other lads just a couple of hours before such a big game. I had done so in the past and saw it had been unhelpful, so this time I decided not to say anything.

I was expected to be mature, because I was 32 years old, a senior member of the team, and I did keep my cool because I felt that was the right thing to do. But inside I wanted to shout. I wanted to stand up and say: *'What is going on here? Hey, Mr Graham, can you tell me why you are doing this, please? Why are you not playing me?'*

It is difficult for me sometimes. When you are the manager you can express yourself when you are happy or unhappy – if you want to shout at players it is easy because you are the person in charge. For a player it is difficult, but I always try to keep my cool.

I tried to think what possible motive Graham could have for leaving me out of the team. There was nothing wrong with my form; in fact it was good. I had trained really hard for this game; I had frightened the Germans in the first leg and, as I said, my experience of European football was surely invaluable. There was only one thing I had done wrong, but surely Graham wouldn't have been so petty to have made that the reason for dropping me – that would have been a case of him cutting off his nose to spite his face.

I am talking about the fact that I had arrived a few minutes late that morning for the team's walk around the town together. I was sharing a room with Jose Dominguez and the alarm call we had booked never came. We woke up late and had to rush down and catch up with the team, who had already set off on their walk. But there had been occasions in the past where somebody had been late for the morning walk and the player concerned hadn't been dropped as a punishment, so surely this could not have been the reason. I can only think

Graham wanted to try something different – but surely Europe is not the place to experiment. If you have something different in your mind you practice it in training, or in a less significant game, but we had not tried it before. It wasn't as if he had dropped a young player; he had dropped me, and for most people it was a critical decision. I wondered if it might have been something personal, but I thought that if he was doing something like this for personal reasons on the day of a big European game, then he was not being very smart.

We left the hotel and went to the Kaiserslautern stadium, and there was more drama ahead. The Germans handed in their team sheet as usual prior to kick-off, not knowing I was out of the Spurs team. After the first leg, they had decided to assign a player to man-mark me in the hope of reducing my threat. But when George Graham handed in our team sheet and the Germans saw I was only on the bench, they changed their line-up, taking out the defender who would have marked me and bringing in an extra attacking midfielder. A UEFA official came to our dressing room to inform us of the change, and to ask Graham if he wanted to make any changes of his own as a result, but he declined, although of course he was not happy that Kaiserslautern had been allowed to alter their team. Spurs later complained to UEFA about the Germans' late alteration but they had not broken any rules – only the spirit of fair play – so Tottenham's appeal fell on deaf ears.

We were warming up before the game when I was taunted by the Kaiserslautern players who had just heard the news. Sforza came up to me and started talking in French.

'What is going on?' he muttered.

I would never criticise the management of my own team to an opponent, so I shrugged my shoulders and told him I didn't know. But then he started laughing.

'Your manager is CRAZY! You are the only player we care about in this team, and now we have been able to change our own team to a more attacking formation. Your manager must be a kamikaze! Say goodbye to the cup, because you are not going to qualify now. Your manager has made a big mistake, he has got it wrong.'

Their baiting wasn't malicious as I think they felt sorry for me, but their spirits had clearly been lifted when they saw our team sheet. As I walked off after the warm-up, I even had a German journalist come up to me to ask if this was some joke Spurs were playing on them.

We held out for almost 90 minutes, defending the one-goal lead from the first leg, but then Kaiserslautern scored a last-minute equaliser and then an injury-time winner to knock us out of the UEFA Cup and leave us feeling totally shattered. I just couldn't believe it. It had been a real dream for me to once again play in Europe, so to go out of the competition at such an early stage was devastating. To make matters worse, Kaiserslautern drew Lens in the third round; that should have been us facing Lens and it meant I had missed the chance to go back and play in my home country, which would have meant an awful lot to me.

Football is not all one-way traffic. If I was a manager who had a player from, say Slovakia, and we were drawn to play a Slovakian team, then I would play him for a bit of heart. I know I am not German but I have played more games in Europe than anyone else in the Spurs team and I couldn't understand why the manager wasn't using my experience. I saw it as a bad decision. I have never had an explanation from George Graham for his team selection that night. The first thing I wanted to do after the game was to ask him why, but there was no point in me going to see him, because I would never get the true answer; I would hear only what he wanted to tell me.

In the dressing room after the game I was a little bit shocked by Graham's reaction. In the previous couple of weeks he had reacted badly after disappointing defeats and I was expecting more of the same. But here he was very sympathetic and he said: 'Well done guys, you did everything you could. Unlucky.' In a way, I saw that as him shouldering the blame for the defeat. The players were devastated and I think he knew there was no point in ranting and raving, which I felt was good management on his part.

I had expected to have more games in Europe but this was the end of a short adventure. This one result affected our whole season – the players were not the same after this game and our confidence never returned.

Shortly after that night in Germany, I received a telephone call from Tottenham chairman Alan Sugar. He took me by surprise – it is not every day you receive a call from your chairman – and my first reaction was to worry that something was wrong. It was a rather baffling conversation.

'Hello, David,' said Sugar. 'I have something to tell you and I want to speak to you; but man-to-man, not over the telephone, so come to my house and we can talk about it.'

'Is there a problem?'

'No, it is nothing to worry about,' he replied.

'Is it about football?'

'Yes,' Sugar said, 'but it is nothing to do with the club. One thing I want you to know is that you mustn't fall into any of George Graham's psychological traps . . . don't be caught out by his mind games. You are important to this club and don't forget you have recently signed a three-year contract with Tottenham. I am happy for you to stay and see it out.'

As I said, the conversation with Sugar left me feeling confused. That was, until the following day, when I had another telephone call, this time from my agent, Chantal Stanley.

'David,' she said, 'don't get carried away by what I am about to tell you, but I think Manchester United want you.'

Chantal had received a call from someone very close to the Premiership champions, asking her if I would be keen to play for them. I have to say I was surprised when she told me, but I am still ambitious and I saw this as the chance to fulfil my dream of playing for one of the biggest clubs in the world. Anyway, after speaking to Chantal, the previous conversation I'd had with Sugar suddenly fell into place. Sugar was always the first to say to me: 'David, we are delighted with you on and off the pitch for Tottenham Hotspur. The image you give to the club is a fantastic image and you are the symbol of Tottenham Hotspur all around the world.'

I realised why he had finished his call to me by reminding me I had recently signed a new contract. I didn't bother to go and see him after that – there was no point. I didn't need to hear him tell me that he had received an offer from Manchester United for me but that he could never let me go. That would have hurt me more.

I almost did play for Manchester United in the 1999/2000 season – as a guest in one game only. However, George Graham put a stop to that. I received a fax from Sir Alex Ferguson inviting me to play in his testimonial match. I went to see Tottenham boss George to ask for his permission, and at first he said: 'I don't see any problem.' But a week before the game he came to me and said: 'I don't want you to play in the testimonial on Monday because we have a game on Wednesday and I want you to concentrate on that.' It was nice to be invited by Sir Alex and I would have been very pleased to play for 45 minutes in his special game, but once George had changed his mind there was nothing I could do or say. Maybe he felt our Worthington Cup third-round game at home to Crewe was more important, which was fair enough, or maybe he just didn't like the idea of me playing – I shall never know the truth.

Of course, I would have loved the chance to play alongside David Beckham, Roy Keane, Paul Scholes and Ryan Giggs. Imagine Dwight Yorke, Andy Cole, Teddy Sheringham and Ole Gunnar Solskjaer on the end of my crosses. I believe if I was playing in a team like that then I would be the focus of a lot more attention, and have a chance of being among the nominations for European Footballer of the Year every season. But it wasn't to be.

There was another, very personal and sentimental reason why a move to Old Trafford appealed to me. I am so passion-ate about my country that I still have this dream in my head that I will get the chance to play for France one more time. It is strange, but I still believe it. It is like a love story: like a lady leaving me in my younger days, depriving me of the oppor-tunity to give her my best years. Then, say seven years later, I would like to meet her again with those extra years of experi-ence behind me and rekindle the love affair. I would no longer be just a boy, I would be a man. I would be able to convey my feelings for her in a different way, because of my maturity and hopefully start the relationship over again. I would love that second chance. Those are my feelings. I like to achieve things in my life, and I don't think I achieved anything where the French team is concerned. The 17 caps I have won are not enough, although it is not a question of having caps, it is a question of playing for my country. It hurts me a lot when I talk about this subject.

CHAPTER FOUR

A Fan-tastic game

'I will never underestimate the importance of the fans.
Without them, we the players would be nothing,
or would have nothing'

Bill Shankly once said famously: 'Football is not a matter of life or death – it is more important than that.' I believe the legendary former Liverpool manager was both right and wrong. Everything in life must be put in the right context. Of course, there are things in life which are more important than football. For example, you are doing a far more important job if you are a surgeon, saving lives. But, in another way, you have people who work very hard during the week and when they go to watch football on Saturday afternoon they want it to take their breath away. For so many people it is the highlight of their week, their bit of escapism which fills a big part of their life. It is a tradition for them to go to the match on Saturday, sitting with all their friends, united in the same cause. They are lads together, going to the pub before or after the game and having a good time.

When they go and sit in the stand they can release all the rage or pent-up frustration of the week they have just endured – maybe something has upset them at work with their boss, or maybe they have had an argument in their relationship. Whatever it is, going to football makes them feel better and helps them release those feelings.

For some people football is like a therapy. I have learned that when a supporter goes to watch a game he cares about the result of his team but he also wants to enjoy it. He wants to walk away saying how fantastic that hour-and-a-half was. I have a great story about some guys I knew who weren't particularly keen on football. But they came to see me once when Paris Saint Germain played Real Madrid in Paris. It was a UEFA Cup tie and the atmosphere in the Parc des Princes was fantastic. We were 3–1 down from the first leg in Spain but I scored one of the goals in a 4–1 victory which took us through. After the game the guys came up to me and had the most amazing look on their faces, like children who had just met Father Christmas. They could hardly speak, except to say: 'That was the most unbelievable experience of our lives!' They had become so wrapped up in the whole event that they had really let themselves go – to the point where they said they didn't recognise themselves, standing up and screaming the players on. This is what we, as footballers, bring to supporters, and this is an essential part of their lives. We give them escapism and a chance to follow a dream.

My philosophy on football is this: First and foremost, I think football is entertainment. I know it is a job and I know we have a lot of responsibility on our shoulders – some players more than others – but football at the end of the day is still a game. That isn't to say I take it lightly, far from it, but when I think about football I think of myself when I was eight years old, playing on a small pitch in St Maxime. For me it was just a game of football without any other interest. Everything in life is important, but to varying degrees. Fans support a certain team and they go to watch football because they enjoy it. But at the end of the day it is still only a game. Obviously it is important to win a game when you are playing in a championship, but when I was playing with my friends it was a learning process. I used to come out of school and play a game of football and, because I loved this game, I was very passionate. I always keep that in my mind. I think of that when people get carried away.

I will never underestimate the importance of the fans. Without them, we the players would be nothing, or would have nothing. I want to share with you one of my favourite pieces of dialogue. It is the opening to the film *The Fan*, a story of baseball starring Robert De Niro and Wesley Snipes. The film begins with De Niro, the demented fan in the film, reciting a poem. Although De Niro's character is an obsessive, whenever I watch this film and hear the opening monologue I still find it moving. Read it for yourselves and I hope you will see what I mean:

> 'Excited and anxious I await my dream,
> to escape, applaud and embrace my team.
> Opening day I always can trust,
> it is just for this high that I crazily lust.
> Return of our hero does bright the days,
> just briefly my troubles get lost in the haze.
> The grace from the field arouses the crowd,
> reflects on the days when I was quite proud.

I'm more entranced than the average fan,
I used to play, you see, and I know I still can.
That time I drove the ball with such loft,
my exit atop shoulders as they carried me off.
This past time and I just fade into one,
expanded upon from father and son.
My boy is young, and awkward for now,
I just need the time and can show him how.
I really am quite close, just a break away,
from straightening things out and being okay.
I can help my team to regain its glory,
with just a little twist to the same old story.
The players say now they play for themselves,
this causes a burning within me that dwells.
The fan is the one who pays for the game,
which bestows all the riches, and welcome fame.
The players will listen but really don't hear,
all the while just hiding behind an invisible tear.
I grow tired now of all this greed,
and chart a course to set things free.'

Any footballer who achieves fame and fortune owes a debt to the fans. When you start out you are unknown, but if you play well they help take you to the top with their adulation for you, they help bring all those headlines. They are part of your life. Not your private life, but they are there every Saturday at the game, they can boo you or applaud you, make you feel good or bad. Sometimes last season I looked at my own relationship with the fans and then compared it with my team-mate Chris Armstrong, who was getting some terrible abuse from the Tottenham supporters. I really felt for him when he was jeered, but when he did something well I was standing there applauding him in the hope the fans would see me and copy me. I wanted them to understand that there is no point abusing someone who needs help, you need to get behind them. Chris Armstrong is a human being and he needed help, but sometimes the fans did not act in the right way, yet in the last third of the season he was one of the most prolific goalscorers in the Premiership and I was pleased for him.

Even though the fans may hand out abuse, you must always give them the recognition they deserve. They are the ones who buy the tickets to watch the team, they buy the shirts and the other merchandise. If you are one of their favourites they have your picture on their bedroom wall and so you are part of their family.

Things like that are very important to understand and when sometimes I see some players not signing an autograph, or just signing it dismissively without even looking at the person asking for it, then it upsets me. It shows a lack of respect, but not just to the fan, to yourself as well. You may think that if you drive a Ferrari it is just because of your status in the game, but if it wasn't for the fans then there would be no money coming into football and you would never get the opportunity to earn so much money. You MUST appreciate the fans.

Sometimes if a player loses a game he forgets about it straight away and looks towards the next one. But the fans may go home and cry, it affects them that much. The result of a football match can make the difference between a person having a good or bad weekend. Some fans don't deserve respect because they give football a bad image, but footballers need to understand that there are many fans out there whose lives depend on their football team and their heroes on the pitch.

Sometimes you are in a hurry and a few fans come up to you and ask for your autograph. You may prefer to go, but you must put yourself in their position and realise how much it means to them. For the sake of staying on for two more minutes, you will make them happy, you will make their day. It is all or nothing to them: if you say 'yes' then they go away with a smile on their face and a spring in their step, but if you say 'no' then you have been responsible for spoiling their day.

I remember the time I was playing golf at Wentworth and when we reached the halfway point there was a fantastic little hut with two girls cooking bacon, sausages, eggs, whatever you wanted. The young caddy who was carrying my bag came to me and said: 'David, those two girls are very shy, but I know they would love to have a picture with you.' I couldn't understand why they were too scared to ask me, so I walked into their hut and said: 'Girls, do you want a picture?' They looked at each other in amazement, but I told them it was no problem and I left them smiling.

I know how much it means, especially to young people, to meet a famous person. I never had this experience when I was a kid because I was in a small village and I never met famous people. But I understand what it means, I can see it in my own son's face if he meets someone important to him. He is a big fan of Manchester United and France goalkeeper Fabien Barthez and of tennis star Andre Agassi (strangely enough, two people who are bald, so I can't understand why he likes them!) and he always wants to ask for autographs. I have had the star-struck feeling myself. My big hero is Michael Jordan, the American basketball star, and when I met him on a golf course once I went up to him and said: 'Michael, I am your number one fan.' I am not scared to tell someone I am a big fan of theirs because if you dream about meeting someone for many years and then one day they are standing in front of you, how will you feel afterwards if you dried up and remained quiet, and didn't make the most of your opportunity? You will go home and say: 'Damn! I missed my chance.'

On a match day at White Hart Lane, the security staff would often come up to me after a game and shake my hand. Why? It was not just because I played for Tottenham, it was also because I gave them my time. Most people think I am arrogant, so it is always a big surprise for them when they meet me to find that I am really very down to earth. They end up walking away saying 'Isn't that David Ginola a lovely person?' So it is sad that they think ALL footballers are arrogant and unapproachable. They judge you without really knowing you as a person, but if they get the chance to meet you they can find out what you are really like and then make up their own minds. Whenever I go to a function, an awards dinner for example, I do not go with a prepared speech. If I have to get up and say a few words I want them to be spontaneous, to come from the heart and reflect how I feel at that moment.

It hurts me that ever since leaving Newcastle I was given a rough reception by the fans when I returned there with Tottenham. The main problem for me is that the fans thought I was leaving because I hated living in the area, and the Geordies are rightly very proud and passionate about their home territory. They forget that I wasn't picked to play in the team for the last four months I was at St James', so my reasons for leaving were based purely on football – nothing else at all. I don't deny it wasn't the best place I have ever had to live in my life; it was a million miles away from what I was used to, but that was not my motive for wanting to leave. I have a lot of friends there and I always had a good time when I went out in the town and mixed with the locals. The people who know me know it isn't true, it is just the fans who do not understand what was going on behind the scenes who felt this way about me.

In a way, and this will sound a little strange, many of the fans who show hatred for me have some kind of admiration for me inside. I discovered this when I was at Paris St Germain and I was able to diffuse a highly volatile situation. We were at the top of the league and we travelled to Bastia, a small club located on the beautiful island of Corsica. When we arrived at the ground there were many banners directing abuse at me. I didn't like these, and as the captain of the team I went to see my chairman. We then went to the Bastia officials and told them that if all the offensive banners were not removed, we would not play the game. So they made the crowd take them down. When we went out to warm up, some of my team-mates were ahead of me in the long tunnel which led from the dressing room on to the pitch, and as they emerged I heard the crowd booing them. But when I reached the pitch and came into view, the noise level rose to a crescendo and was deafening, as the fans vented their torrent of abuse at me. We won the game 2–0, and I scored both the goals and really mesmerised the crowd. It was quite funny because at the start of the game, every time I touched the ball there was a huge 'boooooo!' from the crowd. But as the game went on the home fans began enjoying my skill, the booing got quieter, until near the end of the game when I could hear sections of the crowd actually clapping!

The stadium was being rebuilt so we were changing in portacabins outside the ground. The security people were scared about me going out to the coach, so I was surrounded by minders. There were lots of fans still around, and as I reached the coach a guy who was standing at a nearby bar shouted out: 'Hey, Ginola!' I stopped and said to the security guards: 'Give me five minutes.' They were shocked, and worried for my safety, and didn't want me to go because they would not be able to protect me, but I said to them: 'Don't worry, these people love me.' I walked through the crowd right up to this guy to ask him what his problem was. There was a stunned silence as I stood in front of this man at the little wooden bar in the car park. He was about 45, average build, a typical proud Corsican and I said to him: 'Would you care for something, a drink?' He couldn't believe it but said: 'Can I have a beer please.' I ordered him a beer and said to the other people standing around: 'Guys, anything to drink? I am paying.' They gathered around me in disbelief. I sat there for a few minutes and made friends for life.

'Can I ask you something? Why are you treating me like this? Why can't you be nice? You don't know me and I don't deserve to be abused.'

'David, it is because you are the best,' one man spoke up. 'We are scared of you. Look what you did to us when you came here and won 2–0.'

When it was time to get up and leave they were saying: 'David, please, you should come and play for Bastia, we will give you everything you want.' They then escorted me back to the coach and they were singing: *'Ginola! Ginola!'* as we drove away, waving and clapping. It made me realise that they were booing me because they were afraid that I might play well and harm their team, but when the match was over they had appreciated me as a player. That kind of thing does not compare to the time I was in Paris, and I received hate mail from a Marseille fan, but I shall talk about that later.

The same thing happens to me now in England too. I speak to fans and I know that they respect me as a player, but they don't like me because I don't play for their team – they would like to have my talent at their club. In Paris the two local rivals were Matra Racing and PSG, but there was no serious tradition of rivalry because Matra were a new club, with no real history between them and Paris. It was nothing like the rivalry which exists between Spurs and Arsenal, as that is something which has grown up over a number of years, and I understand the traditions of the two clubs. When I used to live in north London I could not go a day in my life without coming into contact with an Arsenal supporter. But these people were never nasty to me. In fact, I had Arsenal fans who often came up to me and said: 'David, I am an Arsenal fan and I hate Tottenham, but I have to tell you that I think you are fantastic and you should be playing for us instead.'

Getting back to my thoughts on the game, I am scared about football losing its creativity, its freedom and talent. The game is becoming more and more bogged down by tactics and there is no room for freedom of expression. A few years ago the play-makers had a lot of space, but now the tactical play has reduced that. As a supporter of football I want to see players who make me jump off my seat – players like Rivaldo, Gianfranco Zola or Dennis Bergkamp, the ones who make football look so easy. They are the ones I would buy a ticket to watch.

But no matter how talented you are, when you reach a certain level in the game, people have expectations of you and it makes it difficult for you to form relationships in your life. I don't have many friends in football. One of my close ones is Antoine Kombouare, whom I played with in Paris, and who is now a reserve team coach there. We share the same philosophy and he is maybe the only person in my 15-year career who understands me as a person. I see in him a mirror image of myself.

It is very difficult in our job to find people who you can trust. I had some bad experiences in France with people who I gave my heart to. I gave them everything and they stabbed me in the back. For example, after I had the problem with the Bulgaria World Cup qualifying game one of my first managers at Toulon, Roland Cobis, spoke to the press and instead of backing me he said: 'David Ginola? I wouldn't play him in my reserves.' I couldn't believe he could say that.

As a foreign player who makes my living in the English Premier League, I like the fact that a lot of top players have come from abroad to play here. Every club has foreign players and I think it is good when you look at the positive influence they have on the club and how they have helped improve standards in the English game. I think it has helped make English teams more competitive in Europe and English football would lose a lot of its allure if you took away the foreigners. However, if I was the father of a boy who was an apprentice at a big club, I would be concerned about the number of foreigners here as it will make it harder for youngsters to progress. The best ones will get through anyway, but as for the rest, where it was possible a few years ago it will be impossible in a few years. Some players start out as average, but get better throughout their career and this improved quality comes with experience. But, in the future, the clubs will not wait, they will keep the top players and get rid of the average players because there will not be so many places in the first team available. You will have to be good straight away.

I am sure things will be changed in the future because it is not right that teams in the Premiership have seven, eight or nine foreign players in their starting line-ups. It is very important to keep bringing through the young players. You must keep their dream alive. I remember when I was training every day my aim was to reach the first team, but the kids now may feel they have no chance with so many foreigners and so they may decide to go and do something else. You have to find a balance so that you do not kill their dream. It will be harder for them, but that is a fact of life.

I expressed my views on foreign players in the English game when I was invited to speak to the Oxford Union in 1999. People chose their own way of interpreting my comments, but I didn't go there to cause a fuss, I simply accepted the invitation of the Oxford Union who organised it really well and it was a great experience. If some people in the room tried to stir things up, then I cannot be held responsible for that.

We were talking about age, the fact that I wasn't playing in the French team at the age of 33, and I was asked if I felt it should be the same for Alan Shearer and England because of his age. I said: 'Alan Shearer is a big name, but at the moment he is not having a good time for England because he isn't scoring goals. However, people believe in his quality and he is someone who is capable of waking up in a game suddenly and scoring three or four goals. At the moment, because he isn't playing so well, he is staying in the team because of who he is – if he was someone else he would be dropped, but they keep faith with him because they know he is a fantastic player and even if he has a bad time for a while, he can bounce back.'

That was my opinion and I believed it was the truth, but it obviously caused a problem with some people because it made the headlines. I don't think that would have happened in France.

I realise this may sound obvious, but I am in favour of footballers being paid high salaries. I don't just say this because I am a footballer sticking up for my fellow professionals, but I think I can back up my argument with good reasoning.

When it was announced last season that Roy Keane had signed a new contract with Manchester United worth £50,000 a week, it sent a few shockwaves through the game. But not everyone earns that kind of money, only the very top players at the top clubs, and those are the ones who are worth it. So many people outside of football earn a lot of money on the back of the players without giving anything back. When you see the merchandising and the money the clubs earn out of the players, then why shouldn't they earn top money? If you are a top actor you can earn £10 million for one movie – but I never see people saying that is too much money. I am not saying it isn't hard being an actor, but I think it is a lot harder to be a footballer. If a scene in a film is not right, they will do it again ten times if they have to until they get it right. But if you miss a penalty the referee doesn't give you another six chances to score a goal. If I wanted to be an actor tomorrow, it would be possible for me to have a go. But if an actor wanted to be a footballer tomorrow, he couldn't suddenly become one. I started from the age of seven and trained hard to be a footballer. But if I train as an actor from the age of 33, I still have a chance of making it as a good actor after a few years.

I think I could make it as an actor because I always put myself in the position of someone else and that is what acting is about, seeing a role through different eyes. As it happens, I have already been approached to act in films. If I was to pursue that avenue after football, then I would choose very carefully the part I would play. I would never play the role of someone whose character is the opposite of mine, I would have to be close to the role to get into it. I quite fancy myself in films like *Dances with Wolves* with Kevin Costner, or *Legends of the Fall* with Brad Pitt.

The kind of salaries you earn as a sportsman in England are much less than you can earn as a sportsman in America. I never hear people saying basketball players earn too much money – people are happy to pay to go and be entertained by sportsmen, in the same way as they pay to go and see a rock concert. There are 34,000 people going to White Hart Lane to

53

be entertained, so why shouldn't you pay the performers on show good money. The best ones earn the most money, and that makes the younger players strive to be the best.

I like people who excite me, who entertain me. People laugh at entertainers and say they think too much about entertaining and not winning. But if I go to see someone like Michael Jordan he has me jumping on my seat, saying how fantastic he is, and I know he plays to win. He is the only one who can give me that. I watch every single sport when it comes on television, even darts, snooker, cricket and fishing. I am interested in them all, but the only sportsman I saw who took his responsibility in what I call 'the money time', is Jordan. Whenever there were three seconds to go and his team needed a basket, he was the one who asked for the ball and made the shot. He wanted all the responsibility. He showed me the way. I want the responsibility too, so if there is a decisive penalty in the last minute of a crucial match then I want to take it. You have only one life and it is a place for people who dare. People may say I only want to do this to be on the front cover of a magazine or newspaper– but why not? If I am on the front cover it is because I have taken the responsibility and tried to be the best I can. This is not a bad thing. If every single person wants to be on the front cover it is because they want to be successful, and strong, and I don't see any problem with that. The fans deserve something and if they can go home with a happy memory, that is good.

Speaking of penalties, something which has upset me a great deal in recent years is being accused of diving. I look at a lot of games and see so many players diving all over the place without anyone mentioning it. But when it involves me it is always a big issue. It makes me realise that no matter how much people praise me, there are others always looking for a weakness. But I honestly do not dive. I remember in 1999 there was a big controversy when we were playing Wimbledon. Their manager at the time was Joe Kinnear and he really upset me by accusing me of always falling over. That was a terrible thing to say, because I remember the game and I was everywhere. The problem is, when you are a defender playing against me, because I am so fast and twisting and turning my body, you only have to make a faint contact with me and it can knock me off balance and make me fall down. It doesn't have to be a massive foul, but because of the way I manoeuvre my body, one touch can be enough to knock me over. If I made some runs and there was a faint touch, it knocked me over. Like I say, it may not have been a big foul, but it was still a free-kick.

Afterwards, the Wimbledon team blew it out of proportion. Their attitude affected me; of all the things I try in the game, all the positive runs and passes I make, this was the thing people were picking up on. In 1999/2000 I was the most fouled player in the Premiership, the statistics prove it. Yet I could not believe how often there was no referee's whistle. Tottenham never seem to be awarded penalties – in fact, only one was awarded in the team's favour throughout that whole season. I am sorry to say it, but the referees are unfair, and if their judgement is clouded by adverse press then they are not good referees. Even if it isn't a huge foul, it is still a penalty if I am knocked over in the box.

The one refereeing decision which still rankles with me was when I got sent off playing for Newcastle against Arsenal. I shall talk more about this match later, but I had a real personal battle with Lee Dixon and I was being constantly fouled. He was all over me when I had my back to him, waiting to receive the ball, and in my frustration I thrust out an arm which was meant to shake him off. But he went down quite theatrically and the referee saw it as vindictive and ordered me off. In my opinion, I was the victim of an injustice. I was not at all happy with the referee. That contributed to us losing an important game in the title run-in, and I also received a three-match ban for the red card. But because of the way the fixtures fell, I ended up missing almost six weeks. When I came back, I was not the same player, I had lost my rhythm, and I cannot forget that an important refereeing decision – and a bad one in my opinion – had important long-term repercussions for both Newcastle and for me.

To this end I think we need more professional referees. They are not able to see every single incident and I would also be in favour of having an official in the stands watching replays of major incidents and then sending a message to the referee. If a decision wrongly goes against you in the league, then you have enough games over the course of a season to make up for it. But if it happens in a big knockout cup competition, then it can eliminate you and be very costly. The game is too important nowadays in financial terms for clubs to be robbed by a bad refereeing decision.

CHAPTER FIVE

Fame and fortune

'Sometimes it is difficult when people don't realise you
just want to spend a few hours with your wife and
children – they think you are public property
24 hours a day'

If I am being really honest, then I have to say that being a
celebrity is something I don't always enjoy. Don't get me
wrong, I am very grateful for everything I have and I love
meeting people and trying to make them happy. It is just that
being famous interferes with my family life, and that is the one
area in which I wish I could enjoy a little more privacy. It is
always interesting for me whenever I go out in public, to see
the reaction of the people with me to the attention I receive – it
never fails to amuse me. It is flattering to see how women look
at me, and the reaction of the crowd when I arrive somewhere.
I look out the corner of my eye and I can see all the open
mouths. But it is not always me who finds this funny, most of

the time it is the people around me. For example, my wife always laughs when she sees this.

'All these girls think I am living with a sex symbol,' says Coraline, 'but they never see you waking up in the morning, with your hair all over the place – if they did they would soon change their minds! They always see you in good circumstances, but I live with you so it is not the same.'

I think when you live with someone and know them so well, it kills some of the mystique, whereas people who are meeting you for the first time have this fantasy image of you – they dream about where you live, your lifestyle, your sex life. But if you ask my wife she will tell you I am just her husband and the father of her two children, end of story, and she loves me for who I am. She has known me since I was 19, before I had this fame and fortune, and we have grown up together. If she was being interviewed about me for a magazine, I'm sure she would say to all the female readers: 'Leave David alone, because he is just an ordinary guy.'

I am very aware of my responsibilities as a public figure and I give my all when I am at a function, or after a football match. But I care about my privacy. When I go out on my own somewhere I don't mind being surrounded by autograph hunters. But when I am with my family I am very protective of them and I want to devote my time to them. Sometimes it is difficult when people don't realise you just want to spend a few hours with your wife and children – they think you are public property 24 hours a day.

Earlier in the year I took my family to Thorpe Park, the very popular theme park south west of London, and I think the experience we had there summed up my life. We went unannounced, just like any other family might do, but when I arrived I saw the face of the girl behind the cashier's desk light up and I thought: 'Oh no, here we go.' It took 20 minutes to get in after stopping to sign autographs and talk. As we walked in, more and more people recognised me and I could hear them saying 'There's David Ginola!' and I kept getting asked to sign autographs. After half an hour a paparazzi photographer had turned up and started taking pictures, as he hid behind bushes. I decided to confront him.

'I have seen you, so don't try to hide yourself. If you want to take a picture take it in front of me, don't cower in the bushes because you look really silly when you do that. I won't shout at you although I might have the urge to do so because you are not allowing me time with my family.'

Then I went to speak to the woman in charge of the theme park.

'When I arrived you came to me and told me to enjoy myself, but within 30 minutes I see a photographer running around following me.'

She apologised, but it had ruined a nice day out with my family. I am entitled to have this time with my wife and children, but unfortunately it is impossible. Coraline is used to it now, but my son is at the age where he is starting to think about these things and it upsets him. We don't have a great deal of time together so when we do he really wants me for himself and he doesn't understand all these people coming up to me all the time. His view is: 'You have my dad every day, so let me have my dad now.' When I was signing autographs inside Thorpe Park it was hard for us all, because Andrea wanted his daddy to take him on a ride, but I couldn't turn away the young children in front of me asking for my autograph – I did not have the heart to say no. But sometimes I want to say to the parents: 'Can't you please understand, I am with my kids, just like you, and I just want to be able to behave like a normal person.'

I carry my image around with me, but I sometimes wish I could have a mask which gave me a different face when I left the pitch, enabling me to lead a quiet life, to be treated as a person and not like a big-name celebrity. In other words, to be more like everyone else.

A few months ago we went to see Simply Red in concert. When you are with your wife and kids you would sometimes like to be left alone in the corner eating your hot dog and drinking your Coca-Cola, without people saying: 'Look, there's David Ginola, he's eating a hot dog with mustard and onions and drinking a Coca-Cola!' As I have got older, this feeling of having my privacy invaded has grown stronger.

Last year in the summer, I found freedom for almost two weeks. I hired a beautiful boat and went on a cruise with three friends and their wives, no children, just the eight of us and a small crew. There was Thierry Molitor, a friend from my days at the formation centre in Toulon where I studied and trained to become a professional football player. He was a centre-half, and now works for a construction company. There was also Stephane Cohen, a hairdresser and one of the only two people I trust to cut my hair! And the other friend was Olivier Magnan, who owns a restaurant in Guadeloupe, but who was on his honeymoon. They all work hard during the year and this was our chance to relax and unwind.

We started our voyage from St Tropez and followed the French coast into Spain, visiting Majorca and Minorca. We stopped for four days in Ibiza, and when I was walking in the street the people recognised me but didn't hassle me for an autograph. They were just happy to see me: 'Hi David, how are things?' they would shout. 'Are you okay? Enjoy yourself, David!' It was nice that they noticed me without making demands on my time, as if they accepted I was on holiday.

When we were on the boat out at sea it was like being in the middle of nowhere, so I could run around naked for most of the day when I wanted to – just taking care when the women were around! It was like the Kevin Costner film, *Waterworld*, with nobody else alive, just us on our boat in the middle of a sparkling blue sea. Sometimes silence says so much and I couldn't be more happy than I was at that time, in the middle of the sea, surrounded by some of the people who are most important to me – all the things I love the most. I felt like I was living out a beautiful poem that someone had written especially for me. It was very special and these are the moments I appreciate in life.

I am fortunate that my celebrity status brings all kind of opportunities my way, which is why it is important for me to have a good agent, one who cares about their client's image. I am looked after by Chantal Stanley, and we teamed up shortly after I moved to London in 1995. Chantal is French like me, but has lived and worked in London for the past 15 years. When I met her she was already working with many of the French players who were at clubs in England, helping and advising them on everything inside of football and out. I had left my previous agent, Olivier Godalier, and was being represented by a PR company, but I wasn't very happy with what they were doing for me.

As soon as I met Chantal I was struck by how caring a person she was, so I asked her to represent me. We got on very well from the start – she was, and is, very dedicated to me. One of the great things about her is that she is not someone who simply worries how much commission is coming in at the end of the month; her main concern is me and my image. Unlike some football agents, she is very modest and prefers to stay in the background, because she knows that her players are the real stars. The fact that she is a woman working in a male-dominated field does not inhibit her work, as Chantal is very strong-minded . . . and not the kind of person you could walk all over! It is always nice as a man to have an intelligent woman's perspective when you have to make a decision, and I like to think of Chantal as my friend as well as my agent.

Looking after my affairs is a full-time job. Her phone rings all day long and it is not unusual for us to speak five times a day to discuss different engagements or projects. Chantal makes sure that I never have to worry about things. My job is to play football, so she handles all the outside distractions and leaves me free to concentrate on what I do best. She knows that if I am at my best mentally, then I will perform better. She has incredible contacts, and excellent connections in the media and she surrounds herself with good people.

When I finish my playing career I think we will make a good team, as we have big plans for the future. Sometimes I wish I had a clone to help with the workload – imagine, two David Ginolas! Chantal gives me confidence because she has a high opinion of me and tells me I will be even bigger when I retire from football, as I shall have more time to devote to other interests. It is great to have someone working for me who really believes in me and my image.

Chantal is also a talented voice coach for opera singers, and thanks to her I have become a big fan of opera. She works with the Carla Rosa Opera Company in London and often takes me to rehearsals and workshops and I sit there and listen to all the beautiful voices. I am a great fan of opera now and I like to sit on the sofa at home and chill out to the music, which I find very relaxing. I know that Chantal would love to coach me to have a part in one of her touring productions, maybe in the chorus, but I would be afraid of making a fool of myself among such talent. So if I was going to take part, I think I would have to be the producer!

Another dream Chantal has is to arrange a charity concert whereby footballers such as myself sing alongside major opera stars like Luciano Pavarotti. At the moment, I don't think I am good enough to sing alongside someone as gifted as the great tenor (it would be a bit like him playing football alongside me!), but it would certainly be a good laugh if it ever came to fruition. It just shows the wide range of ideas Chantal has.

On the subject of the arts, I was delighted to be asked to become involved in the Monet exhibition which came to the National Gallery in London during 1999. I was invited by the BBC to introduce the paintings and give my own interpretation of them. It was difficult because I don't have all the vocabulary in English to express what I thought was going on in the painter's head when he did the work, especially in front of a camera, but I did my best. When I was interpreting Monet my mind was racing everywhere and it was exciting. I could see how he was not afraid to use a large canvas to express himself, and I could explain how the different colours showed the different moods of the painter day after day. If one day he was happy there was more red and green, and if another day he was in a bad mood there was grey and black.

The Monet exhibition went so well that the National Gallery then invited me to open their Ingres exhibition. I completed a hat-trick of art engagements when the Clore Foundation, in association with the Tate Gallery of Modern Art, asked me to become a patron of 'Artworks' which marked the launch of the National Children's Art Awards. These awards were aimed at all school children throughout Britain, encouraging them to enjoy art directly by visiting the nation's galleries and seeing real works of art. Children were encouraged to submit artwork of their own, and there were more than 45,000 children from 1,500 schools who registered to take part before the closing date of March 1999. I was made an honorary patron of the Clore Foundation, which is a leader in the charity field, and the good work of Sir Charles Clore has been continued by his daughter, Vivien Duffield.

Another interesting invitation I had in 1999 was to open the 35th Notting Hill Carnival. A new initiative was launched, called the Non-Violence Project. This project was already underway in countries such as Sweden, the States and South Africa and is aimed at radically changing attitudes towards violence by inspiring, motivating and engaging young people around the world in positive action against violence. It was quite something for a white man to open an event which is traditionally associated with black people, and I think I showed, in my own small way, that barriers between colour can be overcome.

In America, it is very common for sports people to open a wide variety of events, and I am happy that I was chosen to perform a similar role in this country. Hopefully, it means I am a person who brings a good image to my profession. It was a very emotional moment for me to be presented with the Non-Violence Project Award at the Carnival launch.

The woman who presented me with the award took me by surprise with the speech she made, and I was overwhelmed by her glowing tribute to me and the work I have done in places such as Angola, in my capacity as a United Nations ambassador. And I was honoured with the presentation of their emblem as a souvenir. Martin Luther King's words 'It's not the violence of the few that scares me, but the silence of the many' goes some way to explain why I lend my support to so many humanitarian causes. I also greatly admire the dedication of the British people to charitable causes, and that is one of the reasons I choose to get involved too.

I am often flattered by the wide variety of causes I am asked to help promote. These range from opening a cardiac unit at a hospital and switching on the Regent Street Christmas lights, to being in the body zone at the Millennium Dome representing a healthy body and mind, and being asked by the Home Office and Lord Balsam to back the new anti-hooliganism law which was introduced recently in Britain.

On the subject of law and order, I teamed up with Gary Lineker for an advertising campaign launched by Customs and Excise for Euro 2000. You may have seen the advert which we filmed at Stansted Airport. Gary and I have identical suitcases, mine containing shampoo and his crisps, but the two become mixed up and we both get a shock when we open them in front of customs officials. The idea was to warn people travelling to Euro 2000 to be careful with their luggage, in case others tried to plant drugs on them, for example. I am very proud to say I have never taken drugs of any kind, so this was a campaign I was happy to support.

Among the other benefits of being a celebrity figure are my advertising and modelling contracts. My first taste of this came in my first season at PSG, when I was approached to do my own calendar. My agent at the time thought it would be a good thing for me to do, and it was tastefully done, a mixture of football and glamour. However, I don't think I would do it again, as I do not regard myself as a 'Baywatch' kind of figure. In future, I would only do team calendars.

I then moved on to fashion shoots, and did some work for the Morgan clothes range and did a picture with the model

Carla Bruni. I also posed naked for a magazine called *Glamour*, alongside Yannick Noah. It was a very artistic photograph, very tastefully shot by Mario Testino.

Another photo-related contract was with *Hello!* magazine for two photoshoots. One was Christmas in my home, and the other gave me the chance to have a second honeymoon with Coraline in Bali. We never had a proper honeymoon first time round and this was a nice chance to be together. We were in a beautiful villa overlooking the sea, and we really chilled out, with massages every day and swimming. Time was irrelevant on the island. There were no real set meal times to abide by because there was food and drink laid on whenever we wanted it, any time of the day. I work very hard and it is nice to be able to completely unwind, so this was very enjoyable.

I also joined forces and became friends with Nino Cerruti, who, in my opinion, is one of the best fashion designers in the world. In fact, I signed my contract with him the same day I signed for Newcastle. It was for him that I made my one and only catwalk appearance. Two French rugby players, Emile Ntamack and Laurent Cabannes joined me on the catwalk. It's strange because many people think I have made several catwalk appearances, but that was my first and only one. It was during men's fashion week in Paris at the Ritz hotel. I felt I pulled it off well because I was quite relaxed and cool on stage and a lot of pictures have since been used from that appearance. What nobody realised at the time is that I drank a lot of champagne before going on stage because I was so nervous. Taking a crucial penalty is no problem for me, but appearing on a catwalk is another thing altogether!

This fashion event received mass coverage, with ten rows of photographers – many from England – around the catwalk. At least I managed to look confident, with my chin up and smiling. It was very good to be associated with a company like Cerruti, as they also sponsor Michael Schumacher and the Ferrari Formula One motor racing team. I used to go to Monaco with the Ferrari team and it was a great occasion. I got on very well with Nino's wife, Chantal, who handled all the public relations, and we shared ideas about what pictures would be good to do. I did not renew my contract, however, because the structure of the company later changed, and things just didn't work out for me.

I also did some adverts for Renault cars when I arrived in Newcastle. I love motor racing and was thrilled to receive an invitation to race Alain Menu's Renault Laguna in a British Touring Cars Championship race. Renault invited me as their guest to Brands Hatch to be Menu's co-driver, and also to drive the car. We went to the launch of the new Laguna at the Sports Café in London, and they had made a proper yellow-and-blue driver's suit for me. I had the helmet, the gloves, the boots, everything, and I was ready to make my touring car debut at Brands Hatch.

I asked the permission of my club, Newcastle, if this would be okay. Unfortunately, Newcastle's insurance policy prevented me from participating. As a consolation I was able to go with Jason Plato, Menu's British team-mate, for a spin in a Renault Spider at Silverstone. I hope to get the opportunity to do some rally driving when I am no longer playing football.

When I do hang up my boots I want to take part in the Paris-Dakar rally, one of the toughest rallies in the world, driving across deserts, through forests and all kinds of rough terrain. I love this competition and I would enjoy the adventure.

I also enjoy go-kart racing, but I am too heavy to be really competitive. I am 87 kg but most of the drivers are 60 kg and under. Therefore I would be giving them a significant weight advantage, and this is a telling factor when it comes to cornering because you lose power and it is difficult to accelerate away. I was a guest at the launch of the Daytona Raceway indoor karting track in early 2000, with my Tottenham teammate Jose Dominguez, and I took part in a race. I really enjoyed it, but was beaten by Anthony Davidson, who I believe will go on to become a top Formula One driver.

From advertising for Renault I moved on to L'Oreal, the product with which I seem to be most associated. I would only endorse a product I believe in, and as a matter of fact I bought L'Oreal's 2-in-1 shampoo and conditioner before they ever approached me, because that kind of thing is handy when you are in and out of the shower as often as a footballer, and out of all the products I tried I honestly felt it was the best. I have naturally taken a bit of stick from my colleagues because of what I say at the end of the advert ('Because I'm worth it.') The interesting thing now is that sometimes I will be at an airport and a member of the public will come up to me and say: 'Look, it's the guy from the shampoo advert!' rather than saying: 'Look, it's that footballer.'

These are people who are not interested in football, but they know my face. To them I am not the footballer who does the advert, I am the man from the advert who plays football. And it makes me smile when I hear fans at some football grounds chanting: 'Shampoo, there's only one shampoo!'

L'Oreal are a good company to be associated with, which is why I signed a new contract and agreed to film a new commercial for them for the year 2000. They don't make any unreasonable demands on me. The obvious stipulation is that I cannot cut my hair below a certain length for the duration of my contract. But being a man, at least they can't push me to wear their make-up, for example! When I filmed the adverts I let them colour my hair. This is because my hair has started to go grey. It is a trait I have inherited from my mother, whose hair started to go grey when she was young.

Because of the clause in my L'Oreal contract which says that I cannot cut my hair below a certain length, I could never shave my head à la David Beckham. My first thought was that he must have swapped his contract with Brylcreem for one with Gillette razors! I have a lot of admiration for David as a player. Last season I wanted his shirt for a little boy in France, so I asked our kit man to ask United's kit man to swap shirts, mine for his. I thought this was a fair swap, but he came back and told me that the kit man said David Beckham does not exchange his shirt. I was disappointed by this, and wondered what would have happened if I'd had the chance to ask him for the shirt myself – maybe he would have been happy to have my shirt for his but I never got the chance because he is so closely protected.

It was the L'Oreal advert that got me noticed in America. It was screened in an ad break during the Golden Globe awards ceremony. Afterwards, a reporter from *Newsweek* tracked me down and called my agent, Chantal.

'We need information about David,' he said. 'His advert was shown here at the Golden Globe awards and everyone was raving about him. But they don't know who he is . . . and now everyone wants to know his name.'

So the *Newsweek* reporter came over from America to Tottenham's training ground in Chigwell, Essex, and interviewed me. I featured across two pages in the magazine as a result. He wanted an answer to the question that millions of Americans were now asking themselves: 'Who are you?' I was quite surprised and just responded: 'I am just David, I am from the south of France. I play football for Tottenham Hotspur.' I'm told the Americans had originally bought the L'Oreal advert for six months, but as a result of this interview with me in *Newsweek* they took it for a further six months. It was screened all across the United States and Canada, South America and Europe.

Some friends of my parents went to Austria and said they saw billboards in the street with my picture on them, advertising the shampoo and conditioner. It was a nice feeling to know the advertising campaign had been so successful because when L'Oreal picked me they didn't know how well it would work. I spoke with the boss in France, Mr Rabin, and he told me they had been working with the actress Andi McDowell for ten years, and that he hoped our relationship would last that long too.

Another perk of working for L'Oreal was being invited to the opening of the Cannes film festival two years in a row, L'Oreal being one of the main sponsors of the event. I met all sorts of interesting people, such as the supermodel Kate Moss. But in 2000 the film industry felt there were too many non-movie people attending Cannes, so I stayed away because I didn't want to intrude. Football is a high-profile profession and a lot of players got invited, but I think it was important that the actors kept it as their event and felt at home.

Something completely different for me was appearing as Sacha Distel on a celebrity edition of *Stars in their Eyes*. This is a television programme in which members of the public get the chance to dress up as people who they admire and whose singing voices they resemble. The contestants go behind a screen as themselves and emerge as their heroes. At first, I didn't want to do it, but I discussed it with Chantal and she said she thought it might be interesting. It was a special edition shown on the eve of the new millennium. I thought about it and decided to give it a go.

I didn't do it because I had hopes of starting a career as the new Frank Sinatra, I did it for fun and to show people that footballers have other strings to their bows. It was a very exciting experience, but I was petrified because I was desperate to perform well. I was familiar with the chosen song, 'Raindrops Keep Falling On My Head', and I practised on my own because I didn't have the time like the other celebrity performers to go to Manchester and rehearse. I arrived at the studios on the Sunday lunchtime and after lunch I sang it through with a girl at a piano three or four times. Then it was into make-up and on stage.

Originally I told them I liked Harry Connick Junior and I was going to do a song of his called 'The Recipe for Making Love', but with my French accent the show's producers didn't think it was quite right. I was happy enough with the way things turned out and I know some people might have thought I wasn't very good, but they are the very people who wouldn't have the nerve to do it themselves. I didn't see it as any big deal. Producer Nigel Hall and his team at Granada Studios impressed me with their professionalism, and nothing was too much trouble for them. There was a great party after the show and the atmosphere highlighted how much the people who work on the programme enjoy it. I was amongst the last to leave and I even made presenter Matthew Kelly's day by dancing with his mother!

I also appeared on another television show *Men for Sale*, in which star celebrities are auctioned off to members of the audience. I agreed to 'auction' myself for one reason: because it was raising money for charity. I applaud the fact that lots of wealthy women are happy to go along for a fun night out and bid for their favourite men. But the thing which amazed me was that back home in France they totally misunderstood the purpose of the programme. Here in England, it is simple. A lot of rich women have a good night out and the few who win the bidding get the chance to boast to their friends that they 'bought' David Ginola, or Boyzone singer Ronan Keating, or whichever celebrity they go for.

They don't actually get to take their prize home – and they know that, so there is no way that the woman who won me was ever going to 'own' me for a day, or anything like that. They simply have the satisfaction of knowing they won the bidding, and have donated money to a good cause at the same time.

In France, however, the newspapers picked up on the story and got it all wrong. They actually thought I had prostituted myself for the evening! The way they translated *Men for Sale* was that David Ginola put himself on the market for the richest women in the world – they didn't understand the purpose of the show and thought I was selling myself. It was unbelievable, even a paper like *Le Monde* got it wrong. They just jumped to their own conclusions.

During the summer of 2000 I had to turn down several good offers so that I could have a holiday with my family in Mauritius. For example, the BBC wanted me on their panel for Euro 2000. But if you don't switch off for a month or two, you go out of your mind. There is no point earning money all year round and not taking the time to enjoy it, and as I get older it becomes more important to spend time with my family. That is why we spent a week, just the four of us, in Mauritius and also chilled out in the south of France in June and July. It was also important to get away from it all after visiting Cambodia at the end of May in my capacity as a UN ambassador for the Red Cross.

I have to admit that I worry about money like everyone else. I am not the kind of person who, if for example, owned a profitable company which made a lot money, would hunger after more. I would sell it, and with the money enjoy myself, making my friends and family happy. While I am in demand as a celebrity I believe in maximising the situation to its full potential, because you never know what is around the corner.

I would like enough money to make my family secure. Money doesn't bring happiness, but it can help you to realise some of your dreams. Last year I thought it would be great to have a nice car, so I visited the Aston Martin factory in Newport Pagnell. They showed me everything and I was close to buying a Vantage model. Of course I enjoy driving a nice car, but I am not someone who wants to flaunt my wealth. I am very cautious, so I came home and realised it was not necessary to spend £200,000 on a car at that moment. I would rather save the money now and buy a nice car when I retire to the south of France. The more I earn and save now, the more likely I am to be able to have the freedom to pick and choose what I want later on in life.

Money enables you to achieve your dreams in life and I never stop thinking how lucky I was to be born with this talent. It was a thrill for me to be able to buy my first home in St Maxime. In my earlier years, I had always rented a house there but over my career I saved enough to be able to live in my own home in my town of birth. We built it from scratch and designed everything ourselves. If you look out of the lounge window you can see the sea. Bliss.

I can also remember the thrill I felt when I bought a Porsche. Ever since I was 18, I had been telling myself that I would buy myself a Porsche one day and after nine years in the game that day had arrived. I didn't want to get a loan and pay for it that way, I wanted to wait until I could afford it because then you don't have any financial worries hanging over you.

I don't play the lottery now, but I used to when I was playing for Newcastle. It was because our housekeeper did it every week and she used to get me to join in with her and give her numbers. I used to joke with her that we would win the jackpot and run away together. If I did win the jackpot, say £10 million, I would invest it all in a bank that would give me the best interest. I would play out the rest of my football career and then take a year off with my family and choose what to do with my life.

Money for me means having a choice of what to do, not being a slave to work. It's as simple as that.

There are, of course, other drawbacks to being famous, one of which is being trailed by the paparazzi. Whenever I go to a nightclub, for example, I have to plan my exit almost like a strategic manoeuvre. I make sure there are no girls three metres in front of me or three metres behind. Seriously. I never go out on my own, I always make sure I am with friends, and they make sure that when we enter or leave a place I have one friend in front of me and one behind. This is because a woman I don't know could be innocently walking in or out at the same time as me, and if a photograph was taken of the two of us, it could be manipulated to look like we were together.

I have had two run-ins with photographers, one which didn't turn out too badly for me in the end, and one that did. The first came when I was walking into a club and a photographer started to take my picture. I didn't say anything, I just smiled for him, but he kept on taking shot after shot. So politely I said to him: 'I think that is enough now.' But he just carried on. 'Come on, you have your pictures, that is enough.' But he would not stop, so this time I shouted at him: 'No more!'

That drew the attention of the bouncers who started to come to my aid. I also almost innocuously pushed the photographer away, but he went down theatrically like the proverbial ton of bricks. There was a passer-by on a bicycle who obviously fancied making a name for himself because he rushed over and said to me: 'You pushed him, I saw you push him!' I was angry by now and said to this guy: 'You will get some of the same treatment if you carry on like that!' He carried on protesting: 'I saw what you did, you cannot do that!'

The bouncers calmed down the situation and no further action was taken. But it ruined my night before it had even started. I was too angry to have fun and after a short while I said to myself: 'To hell with this, I am going home'. I wasn't in the mood any more to have a drink and a laugh with my friends. It was a case of me giving an inch, and the photographer taking a mile, and it upset me.

On another occasion, when I first came to England and was less experienced at dealing with the paparazzi, I did make a mistake which I regret. I went to the premiere of the film *Conspiracy Theory* in London with Chelsea defender and my friend Frank Leboeuf and we went on to the party afterwards. It was a very good night. When I came out it was very warm and I was sweating a lot, which I normally do. I was walking out with a polo player who looks a bit like me, and the paparazzi thought he was my brother, so they tried to take our picture. He had a friend with him who was very drunk, and as we were walking to find a taxi there was a photographer following us closely. The polo player's friend then tried to cover my head with his jacket so I couldn't be photographed, but I objected to him doing this and swung my arm to push him away from me.

Unfortunately, the photographer took his picture the moment I was angrily pushing this man away. I had longer hair than now, and was sweating, and my face looked a bit contorted, and so the picture portrayed me in a bad light. But for the paparazzi it was just what they wanted, and the next morning it was splashed across the front page of the *Sun* newspaper with an uncomplimentary headline. I felt I hadn't done anything silly, all I was trying to do was stop someone trying to cover me up. But the picture of me taken at that split-second looked awful.

So after that I knew I had to be careful, and now, whenever I leave a building, I try to walk out with an expression which doesn't show any emotion and just look straight ahead. If someone I am with is talking to me I don't even turn sideways, because I know that even a twist of the head can be made to look bad in a photograph. So, nowadays when I leave an event I walk out and say to the paparazzi: 'Hey guys, how are you?' Or I say: 'Why do you want to take my picture – I am not with a girl, there is no money in it for you, sorry.'

I suppose it was inevitable that, at some point in my life, someone would try to involve me in a sex scandal, and this happened to me in the summer of 1998. I believe I was simply the victim of a woman who wanted to earn some money for herself by claiming she had slept with me. This kind of thing happens every week in the newspapers, to footballers or pop stars or other celebrities, but it is not nice when it happens to you. I never worry too much about myself, I always care about how such lies affect my family, and particularly my wife. I am fortunate that Coraline is not affected by the attention I get from other women. She doesn't believe anything unless she sees it with her own eyes. She would have to see me in bed with another woman before believing something like that – and we both know that will never happen. She takes no notice of what people may say, or what may appear in the newspapers – she is a very smart person and she knows that whatever she hears or reads will be 10 per cent truth and 90 per cent fabrication. It has been the same for years now, wherever we have been. Coraline doesn't check up on me or dig deep into my personal affairs. She doesn't look in my wallet, or check the numbers programmed into the memory of my mobile telephone. She has got me and two children and she is happy, and she believes in me and supports me.

The 'sex scandal' that I got caught up in came during the 1998 World Cup, when I was in France, working for the BBC. I received a phone call on the day before the final telling me that the *News of the World* would be running a story in the morning of how I was supposed to have taken another woman to the house of my friend and team-mate, Jose Dominguez.

I rang Coraline and told her something was going to appear in the paper. She asked me: 'Is it true?' I said 'No' and she said: 'Then that is that.' She didn't care, she accepted my word and dismissed it as the pack of lies it was. The story claimed I had slept with this woman in February, so why was the article appearing in July? The answer was simple, it was done for effect, to sell newspapers, having a French sex symbol who plays football in England embroiled in a scandal on the day France were playing in the World Cup final. It was very clever. I never even saw the newspaper, not because I was hiding from it, but I wouldn't give them the satisfaction of contributing more money to pay this woman. It just amazed me to realise what some people are prepared to do for money, making a profit from something which isn't true. This wouldn't happen in France unless there was undeniable proof, such as a picture of us together. Without that proof, how can you trust someone like this woman? I would have sued the newspaper if I knew it would stop them doing anything like that again, but my advisors told me that even if I sued them and won, it would not stop them from doing something similar in the future if it suited them and would sell papers.

There is one other example that comes to mind of how a newspaper caused me some problems by misinterpreting something I said and deliberately blowing it out of proportion. It happened shortly after I joined Newcastle, in an early interview on Tyneside. I made a big mistake by telling the truth. Some truths are not good for me to tell – they please the journalists but are bad for me.

I was explaining that when I go out in Newcastle there are some very nice girls and I find that they are not as shy as in Paris. Footballers are gods in Newcastle, especially if you play for Newcastle United, and I said that sometimes I meet girls in a bar or a club and I can see by the way they look into my eyes that they want to sleep with me. It was just a feeling I had and it didn't apply to all girls in general. I didn't mean anything by it, but the newspaper made this the main focus of the story.

I didn't get much stick about it, but I realised afterwards that it was not a nice thing for my wife to read. I am just lucky that Coraline is able to rise above everything. She will tell you that her philosophy is simple: 'I have got the husband I always wanted to marry, he has given me two beautiful children and a fantastic lifestyle.' As long as I am a good husband and a good father to my kids, which I like to think I am, then she doesn't worry about what other people think or say. Her only expectation is that when I retire from football I shall be able to spend more time with her and with our children – that is what she is waiting for. Football is my life and that is where we get our money from, so she appreciates that. Yet football is what takes her husband away from her, and so I know she looks forward to a future for us all, away from the game.

CHAPTER SIX

A failure with women

'As a teenager I was shy with women – and,
believe it or not, I'm still shy to this day'

I know some people may find this hard to believe, but my early encounters with women ended in failure – until I met my beautiful wife Coraline. As a teenager I was shy with women – and, believe it or not, I'm still shy to this day. When I was young and met a girl for the first time who I wasn't particularly interested in, I was capable of going up and speaking to her; but when I found someone attractive, I didn't know what to say to her, so I could never make the first move. When I go out on the pitch I know that if my first dribble is successful, then everything will be perfect. But if not, I have my work cut out for the rest of the game, and it was the same with women in my youth. That first contact was always very important to me. If you can make a woman smile with the very first sentence you utter, then that is 80 per cent of the job done, but if she looks at you as if to say: 'What are you talking about?' then you are in trouble. It didn't help that I was a rather puny-looking teenager. While most of my friends had hairs on their chest, I was very thin and under-developed.

The first time I really lost my heart to a girl was at the age of 14, when I was studying at the football academy in Nice. Her name was Bridget Chevallier, and she was beautiful. She was a swimmer, and everybody was in love with her, including me. I didn't even dare imagine that I would one day be close to her, let alone kiss her. She was the cousin of one of my best friends at the formation centre, a polo player called Robert. One day he said: 'Come on, I will introduce you to Bridget.' He took me over to her at school and made the introductions. I was embarrassed and went bright red, but we had a chat about what we were studying and training for, and things went okay. I offered to come and watch her swimming, and she said why not?

So one day I did go and watch her training, and she spotted me afterwards. She seemed pleased that I had gone to see her and after that we ran into each other quite regularly and spoke a lot more. Then one day Robert invited me to dinner at her mum's house. It was heaven. I was deeply and whole-heartedly in love with her, and for the very first time in my life I felt something in my heart for a girl. We stared at each other all through dinner and the way she looked at me I knew she was interested. The next day it was raining and I offered to accompany her to swimming practice. We walked together and reached a place known as 'Lovers' Square'. We stopped and sat on a bench, even though it was pouring with rain, and I kissed her, my very first kiss. It was magnificent and I was jumping around at school all afternoon. I was looking at the other guys and thinking: 'I did it! I really did it!'

I don't know if she was a virgin, but I never even tried to

make love to her. I didn't have a place to take her anyway, as I was in the boarding school and she lived with her mother. The next two weeks were wonderful though – we would meet after school and walk hand-in-hand like lovers do. But then one day she came up to me and said it was over. She said she felt I was smothering her and she wanted her freedom. So that was that. She was probably right, as I was obsessed with her from the moment I laid eyes on her.

The following summer I went home to St Maxime and my friends and I used to spend a lot of time at a holiday campsite because we knew there would be lots of foreign girls visiting. One night there was a disco for the teenagers and I remember there were lots of lovely blonde Scandinavian girls. I met a Belgian girl, however, called Gaetane and we got on very well. A group of us decided to go to the beach, build a fire and cook some food, a kind of teenagers' beach party. My father loaded up his car and provided everything, the grill, the meat, the charcoal, the drinks – what a dad! He helped me get everything ready then left us alone. We were all in and out of the water and having a really good time.

Later in the evening I went for a walk with Gaetane behind some rocks. We were kissing and cuddling, in just our swimming costumes, but it was quite a chilly evening and I was freezing cold. We went skinny-dipping in the sea, and it was like a scene from the film *From Here To Eternity*, with us rolling on the beach and the waves rushing around us. But I was so cold that when it came to trying to make love to her I couldn't manage it – I was a total flop, if you know what I mean! I almost lost my virginity but was beaten by the cold – proving that your first time is not always perfect. We gave up and went back to join the others, and ended up sitting huddled together under a blanket. We saw each other again a few times but never attempted to have sex after that, and then it was time for her to move on. We kept in touch with a few letters to each other, but like most holiday romances it soon fizzled out. Those were my first real experiences with the opposite sex, but I never really thought too much about women in those early teenage years, as I was occupied with so many other things, mainly football, tennis and my other sports, and women only really came into my life a bit later, when my puberty arrived. In the intervening period, until I reached the age of 18, I worked on my physique to help with my football and that gave me more confidence as a person. Then I met Coraline.

I went home again for the summer and was hanging out with my friend Jean-Phillipe. We were on the beach one day, sitting at the bar talking, when all of a sudden I saw the most stunning girl.

'Look at her, she is so beautiful!' I said to Jean-Phillipe.

'Yeah, yeah, we are all desperate over her, but you have got no chance because she is involved with someone, so don't even dream of it.'

I like a challenge so I said: 'What! Who is dreaming? Let me tell you something right now: I will get somewhere with this girl.'

He couldn't see it, and he bet me I wouldn't, so we had a friendly wager.

Nothing more happened that summer, I never spoke to Coraline and she never even looked at me. A year later when I arrived in St Maxime for the holidays, I went to a friend's wedding one Saturday afternoon. We were waiting outside the church for the previous wedding to finish, and when that wedding party came out, Coraline was among the crowd. Before she got into her car, she stopped and stared at me, and I stared back – this was the first time she'd looked at me, and I could tell there was feeling behind the look. I immediately thought back to my bet with Jean-Phillipe a year earlier, and knew I was going to win it.

The following Saturday night her father was organising a fashion show, because he owned a leather-clothing shop, and Coraline was arranging the catwalk and also doing some of the modelling herself. In the afternoon I was having lunch with a group of friends in a Chinese restaurant, and was on the verge of making a move for one of the girls in the group. Coraline was visiting the hairdresser's next door to the restaurant and when she finished she stopped to say hello to her friends, as she knew most of the people I was having lunch with, and it was here that we were introduced to each other for the first time. Some time later, Coraline revealed to me that the only reason she had stopped at the Chinese restaurant was because she knew I was there and she saw it as her chance to be introduced to me, but I didn't know this at the time. She was also checking out this other girl who I was about to start going out with. I knew Coraline was still involved with someone, so I never even thought of making a move at this stage.

We went to the fashion show that night and Coraline, who was working as a model at this time, looked fantastic. The venue for the show was a club on the beach which led out on to the pier. It was a warm summer night and I went to sit on the pier with the other girl and with Jean-Phillipe. The three of us were chatting away, and this girl was cuddling up to me between my outstretched legs, all very cosy. All of a sudden Jean-Phillipe saw Coraline walking along the pier towards us. 'She's coming!' he shouted. With that, I grabbed my girl and pushed her sideways next to Jean-Phillipe, as if to say she wasn't with me – I know it was very rude but I could only think of Coraline's reaction. I asked Coraline to join us and because there wasn't a lot of space she sat right between my outstretched legs, just like the other girl had been doing. I think Jean-Phillipe took one look at us and realised he was going to lose the bet!

While we were sitting and talking, Coraline offered to buy me a drink, so the two of us got up and went to the bar.

'What would you like to drink?' asked Coraline.

'Apricot juice, please,' I replied.

She looked at me, a little surprised. 'Don't you drink alcohol? Most of the guys do.'

'No, I'm a sportsman and I'm not keen on drinking alcohol.'

'Oh, what sport are you doing?'

I told her I was playing football.

'What, you mean you play football on a Sunday afternoon with your friends?'

'No no, I want to make football my job.'

'Is that a job – eleven players running after a ball?'

My heart sank at her reaction but I told her that was what I wanted to do, it was my passion.

We went back to the end of the pier and were alone, as the others had left by then, and we carried on talking. Then her boyfriend came out to tell her he was going home, and to my pleasant surprise she told him to go on ahead without her, and that she would be home later. I knew she was sending him home so she could be with me. We went back inside the club and I wanted to kiss her, but she wouldn't let me – even though I could see she wanted to kiss me too – because she didn't want her friends to see, as it would cause trouble for her with her boyfriend. I suppose she also wanted to get to know me a little better first. She told me that her car was still parked outside the hairdresser's in the town and I offered to walk her back. When we arrived at her car I told her I was about to go for pre-season training to Le Touquet, and I would be away for two weeks. She agreed to meet me when I came back, so I asked her to give me a kiss to wish me good luck. We kissed, a proper kiss, and it was wonderful – and I ran straight to call Jean-Phillipe to tell him he had lost the bet.

I went to the training camp and after that we had a few days off, so I went back to St Maxime and contacted Coraline. We wanted to go somewhere we wouldn't be seen, so we drove to a small town called Cavalaire and spent all day talking. We sat behind some rocks in the marina and kissed. Over time, she gradually eased herself free from her boyfriend and we then started seeing each other properly, but it was at least a month before anything physical happened between us, so I knew it was a serious relationship. I know it sounds strange, but the very first time I saw her I felt she was the one for me.

I was putting pressure on Coraline all the time, even asking her to live with me, but she had just come out of a long-term relationship, so she didn't want to throw herself too deeply into another one straight away. My football took me away for two months, so I didn't see her during that period. But the next time I went back home I was sitting with another girl when Coraline came up to us. I said to the girl I was with: 'Elaine, meet my fiancée, Coraline!' When I said that, Coraline realised what she meant to me, introducing her as my fiancée even though we hadn't seen each other for two months. Coraline didn't know this, but while I was away I had asked my grandmother to walk past the leather shop in St Tropez every day to check up on Coraline, and make sure there were no other men talking to her.

I remember that I told my father about being in love with Coraline before I told my mother. I telephoned home and told my father I was coming to speak to him. I took him into the bedroom and said: 'Daddy, I am in love' and I told him all about her. His reaction was: 'David, love is a beautiful illness!' I think I told him first because I was a little bit apprehensive as to how my mother would react when she found out that her eldest son had another woman in his life other than her. But my parents were very happy for me, and they love Coraline like a daughter, and of course they adore their two grand-children. Even though I am a 'celebrity' my parents don't feel as if they have lost their son. I phone my mother as often as I can to tell her I love her, and I know how proud they are of me as a footballer, and also in my life away from the game.

After a while I left Toulon and moved to Paris. Not long after, I was saddened by the news of the death of my grand-mother and I returned home for the funeral. Coraline saw my car and followed me to the cemetery. She waited for me in her car and when I came out she flashed me with her headlights and we went to have a talk together. Coraline was crying and said: 'I miss you, David.' I was really in love with her and told her to come and spend the weekend in Paris with me, and we had a fabulous time together.

It wasn't long before Coraline got some modelling assign-ments in Paris, so I asked her to come and live with me. The modelling didn't really work out for her, as it wasn't really what she expected and she didn't feel comfortable in the business. I said she didn't have to do it if she didn't want to. She had the choice and she decided to quit and we started living together. The relationship was difficult at first, because I wanted to still have my freedom, to be able to go out with my friends. She didn't enjoy the fact that she would be sitting at home alone and I would not be arriving back until four o'clock in the morn-ing – sometimes smelling of another woman's perfume. In my defence, I can only say I was young and naïve in those days.

EARLY YEARS

Clockwise from top left:
Here I am, a beach babe getting an early taste of the French Riviera, aged 18 months.

I developed a passion for motor cars at an early age – but nobody told me I had to sit down to drive this one!

Horse riding was another one of my early passions, and I used to love the chance of jumping in the saddle.

On the ball, one of my first cup finals when I played for St Raphael, aged 12.

FOOTBALL IN FRANCE

I wonder why they used to call me 'jambes des baguettes' when I played for Matra Racing in Paris?

Who's that Manu? International duty for France with a rather youthful looking Emmanuel Petit, who played for Monaco at that time.

Shielding the ball from my Bordeaux opponent during a game for PSG.

I'm all right, Jacques. Meeting French President Chirac after our 3–0 demolishing of Nantes in the 1993 French Cup Final.

All the president's men. The PSG team are introduced to François Mitterand before the 1995 French Cup final in which we defeated Strasbourg 1–0.

On the wall, as opposed to in the wall, during my French National Service.

On yer bike! Riding pillion on a classic Harley Davidson, with my friend Alain Roche.

One of the happiest days of my life, my marriage to Coraline, in St Maxime, June 1991.

FAMILY MAN

All aboard! Captain Ginola gets ready to set sail. I have a passion for boats and the sea, having been brought up near the coast.

Big brother Sebastien showing why he won't be asked to do any shampoo adverts.

Happy families. A cuddle for mum and dad, my two favourite people.

Clockwise from top:
Gone fishing. Catching crabs in the
south of France is a wonderful way
to relax away from the crowds.

A rather serious pose as I enjoy a
game of petanque.

Are you watching Tiger Woods?
On the tee at my David Ginola
Golf Challenge.

CELEBRITY

If the cap fits! A casual pose from my early modelling portfolio.

Above: Here I am with stars in my eyes, meeting show host Matthew Kelly before being transformed into Sacha Distel.

Left: And you thought I had a lot of hair! Here I am with David Bowie's model wife Imam, at the NetAid charity concert at Wembley in October 1999.

Below: The star of 'Primary Colours', Johnny Hallyday, with his wife Laeticia, meet up with Coraline and me at the Cannes Film Festival.

The tension built up and one day Coraline left the apartment in the middle of the night. She just packed up her clothes and walked out. I was angry and shouted to her: 'If you want to go, then go!' After an hour her mother called me. 'David,' she said, 'even if you don't love my daughter, don't let her be on her own in Paris in the middle of the night.' She told me that Coraline had called her from a telephone box, lost in the city after having walked around for an hour, so I got in my car and went to where she had told her mother she was.

'Come on Coraline, get in the car,' I said on finding her outside the telephone kiosk.

But she refused. 'No, no,' she kept on saying.

'Come on, let's not be silly, come in the car with me.'

She was visibly upset. 'Take me to the airport, take me to Orly so I can go home.'

'No, I am taking you back to the apartment and we can talk about this.'

'I don't want to go there with you,' she said. 'You are too rude to me.'

Suddenly I realised she meant more to me than anything else, and that maybe I did need this stability in my life. I persuaded her to come back home and we talked and talked until we sorted everything out. From then on, I realised I preferred to stay at home with Coraline rather than going out with my friends. They didn't like that and tried hard to break us up, but our bond was too strong. Only a couple of true friends, from Corsica, opened my eyes and told me: 'Coraline really loves you, those other friends are just using you. Don't lose someone who is so important to you.' Until then I had not been able to accept that I was going to spend the rest of my life with this one person, even if I knew it inside. I was trying to put it off until tomorrow, but fortunately I woke up before it was too late.

One regret I have is not doing something special to propose to Coraline. We were living together so it just became a natural progression for us to get married, but I should have done something more romantic. But I shall make up for it in 2001 when we celebrate ten years of marriage, by doing something special with all the people who mean something to me and my wife.

She is half of my success. Knowing myself, if I was with another person I would not have been able to achieve what I have done. Coraline is the opposite of me. She is a steadying influence, and not someone who goes out and throws money around, for example. When I go out of the house I leave a trail of clothes behind me, whereas Coraline is very meticulous, everything is in place. This is good for me, and it is nice to come home to. Coraline is also a very good artist and enjoys painting. I would like to make her feel more confident about her talent because some of her ideas are quite amazing. At the moment she is more concerned about taking care of me and the children to worry about her own interests, so I would like to give her the time in the future to do what she enjoys.

Coraline and I have two children who are very special to us. I believe in treating them the way I was treated when I was young. I saw everything my parents did for me, in terms of giving their love and happiness, and this is what I want to give to my son and daughter. They are so important to me and everything I do is for them. I enjoy being the father of my kids – there is no better moment than when my son or daughter calls me 'papa'.

Everyone has regrets in their life and one of mine is the story of how I missed the birth of our first child, Andrea. When I joined PSG from Brest, Coraline was pregnant and soon after signing I went to Tampa Bay in America for a training camp with the other players. The baby was due on 20 January and I was scheduled to return to Paris two days before, so I thought everything would be okay. Then the manager told us that we were going to have a day trip to Disney World as a treat before we returned. I was in the Mexican Village and called home to see how everything was. Coraline's mother answered the phone.

'David, it is time now. Coraline's waters have broken and we are going to the hospital.'

There was a stunned silence. 'No, not now, not now!' I screamed down the phone.

It was a crazy situation. I was madly shoving coins into a payphone and as I was looking around I could see Mickey Mouse walking around while my wife was going into labour. I asked to speak to Coraline at the same time as I was screaming at my team-mates for more coins. But it was impossible, she was already in labour. It was 10 January and she told me it was freezing cold and raining in Brest, and here I was standing in Florida in shorts and a tee-shirt enjoying 35 degrees of heat. I was in Disney World with Mickey Mouse while my wife was in Brest struggling to give birth to our first child.

I arrived back in France four days after Andrea was born and I went straight to the hospital to see my new son. I went up to the maternity ward in the lift and when the doors opened Coraline was walking right past with the baby. I looked away and said: 'Coraline, I want this to be a special moment. I don't want to see my baby for the first time in a hospital corridor, in front of a lift. Let's go back into the room.' I arrived there with tears in my eyes and when I saw this little person I was really proud, like every father should be. Baby Andrea was no bigger than my two hands; it was an amazing sensation. It is always a bit of a funny story when people ask me where I was when

Andrea was born, and I tell them I was in Disney World. They think 'What the hell was he doing there? You go there with your family, but not with a bunch of footballers!'

So when it was time for Carla to come into the world I made sure I was around to see the birth. I was determined to be there after missing out on the birth of Andrea. I felt ashamed that I had been with my team-mates, miles away from home, when my first child was born. The doctors had decided to induce Carla so I knew she would be arriving on the afternoon of 3 October. I went into training in Paris in the morning, but I couldn't concentrate so I just said to everyone: 'I am going now, don't ask me anything!' I went home and took Coraline to the hospital while her mother looked after Andrea. I was able to experience everything I missed the first time around. I was holding her hand and I was there when my daughter was born. It was truly a moment of extraordinary emotion.

CHAPTER SEVEN

There's no place like home

*'I lived for my Saturday afternoons when I could play
football. The rest of the week was like a waste of time to me'*

Legend tells the story of two lovers, Maxime and Tropez, who
lived together in Provence, a region in the South of France that
sprawls along the Côte D'Azur – the blue coast. One day the
lovers had a terrible argument which meant they would never
speak again, and Tropez went to live on the other side of the
bay so they would not have to be in the same place any more.
So were born St Maxime and St Tropez, the two places where
I spent my childhood. They became two completely different
towns. St Tropez is a famous resort where most of the richest
people in the world go to spend time in their beautiful houses,
driving their beautiful cars and living a beautiful lifestyle, while
St Maxime is a quieter place, more for families, which lives in
the shadow of its more extravagant neighbour. They are both
lovely places and really complement each other well. In the

winter the whole area is peaceful and unspoilt. Then in the summer it is transformed, overwhelmed by vibrant colour, vivid lights and vivacious crowds. St Tropez is a fishing village whose winter population of 10,000 expands almost ten-fold in the summer, creating an amazing ambience and atmosphere. It is infamous for its summer parties, many of which are world-renowned. We can barely recognise our home towns in the summer because there are so many people, so many visitors with all the luxury yachts moored in the harbour.

The woman who put St Tropez on the map as a playground for the rich and famous was the film star and sex symbol, Brigitte Bardot. She thought it was a beautiful, quiet village with a lovely setting, so she built a house which she named La Madrague, in a little bay called Canoubiers. She went out with Gunther Sachs and it was the stories of their parties which soon spread around Europe. As more and more people flocked to the area to see what all the fuss was about, it led to the opening of several bars and restaurants, and so the village grew into a summer resort. At that time, in the early 1970s, it was a healthy resort, because there was no pollution. But nowadays hundreds of boats and yachts come in and out of the bay bringing with them all their rubbish – it makes me sad that in the year 2000 a beautiful beach like the one in St Tropez often has to be closed because of water pollution.

Although I was born in Gassin, in the hills on the outskirts of St Tropez, my family home was in St Maxime. My father Rene and mother Mireille saved all their money so they could buy a plot of land, and on this plot they built their own house, with their own hands. To keep the costs down in those days, houses were built by all the family, friends and neighbours. So one of my uncles did the plumbing, for example, while another was a craftsman who did all the woodwork, from the doors, to the roof, to the floor. It was a small, two-storey house, with a studio downstairs which was rented out in the summer to bring in a little extra money. The studio had its own bedroom, lounge, kitchen, bathroom and garden, so it was an ideal holiday home for vacationers for two months in the summer. It may not have been a really beautiful house in terms of grandeur, but for me it will always be the best one in my life – a proper family home, because my parents worked hard to make sure we grew up in a nice environment. They still live just as happily there today, and I couldn't bear to see them sell it.

I shared a room with my brother Sebastien, who is four years younger than me. My parents had their own bedroom, there was another room for us to study in, plus a lounge, kitchen and bathroom. A lovely little garden surrounded the house and I have fond memories of a cherry tree in the middle of the garden. I recall climbing the tree to eat the big cherries that grew on it, climbing back down again with the red cherry juice stained around my mouth. There was also a fig tree, so if I wasn't eating the cherries I could eat lovely figs instead. I remember in later years that the cherry tree had to be cut down, and that was one of the saddest days of my childhood life! But in the garden on the top level of the house there is still a tree there which I planted many years ago. It has grown tall and my parents proudly refer to it as 'David's tree'. The garden on the level below was also my first football pitch, as it was here I kicked a football with my brother and all the neighbours.

When I look back now at where I lived I can remember that it was a very close community, in which everybody knew each other for years and shared a cup of coffee together or borrowed a cup of salt, and forever helped each other out. My memories of the place are that it was not very big, and it was easy to get around, with virtually no traffic. I travelled everywhere on my treasured bicycle, one of my early Christmas presents, and it never took more than five minutes to reach anywhere – the harbour, the shops or my school. My grandparents also lived in St Tropez and I could easily travel the 12 km from my house to theirs. Everything was accessible and it was perfectly safe for a small child to ride everywhere on his bicycle. It was a perfect place to grow up. The summer time was brilliant and in the winter we were two hours from a skiing resort, so we could indulge in another passion.

I will never lose touch with my roots and occasionally I still have flashbacks to when I was a teenager. When I first went to Nice, I loved to go out on to the football pitch first thing in the morning and breathe in the smell of the freshly-cut grass. Then I would put a leather ball to my nose and smell that too, just appreciating the smell of the things I loved. So some mornings when I arrived at Tottenham's training ground in Chigwell, I would stand there on the grass and take a ball and inhale. The two great smells let my mind drift back to 20 years ago and all those moments when I have struggled, and how I have come through them. It is important to relish the little things, the things which gave me the passion for football, the grass and the ball.

I was – and still am – very close to both my paternal grand-parents, Julliette and Desire, who are now still living in St Tropez at the golden age of 88. They are brilliant, and I have loved listening to all their stories over the years. The thing that makes me happy is that after so many years of working hard, they are now able to afford to go to the finest restaurants every week, and enjoy their late years together. I love them very much and there is nothing more I would not want in the world than their happiness. Nobody can be more proud of me than my grandfather and my grandmother. My grandfather has kept several scrapbooks full of newspaper cuttings all about my career over the years. He is the only one who has pictures and stories from when I first played football at the age of five. Coraline now sends him cuttings from England and he sits in a little office in his house with his scissors and glue and meticulously updates his books, with the place and date of the relevant picture or article. Every time I go and visit them we open the books and I sit with him and talk about the things in them. I feel alive when I see my grandparents, I feel loved. My grandmother is like the traditional fisherwoman: 'Buy my fish, my fish is the best!' Everything is black and white to her, there is no in-between. She either loves you or she doesn't – and you know about it if she doesn't. She is very straightforward, but very fair, not a hypocrite. She can be in the car and another driver can be annoying her, and she will let fly with an angry tirade; it's a hilarious sight. It always stirs emotions of affection in me when I talk about my grandparents.

One of my happiest memories is of my grandfather's boat, and the two of us would spend many a weekend on the sea, diving for shells. For the people in the south of France it is very important to have a boat. As well as its practical uses, such as fishing, it gives you the freedom on your days off to go to different places. My grandfather put all his money into his boat, and it was his pride and joy. It was 30 feet long, with beautiful wood panelling. It had a cabin, toilet, and a kitchen, and we spent many Sunday afternoons on this boat. He named it Dadibanou, which was a combination of the two pet names the family had for Sebastien and me. Sebastien could not pronounce my name as a baby, and called me 'Dadi' instead of David, while he was affectionately known as 'Banou'. I used to get so excited on a Saturday night that I couldn't sleep.

Weekends were so important to me. On a Friday night I would pray for good weather on the following day so I could play football, then I would do the same again on the Saturday night, praying for good weather so we could go on the boat with a blue sky and immaculate sea. It was a beautiful setting, going to the marina and getting the boat ready. Then we would sail off to a quiet beach somewhere, go fishing and swimming and then cook and eat the food we had prepared. People in the south of France know what is important for them, they decide early. They work for a house, then if they want a boat they work to buy a boat. Some people spend all their money travelling around the world. My grandmother has never been on an aeroplane, she has never wanted to nor felt the need, and my grandparents were happy to put all their money into their house and their boat. These were their luxuries.

My father and mother both worked in a factory situated just two minutes from the entrance to St Tropez which built torpedoes for submarines. My mother studied for exams, but my father started working in the factory from the age of 14. If you speak to anyone from this era you will find that they all worked in this factory at one time or another, it was just a natural progression for them to go there and start earning money as soon as they left school. My grandfather worked in this factory, my father worked in it, my cousins worked in it, and if I had not been blessed with a talent for playing football then I am sure I, too, would have ended up working in this same factory, making torpedoes. It was for kids who had no other opportunities in life, a ready-made work place on your doorstep, allowing you to stay on in your homeland. Unless you were someone who opened a tourist attraction in St Tropez, there was no other industry for you. My mother and father worked very hard. I have happy memories of how close they were. At six o'clock every morning I would hear my father take coffee and biscuits to my mother in bed, before kissing her goodbye and catching the bus to work.

Although my mother is French, where she hails from is right on the Italian border and there is a strong Italian influence. Our characters are very much alike – she shouts, I shout. Every Sunday we would spend from 9.30 in the morning until one o'clock in the kitchen. It was a ritual. We often cooked pasta – but not pasta from the packet, this was real, fresh pasta – and we baked cakes. Sunday was the family day and because we were not overflowing with money to buy ingredients we would prepare our own meal with sauces and wine, real Provençale, healthy food. Then my father, mother, brother and I would sit around the table and enjoy it. Afterwards we would go for a walk on the beach, or into the forest and collect mushrooms. I learned how to cook and now, with my family, I do the same. My children have their hands in the flour and we bake together. It is very important to me and stems from my family's Italian origins – my father's family are from Genoa. In Italy everything revolves around 'la mamma, la pasta, I bambini'. It's a large part of their culture. I was, and still am, very close to my mum. I remember that if I did badly in a test at school I would lie awake in bed, crying and worrying, unable to go to sleep. She would hear me and come in to my room to see what was wrong. I would say: 'Mummy, I scored only two out of 20 in my maths test today,' and she would tell me: 'Everything will be okay, you will do better next time. Always remember to tell the truth, because then you shall sleep better.' In my life, whenever I have found myself in a bad position, I have come out bigger and stronger as a person, as if some force inside me took over automatically and helped me through. My strong mind has taken care of me without me having to push myself.

My first memory of football is fixed not just in my brain, but also in my nose. My father was a defender for our local team, Association Sportive Maximoise (ASM), and my mother would take me to watch him play every Sunday afternoon. Through our shared love of football, a strong bond was formed between my father and me. I was allowed the treat of accompanying my father into the dressing room, where I was captivated by the heady smell of pure camphor oil which they used to rub on their legs. That smell meant everything – better than perfume – and I used to sit near my father, watching him get changed and rubbing the oil on his legs. I was exhilarated by the special aroma and would tell myself: 'One day, I want to have this oil on my legs as well.' I didn't have to wait too long for this early ambition to be realised as when I was seven I asked my father to rub some oil on to my small thighs one day before a game I was playing for St Maxime in the Gulf Championships. It made me feel like a real footballer for the first time in his life and I walked on to that pitch with my chest puffed out, so proud. I always stood out on the pitch anyway, as I was dribbling past everyone and scoring six or seven goals in a game.

My father played at right back for ASM and continued until he was 38 years old. In some ways I suppose that is ironic, as he would have had to mark me if we'd ever played against each other! As soon as I was old enough to leave the house on my own I would ride my bicycle to ASM's home ground, the Stade Gerard Rossi, which almost became my second home. The grass had worn away from the pitch, there were tiny stands, a cramped dressing room and a little bar selling crisps for the ground, but to a small boy like me this was my Parc des Princes, my Wembley.

I was passionate about football from an early age. From

about two years old, as soon as I could walk, I was kicking a ball about. I have vivid memories of loving football from the moment I figured out how this plastic round thing could move – I think I was born to play football. It was my father who introduced me to the game when one day he just kicked me a football. We played together and he asked me what I thought. I replied: 'Yes, I like it,' and from then on I was never without a football tucked under my arm, always in the garden practising my skills. My father never pushed me, he was happy to let me develop at my own pace, but then he never needed to push me because I was that keen. He always said: 'My son will do what he wants to do in his life.' But I am sure he was always desper- ate for me to become a professional player, as it would help make up for the opportunity which passed him by in his youth. He always had dreams to be a professional footballer himself, but when he was growing up in the mid-1940s, just after the War, life was too difficult to think of making a living as a football player and he had to work hard instead – it was just too unrealistic in that era to think beyond earning the next few francs. People needed security and money to feed their family, and I am sure that if he had told my grandmother he wanted to pursue a career playing football, she would have replied: 'No chance, you don't live in a big city and you have to work because money is too important.' At this time there was not so much money in football, and living in St Tropez was too far away from a big city like Paris or Bordeaux, where you had more of a chance to play football. I remember how my grand- parents took me to training sessions or trials when my parents were at work and I was in the back of the car leaning forward between them, and my grandmother would say: 'Why are you bothering with all this football nonsense? It won't pay. Why don't you get on the beach, become a beach manager?' And I would reply: 'Mamie, when I'm a star, you'll be so proud of me.' She still remembers that conversation today. My parents have always worried about what people think of me, and still do so today. When I was young, people came to look at me and said to my mum: 'What a lovely girl,' because I had these lovely eyes, and in the end I got so fed up with it that I would just pull my pants down to show them their mistake. They would then say: 'Oh, sorry, what a lovely little boy.' It is important for me to send a message to other parents by telling them how my own mother and father never put pressure on my by pushing me, they were always there for me every time I needed them and even when I didn't. My father never said: 'You HAVE to become a footballer,' he trusted my quality and he let things take care of themselves.

I know that when I was offered my first professional contract it was as much a dream come true for him as it was for me, and he has remained so proud ever since. He was my major influence early on and provided me with the right foundation to do what I do today – he gave me the hunger for football. When people spoke to him about me, they said: 'Rene, where does David get his skills from, because you were awful! You couldn't do one quarter of the things your son can do!' But on the pitch he gave 150 per cent. They called him 'Atilla' because the grass never grew under his feet and if the ball got past him then the man didn't. The doctor who brought me into this world was a fantastic artist, and he used to draw adverts around the town to publicise the weekend game. I always remember seeing one of my father, the big, strong defender, holding a tiny baby, me, as the advert for the game ahead. After all those years when I used to stand on the touchline watching him, the roles were reversed and he used to come to watch me play every weekend. He was always very positive to me but made sure I kept my feet on the ground, and his wisest words of advice were: 'Don't lose sight of what is important in life.'

My father never had to push me, like other fathers might have to do with their children, but I do remember how he needed to give me a kick up the backside to get me going in matches. I always say I was like a diesel engine, I needed a few minutes to get warmed up. I used to stand in the middle of the pitch and watch the first ten minutes pass me by, taking in everything around me. My father used to watch on the side and suddenly he would shout: 'Hey, David, the game is on, you know!' He would tap his watch and tell me it was time to get started, and that did the trick as I snapped into action and began popping up all over the field.

I think my talent is just a gift I was born with. I have always had the ability to pick up a trick quickly and I can learn how to do something in just a couple of attempts. I played football every evening in the street outside my house with my friends. In the summer we would kick the ball around for hours, until the sky darkened at about 10.30 pm. The game was interrupted only if a car came by and we all rushed to the side of the road until it passed. Sometimes we played against a nearby wall, marking out goals and inventing rules; or else, not far from my house there was a patch of ground near a river which belonged to a holiday camp. It was used as a play area for the guests and it was an ideal pitch for us. We scratched out goals in the ground and had our own little stadium to play in. I still see kids with footballs in the same places now, although it has since been re-laid with Astroturf. It was surrounded by a vineyard, so in the summer we would stop on our way home and pick the big, sweet grapes to eat. There were also peach trees, so we picked lovely ripe peaches too. The other thing we used as our goal sometimes was the gateway to my house. The gap between the gates was perfect. The only trouble was that the windows to the house were directly behind, and I lost count of the number of times we smashed them. We used to close the shutters on the broken windows, leaving my mother to find an unpleasant surprise to greet her the next day.

My mother will tell you that she knew I was going to be a footballer from the moment she first felt me inside her stomach. She could feel me kicking all the time, I had such powerful feet. Then when I was born and she took me out walking, an old man came up and told her I was going to grow up and be very big and strong – he could tell this because I had such big hands. Maybe I should have become a goalkeeper with such big hands, but that wasn't my game, I preferred to be dribbling with the ball and I would score goals rather than save them. I demonstrated some skills very early on, from the age of about five, and my parents could tell I had something by the way I would shoot the ball.

My parents still have my very first pair of football boots. They are tiny, but perfectly formed. They are black with moulded studs and are so small they fit in the palm of your hand. They were bought for me by a friend of my father, Marc Bourrier, who was the coach at St Maxime. He had a son the same age as me and we used to play together, so he bought us a pair each. I treasured those boots and used to go to bed with them every night. It was only once I was asleep that my parents would come into my room and prise them away from me.

Although I enjoyed my kickabouts, nothing can take the place of competition. I lived for my Saturday afternoons when I could play football. The rest of the week was like a waste of time to me and the most important thing was a game on a Saturday. Even at seven years of age I had my routine. My father did everything to make sure my kit was preened, my boots gleaming, my towel folded and my bag prepared. It was very important for me to feel good, to look elegant. I had to be immaculate, right down to the little bit of lace turned over the top of my socks. My parents always did their best to give us what we wanted, within reason, such as the right football boots, because they were living for their children, and we appreciated what we had. When Saturday came I would wait in the kitchen and focus on the game ahead. I sat on the table, concentrating, staring straight ahead, miles away. If the weather was bad my father would come in and say: 'David, sorry, no game today.' I would run and lock myself in my bedroom, crying all afternoon.

I wanted to look like Michel Platini, my boyhood hero. I used to call him 'the curly-haired one' and I wanted to have curly hair, just like him! I used to say to my mother: 'Why can't I have curly hair, like Platini?' and I used to ask her to try and curl my hair with her tongs. I had pictures of him all over my bedroom wall, and tried to model the way I looked on him.

I want to win everything. I was, and still am, a very bad loser. I prefer the game to have an edge, with rules and a referee. I want competitiveness all the time. Whether it be tennis, golf, or a game of cards, I need to win. It must be a pain in the neck for my friends! They might say: 'Hey, let's just have a good time.' But if they want to have fun they will have to find someone else to play with – although I don't necessarily think it is a bad thing that I am a bad loser. My parents were shocked sometimes because I was always ready to fight for my cause. They would say: 'David, calm down, sometimes you have to compromise.' But I was stubborn and would simply say: 'No.' I cried so many times because for me it was impossible to lose. If I played tennis for example against someone much better than me, I never knew when I was beaten. I would cover every inch of the court to return that ball – my father couldn't believe it. I would be so annoyed if I lost the first set I would try even harder, and that would frustrate the guy on the other side of the net so much that he sometimes would give up.

I don't want this to come out in the wrong way, but I was the kind of child who was good at all physical pursuits. Everything I tried I took to naturally and was successful. Every winter we went skiing and I entered some slalom competitions. I was good, and so when I was 13 I was approached and asked to go to a sports and study centre in Moutier to train to become a professional skier. I actually wanted to be a skier at this time, but then when I went back to St Maxime and started playing football I knew that was what I really wanted to do. At school I played handball, volleyball, tennis, golf, and I was good at all of them. I really had a choice of what I could do, but football was my main passion. It must have been hard for my parents to know if I was making the right decision when I had so many choices.

I used to sulk if I didn't get my own way and made my parents' lives a misery at times. One time I wanted a new skateboard, so I got into a fit and a sulk. I wanted everything and I wanted it yesterday – I am still like that – and after a while they just couldn't take it anymore and gave in. My parents still have three of my old skateboards at the house. When I wanted things I described them, drew them on paper, cut them out for my parents to see. I was very particular, very fussy. Looking back I can see how at times I must have been a difficult child.

My father always said that was the difference between me and my brother, Sebastien. I never had to be urged by my parents to do anything, whereas with him it was always: 'Come on, you have to do this.' He would sigh and say: 'Oh, okay then.' But he had ability too, and the same opportunities as

me. He played as a centre back and had a lot of the right qualities, but mentally he didn't want it. When I watched him play
he surprised me because he was very tough on the pitch – the
contrary to me. He was a hard defender, always tackling. He
was a very good tennis player but to show you a comparison
with me, if he was two sets up and 5–0 ahead in the third, my
father used to say: 'He will lose the game.' He doesn't have the
killer instinct to want to walk on his opponent rather than lose.
You have to have that cutting edge if you are going to make it
to the top. Sebastien's potential football career was cut short by
injury, so my parents encouraged him to try other sports. He
excelled at water sports and is now a qualified sailing coach,
although he is able to teach all sports.

My brother lives in my shadow all the time and probably the
only problem I have in my life now is that I don't really know
him, but that stems from the fact that I left home at 13, while
he was only nine at the time. This is something I shall regret
until I die. We never got the chance to form that bond between
two brothers going into their teenage years together, helping
each other. If I had stayed in St Maxime instead of going to
Nice, I would have been close to him and helped him out.
When I was 17 and he was 13, I could have talked to him about
girls, or other things important to a teenager. But when you
live in a small village and have an opportunity to go to a big
city and try to become a football player with a professional
team, it is something you cannot refuse. I think that my
parents gave me more of their attention, although it was not
something they were conscious of, because they spent every
weekend travelling to Nice to see me, and I always worried
about how they could find the right balance between what they
should do for their two sons who were separated. My brother
lived his own life and formed a relationship with a girl, Isabel.

She was from Monaco but she came to live in the studio in our house, so they could be together. Her parents ran a tourist attraction, the trains which tour Monaco, and eventually they asked Sebastien and Isabel if they would like to go and live there and run the business. They accepted the offer and now run a successful family business. They were married in January 2000 and are very happy. You can never get the past back, and I feel a little bit guilty about the lost years with my brother, but we are much closer now. My brother is just like me and we have the same expressions and features, although he has short hair.

When I was aged nine and at school, my teacher set us an essay topic with the question: 'What do you want to be when you grow up?' Most of the kids talked about being a fireman, doctor, hairdresser or air hostess, things like that. But I said I wanted to become a footballer. I said things like I wanted to earn money and buy a house for my parents. I wrote: 'Above all I want to play football, to be a professional in a big team, like St Etienne. I would like to be on the pitch with my friends, preparing for the big matches with our coach, who would give us advice for defeating our opponents and finishing first in the championship. It is only a dream, but I hope it will come true.'

My teacher was very friendly with my parents and told them: 'David wrote an essay saying his ambition was to become a football player. This is the first time in my whole career I have ever heard of a child saying this.' That was because in our village the opportunity to become a footballer just didn't present itself. She saw in me at nine years old the determination in me to fulfil my dream, and if you talk to her today she will tell you that she and her husband, who was also a teacher there, always believed I would become a footballer, because they saw I had it in me when they used to watch me in the school playground from the window, practising and playing with a ball all the time. One of the things which inspired me to write that essay was watching a classic European Cup tie on television. It was St Etienne – the team who were doing well in France and Europe who we supported – against Liverpool, with Kevin Keegan, Terry McDermott and Co. I always wanted to play for teams I saw on TV and I was convinced St Etienne were the team for me. They beat a vintage Liverpool team 1–0 in France before going down 3–1 at Anfield. The football throughout the tie was beautiful, and little did I know then that one of the Liverpool goalscorers would have such an impact on my life almost 20 years later.

The first time I fell in innocent love was at school – with my English teacher Madame Bonnemain. She was beautiful to me, the way she spoke, the way she moved on the raised platform in class like a dancer. She was brunette and had a lovely body, with nice eyes and a pretty face. I used to sit in the front row of her class and stare at her all the time, to the point where it unnerved her. Whenever she asked a question my hand would be the first in the air, urging her to choose me. She knew I was staring into her eyes and so she used to look back into mine, but it was always she who had to turn away first and look at the floor. She even called my parents to tell them that I made her feel a bit uncomfortable and asked them to have a word with me. My schoolboy crush on her certainly made me more interested in learning English. I liked History and Geography too, with all the colourful maps and learning about the resources of different countries, because I was always curious for knowledge, but the teachers of those subjects never had the same appeal as Madame Bonnemain – mainly because they were males!

I had a good all-round education – mathematics, physics,

natural science, philosophy and French literature, such as Charles Baudelaire, Artur Rimbaud, Alexandre Dumas and Jean-Paul Sartre. My philosophy teacher thought I was something of a poet, as when I wrote, my thoughts would spring off in every direction. When I took my exams, my text was a poem by Baudelaire called 'L'Albatross', all about the destiny of the poet. I had to explain what the author meant, and analyse why he said it. I found I had a flair for this; I can read something and understand the context very quickly.

I think the things I learned as part of my education were important. Now I can have a conversation with anyone about anything. I am interested in historical stories and real-life stories, and I like looking deep beneath the surface. My favourite films include *Schindler's List*, *The Mission* and *JFK*, because they are based on real events which I find fascinating. Everybody should know the history of their country, the wars and the problems it has faced. I think it is an important part of life and I cannot believe that some children in France do not know the history of the French nation.

If I was going to carry on studying rather than become a footballer, then I would have liked to have been a lawyer. I would enjoy fighting for justice and think I would be very good at standing in front of a jury and arguing my client's case. The one problem is that I would have to accept in my own mind that my client was innocent, because if I knew the person was guilty of a serious crime, such as being a rapist or a paedophile, then I would not be able to live with myself if I defended them. People who abuse children deserve to be locked away forever. I feel so strongly about this that I can sympathise with fathers who seek their own retribution even when it means going to jail.

Another passion of mine as a boy was comic heroes. I used

to spend every single franc of my pocket money on my favourite super-hero comics, and somewhere in my parents house there is a box full of these old comics. I loved them all – X-man, Captain America, Iron Man, Silver Surfer, Spiderman, Daredevil. I loved reading the stories of the Fantastic Four. I was good at drawing and I would take my time drawing all my favourite characters, throwing the sheets of paper away and starting again until I got it right. I loved the power and strength of these characters and in my head I wished I could be one of them. I think I would have liked to have been the Silver Surfer, because he was always calm, but had all the powers. But I hated dressing up, so I never tried to wear any of their outfits. I was a stubborn child and I remember I was invited to a fancy-dress party once. My mother tried to draw a moustache on me as part of my costume, but I fought with her and cried because I didn't want her to. Eventually I gave in, and liked it, and that was typical of me, always saying no, but then when I did relent I usually liked whatever it was. When I wanted something badly, I made my parents' life a misery. One time I wanted a skateboard but they said no. I carried on and on at them until finally they gave in and I got my way, but when I think about it now I am not proud of how I behaved.

When I was 11 years old I was invited to play in an international football tournament for a team from St Raphael, a nearby town, and this was when I had my first experience of playing as a 'ringer'. Officially I was not allowed to compete because I was registered with St Maxime, but the calibre of the opposition included teams representing AC Milan and Barcelona. I really wanted to play in the competition so I played under a false licence, taking on the mantle of a boy named Eric Boyer, who was registered to play but unable to. I really turned on the style as we won the event. There was an awards ceremony and all the teams lined up on the pitch. I was messing around with some of the other players while all the formalities were taking place. Then it was time for the Player of the Tournament trophy to be awarded: 'The player of the tournament is ... Eric Boyer!' came the announcement over the tannoy. Of course, I forgot this was me, so I carried on talking. 'Step forward, Eric Boyer from St Raphael!' came the announcement again. Suddenly one of the other players realised what was happening and elbowed me in the ribs. I shot both my arms up in the air and shouted: 'Yes, it is me, I am Eric, I shall collect my trophy!' To make matters worse, although it only adds to the humour of the story, one of the scouts from Milan thought I had played so well that he started asking where he could find the parents of Eric Boyer, to find out if they would be interested in letting their son sign for the Italian giants. I was ushered away quickly and quietly, but I hear that to this day Eric Boyer has been able to tell his children how the mighty AC Milan once tried to sign him as a schoolboy!

I had to wait only two more years before I did get my big break, and the chance to sign for another professional club. Each year there is a regional selection and a scout from Nice named Eugene Centurion came to watch me play. He was a big man and had a droopy moustache which made him look like Charles Bronson, and he scared me a little. But he liked what he saw and at the end of the trial he came up to me and asked if my parents were there, as he wanted to speak with them. My heart was beating faster than I had ever known before. I told him that my grandparents had come to collect me, and that he could talk to them. He arranged to visit my house so he could ask my parents if Nice could sign me for their 'centre de formation' a kind of football academy. He had to come to my house twice, because my parents were out the first time, and the second time I was listening at the door as he told my mother and father how much he wanted me. It was a professional club, in France, not too far away and I was very excited. My father was obviously interested, but both he and my mother were concerned it would interfere with my education; as a 13-year-old there was no guarantee I would make the grade. The scout explained that I would still attend a normal school, but I would be coached at the club in the evenings and play for them at weekends.

Mr Centurion told my parents: 'Opportunity usually comes knocking on your door only once in life, never usually twice. However, I have come knocking twice and I want you to please think about it, because I will not be back a third time. I urge you not to waste this chance.' I heard my mother at first say 'No' and I could see my dream slipping away, so I came into the room and said: 'Mummy, you must let me try – please.' I begged them to say yes and to let me go. My parents wanted me to stay at home and carry on like I was, but I was watching professional players on television and I couldn't imagine a better opportunity than this. My parents later told me that they felt this was the turning point in my life, when Mr Centurion warned them not to turn away Lady Luck, in case she never came knocking again. I was determined to try, but when I look back I sometimes wonder if I made the right choice. I was only 13 years old and at first I thought I would have no problem moving away, as Nice is only an hour from St Maxime. But at that age you do not have the necessary experience to make a sound judgement on your career and maybe it was an unwise choice because I wasn't mature enough for it.

Now, at the age of 33, I realise that if I could do it all again I would make a different choice. I would definitely have tried, but I would have gone later, maybe after a couple more years in St Maxime. I was a child, not really an adult yet in body and mind and with the benefit of hindsight it was too big a decision for a naïve youngster to make. It was time to fend for myself and most of my new friends in Nice were more mature than me. There is a big difference between growing up in the city and in a village. When I arrived in Nice I felt like one of the cinema characters from Smalltown, USA, who wanders goggle-eyed around the New York metropolis. If I have something to say to parents now who want to put their children through a football apprenticeship, I would say wait until you are sure they are old enough to cope. The one positive thing to come out of it was that it made me stronger. I toughened up to some extent and was no longer such an innocent. Experiencing confrontation also game me a certain maturity.

I owe a big debt of gratitude to Eugene Centurion, because he was the man who discovered me. He later left Nice, but after I was rejected by the club and then made it as a success he was invited back by the chairman, Mr Innocentini, who recognised his talent-spotting ability. Eugene is now the assistant manager at Nice and is in regular contact with my parents. He tells them how proud he is of me, and the fact that he saw my potential all those years ago.

As I said, the apprenticeship at Nice played a big part in building my character. But there was another experience which also moulded me into the person I am today. That came when I was 20, in my first year with Matra Racing in Paris, and I was called up for my year of national service.

In France military service used to be compulsory. It was regarded as important to contribute in order not to be seen as unpatriotic. However, professional footballers were given the option of exemption from service and I could very easily have made that choice. I knew my parents wanted me to do my national service – my mother thought I might need the experience in case I didn't make it as a footballer – and I was happy to go through with it when I went for my interview. I was seen by the sergeant in charge.

'I see you are a footballer, so I shall sign your exemption certificate.'

'No, that's not what I want,' I said.

He was somewhat taken aback. 'Are you sure? Most footballers do not bother.'

But I insisted: 'Yes, I am sure.'

I started in the winter, and was assigned to a special battalion for professional sportsmen. We were at the army base from Monday to Thursday and then had the weekend off to play our sports. But the first three weeks were spent training like any other regular soldier and it was a bit of a culture shock for me. I had to have my hair shaved very short, and then cut every week to keep it that way, as well as always being clean-shaven. We were woken every morning at 6.30 and had to attend the drill where the flag was raised. Every day we were taught how to march together in step, 'One-Two, One-Two' and how to stand to attention and present arms. I didn't like any of it and couldn't apply myself to the training. I do not like taking orders, and I hated being called 'Ginola', rather than 'David' or 'Monsieur Ginola'.

During these three weeks I had a game on a Wednesday night for Matra away to Strasbourg, so was released from the army for the day. I played brilliantly and scored with a fantastic free-kick. I caught a plane home and arrived at 1.30 am feeling happy after my night's work. But I was greeted with some shock news from Coraline, who was living with me in Paris.

'David, the army have phoned. You must return to the base,' she said.

'Yes, of course I will, in the morning.'

'No, they want you back NOW.'

Even though I had just travelled through the night returning from the game and was exhausted, I knew there was no compromise. If I was in the army, I had to behave properly or not at all. So I got in my car and returned to base. I parked at the front gates and had to walk to my barracks, which were a mile from the entrance. When I got inside, all the lights were on and the rest of the guys were standing by their beds in full uniform and boots, holding their guns and wearing their backpacks.

'What is going on?' I asked the sergeant.

'Get ready,' he told me. 'We are going for a 10 km hike.'

'But I have just come back from playing a game,' I protested.

'Then this shall be your warm-down.'

It was 3 am by the time I had donned my uniform and boots and prepared my gun and backpack, and then we set off on our hike. The exercise was meant to show us what it would be like if we were on manoeuvres, in the forest, and every so often we had to dive in the bushes, which was not very pleasant as there was ice on the ground. We eventually arrived at our destination, where we were told we could have an hour's rest before the truck came to take us back to base. I sat down and lay against a tree, and although my body was warm from the exercise I wrapped my coat around myself and fell asleep.

After an hour I was woken up so that we could go back. My body temperature had dropped dramatically and no matter what I did, I could not stop my teeth from chattering. I was freezing. Then came the 'good' news: There was no truck to take us back, so we had to walk! Somehow I managed to get myself up and moving again, but I lagged at the back of the group, about 100 metres behind everyone else. One of my friends was a Maori javelin thrower and he stayed at the back with me, to help keep me going. I arrived back, suffering from severe cramp and fatigue, but I was still in one piece.

My other memorable experience came in the December when we went on a tour, spending 15 days in India, 12 days in Zaire and 10 days in Morocco. It was a great adventure. I played for the army football team and in Morocco we took part in an international tournament, reaching the semi-finals before losing to the hosts. It came to New Year's Eve and we were feeling a bit fed up with the strict regime, the food and the conditions, so three of us decided to bunk out after dark and go out on the town. There was me, Michele Pavon who is now captain of Bordeaux, and Patrick Valery, who used to play for Blackburn, and we got our guide to take us to the best restaurant in Casablanca, where we dined on lobster, then on to the best nightclub. We walked back to our lodgings on the university campus, by which time it was 6 am. Unfortunately for us, the manager of our team – who was none other than Roger Lemerre, the current manager of the French national team – noticed we had gone missing, and reported us to the sergeant.

The next morning the whole squad were summoned to a meeting in the amphitheatre. We were berated about the behaviour of three members who had broken curfew. The three of us couldn't help but laugh, until the sergeant blasted: 'What is so funny? We are talking about you!' We were told that we would be sanctioned when we returned to Paris. I think it was because we had lost in the semi-finals of the tour-nament and they were trying to make examples of us. A special report was sent to the colonel and we were called before him to explain ourselves.

We were in serious trouble. I felt that it was all a bit unjust. After all, it wasn't as if we had murdered anyone, we had simply gone for a night out. But the colonel told us he was considering sending us to Baden Baden to finish our national service. I was shaking, because that would have meant the end of our footballing careers. The seriousness of the situation hit me and I knew drastic measures were needed, so I stepped forward and spoke to the colonel.

In a very soft voice I said: 'Sir, I respect that you have the power to give us this punishment, and that you are considering doing so. I agree that we were wrong to go out celebrating the way we did, and we made a mistake. But please, did you never make one mistake in your life when you were just 20 years old? Okay, we went out, but we did nothing bad and did not tarnish the name of the army, and yet you want to send us to Baden Baden. If you do this you will finish our careers as footballers and you might forever have that on your conscience. Please, remember that we are still only young. Please, remember what you were like when you were 20 and just, please, bear all this in mind before you sanction us.'

We were sent to the canteen while our futures were decided, but I had managed to touch the heart of the colonel with my plea, and they knew that we were not bad guys really. Our punishment was still tough, although not one that would wreck our precious football careers. Instead of being given a 15-day break with our families at home which everyone was entitled to, the three of us had to stay behind and clean the entire building. We were not allowed out at all during the 15 days. I couldn't believe it, but we had no choice. After all, this was the army we were dealing with – they could throw you in jail if you did something wrong – and we had to take our punishment and learn our lesson.

I finished my 12 months and I remember my release day being one of the happiest days of my life. But now I look back on the whole army experience as a positive thing in my life because it helped build me as a person. I did things that I would not normally have done in my life, such as stripping a gun to pieces and putting it back together again, and shooting at targets. It also instilled a discipline in me, such as waking up every day at the same time, making my own bed, shaving every day. And it was also good to be a type of ambassador for my country, as well as visiting amazing places such as India, Goa and Brazil. In all, it was a positive experience that prepared me for the challenging times ahead.

CHAPTER EIGHT

Rejection and resurgence

'Daddy, what will I do now? . . . football has not offered
me anything, so what will happen?'

My career as a professional footballer might well have been
over before it even started, for I suffered the first major disappointment in my life when, as a 16-year-old, I was rejected by
OGC Nice and told I had no future in the game. And that is the
kind of crushing experience I shall never forget.

It came at the end of a three-year period studying in Nice,
while I was associated with the football club there. I was sent to
the Parc Imperial boarding school at the age of 13 to study for
a proper education. It was a very nice school and catered for
tennis, judo and football. I was having lessons in the morning,
lessons in the afternoon and then playing my football in the
evening. A minibus would come to the school and pick us
up for the 30-minute journey back to Nice so we could train. I
was like a normal student, rather than being at a sports centre

mixing an education part-time with playing my sport; my father and mother wanted me to have proper schooling while I was associated with Nice as a teenager.

When most kids arrive at a football club as youth apprentices their minds are not focused on geography or mathematics, they want to be on the football pitch playing with a ball. It was difficult for me because I wanted to train every day, so I looked forward to school holidays when I could train full-time with the other apprentices. At the weekends I was playing in the second reserve team, which is common in France. It was still a good level of football, and I was expecting one day to step up to the reserves.

My parents were very supportive of me while I was studying at the formation centre. They came to visit me every weekend, with Sebastien in tow, to watch me play football. After the game we would go into the centre of the village and sit on a bench, and they would help me with my homework. While my father played with Sebastien in the square, my mother would help me with my work, so I had everything ready for the Monday when I went back to the boarding school.

My body was not very well developed at that stage. I was not very strong or mature and had the nickname 'Jambes des baguettes' – which is a thin stick of French bread, snapping easily in half when you break it up. Even though I looked like a baby I could still do incredible tricks with the ball, but thanks to my slight frame I was also easy to knock off it.

I spent my three years in school doing just enough to get by. I passed every year with average marks – no more, no less, just the minimum required to move on to the next level. The last year I took my Baccalaureate (equivalent of A-levels) but I struggled and failed. It was at the end of this academic year that my father and I were waiting for news from Nice as to what kind of contract I would be offered, so I could start as a full-time apprentice.

My father came to Nice that summer but nobody came from the club to talk to him, or to me. So he decided to go to the club to find out what was happening. He spoke to Pierre Alonzo who was in charge of the reserves at the time, although he was speaking on behalf of the club and the first-team coaches.

'It is very simple, Mr Ginola,' said Alonzo. 'We don't see your son becoming a professional footballer. We don't envisage David playing in the first team in the next three years, so we cannot accept him. I am sorry, but we don't want him.'

My father was angry. 'What is this all about? You mean to say you won't give David any contract? While he has been at school for the past three years, you have never given him a proper chance. He has been unable to train full-time with you because it was important for him to have an education, but this is what he wants to do now. It is surely not too late. He was a part of the club for the last three years and it would be nice to give him a chance to work at it properly.'

But Mr Alonzo said I wasn't wanted, so my father came back to see me, as I had been waiting outside.

'Daddy, what is going on?' I quizzed him.

'David, they don't want to keep you at the club.'

I was distraught and started to cry in his arms. It was the first real moment in life when, as a child, you realise it's a tough world out there and that you have to fight very hard to achieve what you want. Nobody will give you any gifts or help you. No matter how hard you might work, if people don't think you are worth it they will drop you like a stone.

As we were about to drive away we met the chairman of the club, Mr Innocentini. My father said goodbye to him and he asked why we were going. When my father told him we were going home because they didn't want me, he appeared to be very disappointed. When I went back to the club as a successful player a few years later, he told me he felt angry at what had happened, but I shall come to that later.

As we drove off in the car, my life appeared to be falling apart in front of me.

'Daddy, what will I do now? I didn't succeed in my Baccalaureate, football has not offered me anything, so what will happen?'

'Do not worry,' he said.

A few days later he called Mr Pieri, who was in charge of recruiting the kids in Toulon. He told my father that Toulon were having a training camp, which was a trial for all the potential signings, so they could select the best youngsters from the area. He told my father it would be no problem for me to attend the trial, and that news started to rebuild my confidence.

I did fantastically well at the training camp. I was scoring goals and doing amazing things on the pitch and people were taking notice. The manager of the first team, Christian Dalger, was watching the kids and he later told me that having seen me play that day he put two red lines underneath my name to highlight me, because I was the one player he was interested in. He said to his colleagues: 'We must sign this kid, he's amazing' and someone told him I had been let go by Nice. He couldn't believe it. As a player he had been very skilful and very talented and I think perhaps he recognised something of himself in me that day.

At the end of the trial my father was called into the office, while I was left waiting nervously outside, because I was still under 18 and therefore not allowed to represent myself. In

France there are three contract stages: a two-year Under-17 contract, a two-year Under-19 contract and then a professional contract. My father came out smiling.

'What is going on?' I asked.

'They wanted to offer you a two-year Under-19 contract, but I had to point out you were still at the Under-17 stage,' he said. 'So they offered you that contract instead!'

I signed right away and we went back home and drank champagne to celebrate. I was so happy for my father, because if I hadn't found a club he would have been so miserable for me and felt guilty about the situation. He knew I was very good and he didn't want me to waste my talent. We had come from the depths of despair at Nice to a fresh start somewhere else. I never thought it would happen for me after the rejection by Nice, so I knew this was now my big chance. It was such a boost for me to know that my career could now start properly. My whole village was very proud of me, because I was the first kid to have gone this far in football from the whole area.

I played regularly in the reserves in the French third division and I did incredibly well in the number 10 shirt. In France, wearing the number 10 means you are the playmaker. It was the number worn by the great French stars, such as Raymond Kopa and Michel Platini, and of course great players around the world too, such as Pele, Maradona, Glenn Hoddle, Gianni Rivera, Giancarlo Antognoni – all the players you admire (although Johan Cruyff for whatever reason wore number 14, my number at Tottenham). When I first started playing in a football team at the age of eight, everybody wanted to wear the number 10. It signified the best player in the team.

At this time I also started to grow up physically, very quickly, and the shape of my body changed completely in that first year. I was able to hold my own in the reserves, especially with the added bonus of my good technique. I had been working on my body anyway in my last year at the Parc Imperial by joining some of the other sportsmen at night when they went weight training. I continued this to help define my body and give me some muscles, and it was paying off.

The club had more of a family atmosphere than Nice. There was an emphasis on encouragement, and from day one everyone believed in me, which was a refreshing change after the negative vibes in Nice.

I went from strength to strength, and during my second year the manager of the first team, Christian Dalger, had a problem in midfield, so he came to see the reserve team manager, Gaby Robert, to ask him to recommend a player he could take into the first-team squad. He was told that if he had to pick someone for the first-team midfield, then I was the one, because I had been performing magnificently in every game for the reserves.

I was asleep in my room when I was woken by the caretaker of the dormitory and told that Gaby Robert wanted to see me. I was terrified and kept asking myself what I had done wrong. I went and knocked on the door.

'Come in and sit down. David, I have something to tell you.'

I was sitting there thinking: 'Come on, give it to me, tell me what I have done wrong . . .'

'Tomorrow morning, you go to play with the first team because Christian Dalger wants you in his squad for Saturday.'

I remained very calm and composed all the time I was in his office, but the moment I stepped outside I let out a whoop of delight. I ran and phoned home and my family were over the moon. It was a pivotal point in my career, as from that moment on, I never left the first-team squad.

I did have one lucky escape during my time at Toulon, as I was nearly thrown out of the club lodgings after getting caught smoking in the sleeping quarters one night. To look back on it now is funny. After lights out, I lit up a cigarette and enjoyed a smoke, before stubbing out the butt in the cap of my shaving mousse and putting the can in my locker. We went to sleep but after a while I was woken by a strange smell. I put on the light and saw to my horror that the room was engulfed in smoke! Then the smoke alarms went off and before we realised it the fire brigade had come rushing into the building. Everyone was wondering what was happening, so I had to own up to smoking a cigarette. Gaby Robert summoned my parents for a meeting and I was almost expelled. My parents told me I was on a final warning. It certainly made me think but although it was a scare I still carried on having a sneaky cigarette now and again – I just made sure I never got caught!

Gaby cut a frightening figure for the youngsters at Toulon. He wasn't the type to shout and rant, but he had a certain coolness and wisdom that demanded respect. The kid he taught hasn't forgotten his lessons.

Because I had been promoted to the first team set-up, training with the senior professionals every day, it meant that I had a different regime to the rest of the apprentices I was living with. For example, I would have a day off after a game and could relax in the room, which didn't coincide with someone like Frank Leboeuf who was sharing the same accommodation as me but playing for the reserves. I was then given a room on my own by Gaby Robert, because my timetable was now different. I started at 10 am instead of 9 am, I did only one training session, I got more days off, and I needed to sleep more – but I still had my duties in the building. In France we don't clean boots, but I had to take my turn on the rota to clean the dinner tables, wash the floors, and clean all the cutlery, crockery and glassware.

I made my first appearance coming on as a substitute against Metz, shortly before the end of a 2–0 victory to Toulon. But I prefer to date the launch-pad of my career as my full French league debut for Toulon, which probably couldn't have been more testing. It came against the reigning champions Girondins de Bordeaux, who were the best team in France at the time. The equivalent in England would be making your debut for a small club like Charlton Athletic at Manchester United. Bordeaux were used to playing in Europe and nearly all their players were internationals. When I was in the dressing room putting on my shirt, I knew that this was it, this was the start. At Bordeaux's Parc Lescure you have to walk through a long corridor of about 150 yards underneath the ground before you go up the steps and on to the pitch, to be greeted by the enormous roar of the crowd. I felt I had arrived at last.

It was such an emotional occasion that I just couldn't seem to relax. I have never really shared with many people the emotion of these moments. I was looking at the players around me in the Bordeaux team, and they were the same guys I had watched on the television playing in the European Cup. They had some of the stars of French football, including Alain Giresse, Jean Tigana, Thierry Tusseau, Horst Hrubesch, Dominique Dropsy, Patrick Battiston, Zlatko Vujevic – it was just a great team. I was given the right midfield slot and told that I was in charge of that side of the pitch. My aim was simply to follow every single step of the manager's instructions. Bordeaux were the top team at home playing against one of the bottom teams, so not surprisingly I spent a large amount of time defending, rather than showing my skills in the attacking third of the pitch, although I had a few opportunities to show what I was capable of. It may sound strange to people reading this now, but I can tell you I was defending very well – tackling, tracking back, the lot! We lost as expected, 3–0, but all the journalists afterwards were interested in the skilful 18-year-old making his debut for Toulon. My family had not been able to make the trip, but they were there for my next game, at home to Monaco, another of the leading clubs. When I came on to the pitch and waved to my father and mother in the stands, it was such a proud moment.

My life was changing even more off the pitch too, as I left my club accommodation and rented a lovely little apartment in a little fishing village called Sanary-Sur-Mer. It was my own little cocoon, with the sea 200 yards away, and lots of nice restaurants around the marina. At first I took the bus to training every morning because I was too young to have a driving licence. I had more money as I was picking up bonuses from the games, so as soon as I was old enough I bought my first car. I was training in the morning then going back to the harbour to eat. I knew everyone and I was the pride of the village, so it was a happy time even if the results weren't going so well. I had what I wanted, the apartment, the girls, the independence, and I lived it up, although I never forgot the fact that my first challenge in life was to sign as a professional player.

In my debut season for the Toulon first team I went back to play a game against OGC Nice. I would be meeting the people who told me I was not going to be able to make it as a professional footballer in three years, yet this was only two years down the line.

I arrived at the Stade du Ray and I noticed immediately those associated with the club were not comfortable looking me in the eye, so they stared at the floor as they walked past me. Some of them were even unsure it was me, as I had changed so much physically. My father said: 'David, be proud, proud of what you have achieved so far.' The only person who came up to me was the Nice chairman, Mr Innocentini.

'David, what a shame for us. We showed a lack of professionalism in the way we treated you at this club and I am very happy for you and very glad for your father. You have got what you deserved. Unfortunately for us we were not patient at all and couldn't wait – I could but the coaches didn't want to wait a year or two for you. Because of that you went away, we'd paid for your study and had you for three years and we got nothing in return as a result of our own foolishness.'

I hadn't played too many times in Nice's Stade du Ray, and I stuck out my chest as I walked on to the pitch in another team's colours. The game started and I played brilliantly, teasing players all over the pitch and drawing chants of 'Ole!' from the crowd every time I nutmegged a bemused opponent. I scored one goal and made another as we won 2–1.

I understand the Nice chairman had the manager and all the coaches in his office on the Monday morning for a special meeting and gave them hell about me.

'Did you see that David Ginola on Saturday? What do you think?'

They all agreed I was a great player so the chairman continued. 'This guy should be playing for us, right here, right now! I paid everything for him, only for you to turn round at the end and tell him and his father that he would not be a professional footballer in three years. You didn't even try him for a year at least, to make sure in your mind you were right to say no.'

The manager of Nice at the time was Nenad Bjekovic, a famous Yugoslav who had been a first-team player at the time I was discarded. After that meeting with the chairman, Bjekovic gave an interview in a newspaper saying what a mistake the club had made with me, and that was the first thing to really give me a feeling of pride at becoming a professional football player. It was so important for me to prove myself to those people, who had treated my father and I so arrogantly. They treated the best players in the club as Gods and the rest as rubbish, yet we were all trying so hard. It was a huge victory for me over the doubters who didn't believe in me.

I think it says a lot about the way they ran the club that not one of their young players at the time came through and made it as a professional. I was one of five players at the boarding school who were expected to make the grade, and the four others were all rated much higher than me. Yet I was the only one to succeed.

A few years later I went back to the boarding school to see some of the teachers. The same thing happened with Yannick Noah the tennis player, as he was also a graduate of the school just before me. I spoke to him about it later and we both agreed we were proud to have started out at the Parc Imperial. I knocked on the door to see my teachers and they couldn't believe it was me, and all the kids in the classroom went wild with delight. I was very happy to go back there having made a success out of my life.

I stopped at the gates and said to myself: 'The last time I passed through these gates I had floods of tears in my eyes, feeling destroyed. Now I am walking in with a big smile on my face, knowing I spent three years of my life here. Maybe those years made me mentally strong, and capable of proving my detractors wrong.'

I was called up to play for France's Under-21 team and by a beautiful twist of fate I was reunited with the man who bought me my first pair of football boots. The coach was Marc

Bourrier who, when he was the manager of Association Sportive Maximoise years before, obtained a tiny pair of football boots for Rene Ginola's son. Marc was a very good friend of my father and I was close to his son, Jean-Marc. We used to play together as three-year-olds when we were finding our footballing feet and our fathers were playing for ASM. So I had an extra incentive to play well when I was given my international break for the Under-21s. It was a happy moment for both families.

I pulled on the famous blue shirt of France for the first time in the annual Under-21 international festival of Toulon. For two years running I represented my country in that competition and both years we won. The first time we beat Bulgaria in the final, and I was voted Player of the Tournament. The second time we played against England in the final, whose stars were Paul Gascoigne, David Rocastle and Michael Thomas.

Toulon didn't want to wait for me to finish my apprenticeship because I had made such progress, so they offered me professional terms at the end of the year. I was earning the equivalent of a basic £2,200 a month, and although this was a good enough salary for a first professional five-year contract – what with the bonuses and appearance money – it wasn't good enough for me because I was enjoying a good lifestyle and spending it faster than I was earning it! At the end of the month my bank statement was always in the red and it scared my parents. They used to say: 'We are earning less than you, but we still have to give you money!'

Toulon was an ideal stepping stone for me, and a gentle introduction to the world of professional football. We were an average team, never challenging but never struggling either. I was able to play in the First Division without feeling too much pressure, and with the added advantage of having the anonymity so I could be a bit wild off the pitch as well. I recall we were training one day for the start of the new season, in 35 degree heat. We had a session in the morning, went to hang out on the beach at lunchtime, had another session in the afternoon, then in the evening there was a party on the beach. In a way, it wasn't the beginning of my professional life. Toulon was a little team and I was still too young to fully appreciate my circumstances. It was only when I went to Paris that I realised what the life of a professional was really like.

I left Toulon after one more year. The club never had any great financial support; they always needed to sell their best player at the end of the season so they could ensure survival for the following year. I had played a game in my first season in Paris against Matra Racing and the manager was Artur Jorge, the man who coached Switzerland at Euro '96. I did very well and he went to his board and said if they wanted to recruit some great players, then they should buy David Ginola. So they did, and it was a good deal for Toulon because Matra bought out the remaining four years of my contract.

Initially I was sad to leave Toulon but I was also excited about moving to a better environment with better players. It was a very big challenge for me because Matra Racing Paris were one of the biggest clubs in the country at this time, because the chairman Mr La Gardere was also chairman of Matra, a massive electronics company. He had bought most of the French national team players, plus the Uruguayan Enzo Francescoli, former Spanish international Luis Fernandez – who would later be my coach at PSG – and some of the top Africans. I knew it was going to be difficult, at the tender age of 20, to impose myself in such an accomplished team.

We had a strong squad of 30 players and in the pre-season we went to Holland. In the practice matches Artur Jorge

picked his probable starting eleven against the next eleven –
and I was pleasantly surprised to find myself in the starting
line-up. Some people in my life think things have come easily
to me, but I was working so hard at this time for my success.
I was looking at the B-team and they were all internationals, so
I knew I had to work very hard to keep my place. But it was
hard for all those internationals to get on well together, with 30
top players competing for only 11 places. I played 34 games
out of 38 in that 1987/88 season, while some of the more experienced players were left on the bench, so I was pretty pleased
with myself.

I can recall a funny experience involving Luis Fernandez
which really opened my naïve Southern eyes. Not long after
joining the club I arrived in the car park in my new car, a black
Peugeot 205 GTI, which I was proud of. I got out and saw the
other cars – Ferraris, Porsches, four-wheel drives, and other
beautiful vehicles. Matra was a rich club with big salaries
thanks to the chairman taking it to new levels, a kind of Jack
Walker figure of the French league if you like. I was admiring
the Porsche Carrera of Luis Fernandez when he came out and
said to me: 'One day when you get a car like this, it will mean
you are successful.' These words from a great player gave me
an immediate insight into the benefits of success.

Matra was testing at first. Not only did I have to adjust to a
big club with great players, I also had to find my way around
Paris, the Big Apple of France. For a Southerner to move to the
capital is something else and it wasn't like just changing clubs,
it was like changing country. Moving to Paris for the first time,
I felt like some peasant going to the big city. It was a big surprise – the constant buzz, the traffic, the crowds of faceless
people, the sheer size, the culture, the bright lights and the
unique flavour of a 24-hour city. I wasn't really prepared for

my new life and in football you have little time to adapt. I didn't even have time to think about missing my home or my family. The difference between Toulon and Matra was the difference between a club trying to survive and a club trying to win things.

Professionally, though, I was much more focused. I had to concentrate more, each day. It woke me up and my mind was immediately centred on the training ahead. There was more pressure and I had to be more aware of my responsibility, giving my best all the time.

For a short while I was surrounded by some hangers-on, bad people. They were just individuals whom I had come across during my time at the club after matches. One was a so-called friend from childhood, and others were friends of his. They liked to hang around with me because I attracted women for them wherever we went. People recognised me when we went to clubs and restaurants and I was given VIP treatment. This entourage enjoyed all the advantages of my success – I opened doors for them, both socially and in their business. We had a few good months together, all the lads, but then during this time Coraline came to Paris and I didn't want to go out clubbing any more, I wanted to stay at home and spend time with her instead. But this spoiled things for my 'friends' and they tried hard to split us up, although if they had been true friends they would have understood me. That was when I realised they were bad for me and I was soon back on the right track. The one thing about me is that in my life I always know when I am going too far and straying from the right path and I correct that immediately. I have always known my limit. Fame brings with it fake relationships, but Coraline helped me a lot with this, because she is very good at assessing people and determining whether or not they are genuine. My agent, Chantal, is another who is very good at this, and always helps me decide who I should be mixing with and those I'm better off avoiding.

We had a bad time at Matra. The first season was difficult because there wasn't a very good atmosphere in the team. Artur Jorge left the club in heart-rending circumstances as his wife was taken very ill. The reins were taken up by his assistants, but they didn't have the same experience and managerial flair. Because the team was struggling, the chairman was advised to withdraw his financial support, as the negative aspects of the club were affecting his business reputation – he couldn't afford to be associated with an unsuccessful team. In my second season the 'Matra' was dropped from the team name and we became just Racing Paris. Also, the team was reduced to just young inexperienced players, as the big stars left when the sponsorship disappeared, and we lost our great training facilities because we couldn't afford to keep them.

The season did have one highlight. We reached the French Cup final in 1990 having beaten mighty Marseille 3–2 in the semi-final, in the Velodrome. The odds against us beating them were huge, as they were playing in the European Cup and we were minnows in comparison. We had a big party afterwards. In the final we faced Montpellier HSC who boasted Eric Cantona and Laurent Blanc. I scored, but so did both of them as we lost 2–1 in extra time. Nevertheless it had been great to reach the French Cup final, especially in such a poor season which ended with us being relegated from the First Division.

I didn't want to play in the Second Division but it was difficult for me to get out of the club because Racing had bought out my five-year contract. The club had money problems and needed to sell players, but they put a ridiculous price on my head which scared off any potential buyers, who ended up looking elsewhere for their summer signings. By the time they relented and were prepared to accept a more realistic fee for me, it was too late to join a big club, and the only one who came in for me was Brest Armorique.

I remember that when we had played them during the season I was sitting in the back of the coach saying: 'I would never come to play for a club like this.' Yet here I was signing for the club that offered me my only escape route. Brest is in Brittany, in the north of France. When I began to play football I planned to draw a geographical line at Paris. I had no intentions of going further north – and here I was in Brest, a town with the same weather as Newcastle! I was living with Coraline at the time and when I told her we were leaving Paris to go to Brest it was like we were taking a step down. Brest is a poor town and there are very few diversions, unlike Paris; in fact it is famous for its potato fields! But they were in the First Division which was what mattered and in footballing terms I had no real complaints. In the first season we played really well and were top of the league for four months, before eventually finishing the season in sixth place, just missing out on Europe. We were a very young team and the former France goalkeeper Bernard Lama, Bernard Ferrer, and midfielder Correntin Martins were thriving in the promising side we had. I was playing number 10 again, the playmaker. It was good to go there and work hard in a warm and friendly atmosphere and I didn't think I could be so happy. The players developed a very close bond because of the environment and I formed a good friendship with Bernard Lama, who was my room-mate. I have fond memories of the hours we spent staying at the team's training camp before games. We would sit outside on the balcony, watching the sea with the sound of Bernard's reggae music providing a perfect backdrop.

The team was doing well and I as an individual was in

fantastic form, scoring lots of goals, and earning rave reviews in *L'Equipe*. Each Monday morning player ratings were published in the press and I was top of the league. I worked so hard that I won my first full French cap, only the second time a player from Brest had been selected for the national team. Brest was a small club, like Wimbledon in England, and I never dreamed I'd be called up. The call came for me before a European Championship qualifier against Albania at the Qemal Stafa stadium in Tirana, on 7 November 1990. It was another example of how every time in my life when I was in trouble, I came out bigger and stronger.

I remember the scene very clearly. I was at an army training camp and we were all sitting around having dinner. The phone rang and our trainer Slavo Muslin went off to answer it, spent a few moments chatting, then came back to the table while we were all still eating.

'I have some good news. David has been selected for the French national squad,' he announced.

I practically choked on my soup. 'Come on, are you joking or what?'

'Absolutely not. That was Michel Platini on the phone and he has selected you.'

My heart went 'boom' and all the players gave me a standing ovation, it was brilliant. Platini was my idol, probably the best player to have come out of France, the only French footballer known throughout the world. There are only a few in that class – Pele, Maradona, Cruyff, and Beckenbauer. They were exceptional players, each with unique gifts, and all had reached the peak in our profession. Platini was an idol for my whole generation. He played for France in four major competitions, the World Cups in 1978 and 1982, the European Championship in 1984 and the World Cup again in 1986. That 1984 team in particular was great, but Platini stood out. He didn't have the best body shape ever seen, but in terms of skill, vision, and ability, he was remarkable. The thing I remember most about him is not his ability to dribble – like Pele, or Maradona, or Cruyff say – but the fact that he could pick up the ball 50 yards from goal and lay it at the feet of the striker to score a goal. He was a wonderful playmaker, deadly from free-kicks and had such a great touch. He was fantastic. There was that magic midfield quartet in the 1984 French national team: Platini, Jean Tigana, Alain Giresse and Luis Fernandez.

I arrived at the national team headquarters, the wide-eyed new recruit. There I was in that situation again of being among all the stars, and I felt like a child who had discovered the world. I stayed quietly in the corner, the youngest member of the team, but Michel Platini told me to think like a man, to be confident, to cover plenty of ground on the pitch and to play my normal game. The experience of going to Tirana was a real eye-opener. The hotel was of a very poor standard, and it was a very run-down country. Every day on the coach to the training ground we were surrounded by bunkers by the roadside. You saw kids playing in the mud and it made me realise these people had nothing. They all came up to us asking for money, and for our clothes – they wanted our tracksuits and our shoes, because they had never seen brand new clothes on people.

It was not a memorable game. The pitch was awful, but France won 1–0 thanks to a goal from Basile Boli and although my debut went well, it was to be almost another two years before I won my second cap.

Although Brest finished sixth in the league, we were relegated because of financial irregularities and the club was declared bankrupt. Throughout the season there had been a good atmosphere among good players, but nobody had any idea about the money situation – it was all swept under the carpet.

Because the chairman of Brest, Francois Yvinec, had financial problems, he asked a renowned Paris business wheeler-dealer, Charly Chaker to come and help him run the club. Chaker brought with him Phillipe Legorju to watch the players. Legorju was from the French special police force, the GIGN – the crack outfit which was the equivalent of the SAS – and during the winter break he took us to an army training camp just outside Le Mans for four days. It was in the middle of nowhere, with just a river and trees. We went through all the routines that the army goes through, including the tough assault course, and we all had to fire a .357 Magnum gun. You have to be strong and focused to resist the recoil of that deadly weapon. Legorju demonstrated by shooting at one of his colleagues who wore a bullet-proof vest, something which sent shivers through my body. We were also set a major task which was to prove an important lesson in bonding.

The squad of players was divided into two teams. Both teams were taken at night deep into the countryside and left at separate points. Each team was given only three things – a compass, a torch and half a map – and it was very scary because it was in the dark and we were miles from anywhere. There was a meeting point on the map where both teams had to rendezvous, then they would swap maps and find their way back to where each other had started out and eventually be picked up.

I took charge of my team and it was an amazing experience. We had to negotiate fields with cows in them and jump over fences with dogs chasing us. We had to cross a river using some rope and inner tubes which was a good test of our improvisation skills. We did very well because there were a few differences of opinion with people wanting to choose to go different ways, so it was all about making decisions as a team. It may have had nothing to do with playing football but it worked wonders for promoting team spirit and cementing a bond between the players, which I am sure helped us to go on and finish the season so well. At the end of the exercise we went back to the hotel sharing plenty of stories and plenty of laughs. It was a good idea, and if I was a manager I would do something like that in pre-season because I got so much out of it as a player. I was really enjoying myself with my Brest team-mates, although I had to leave after two days as this was when the call came through telling me I had been called up for the French national team, and it was Phillipe Legorju who drove me to Clairefontaine to join the rest of the squad.

Being relegated after we had worked so hard to finish sixth left another bitter taste in the mouth. The only assets the club had were us, the players, and Brest needed someone to come in and invest in the club, to turn it around and achieve some sort of stability. Instead, a couple of 'entrepreneurs' who owned a small airline company in Brittany tried to buy the club for the equivalent of £1. It would have been fine if they had planned to invest money into rebuilding it, but they simply wanted to sell all the assets – the players – and pocket all the money for themselves.

The players were really worried, and as it was we hadn't been paid for three months. Their plan was so unfair that the only thing we could do was to fight them in court. I took on the responsibility of being the spokesman for the players, because I felt I was the only one with the determination, power and profile to get us noticed and be heard. I felt most of the other people at the club were hiding from the responsibility, although the coach at the time, Jacky Castellan, was very understanding. Together with a lawyer, I represented every single player, from the first teamers to the youths. When judgement day arrived I went to a court tribunal with a huge file to defend the players against the businessmen who wanted to buy the club. I tried to explain our situation to the woman judge.

'We deserve our freedom because we have been abused by the club. If these people want to come and invest millions to clear the debts of the club, then the players will stay and play for them. But they don't want to put any money in, they just want to take advantage of the assets, and we don't want that, we want to fight against that.'

I told her I wanted all the players to be free, not just the professionals but also I wanted the formation centre – which is where the youths trained – to remain open for at least another year so the young players could have time to sort out their future. Both sides of the argument were presented and then the hearing was adjourned while the judge deliberated before announcing her verdict later that day.

I went back to my home and sat in my lounge with Coraline, just waiting, almost like the condemned man awaiting a reprieve. The phone rang and Coraline answered. It was the lawyer, so she handed the phone to me. 'Well?' I said, not sure whether I wanted to hear the reply. But then came the three magical words: 'You are free.'

We had won! The club was put into liquidation and all the players were free to go. Just as important, the formation centre was kept open for another year, to be funded by the local council. Poor Brest, the club was stripped of its professional status after a tragic farce.

All the players started to look for transfers, joining clubs like Monaco and Nantes. I had offers from every big club in France, and I spoke to the major chairmen such as Bernard

Tapie at Marseille, Jean-Didier Lange of Bordeaux and Monaco's Jean-Louis Campora, and of course PSG. Some time after this saga I received a letter from a player named Erwan Manach, who had been the centre-back in our team. He wanted to thank me for all I had done for him. He was newly married with a baby and felt that he wouldn't have survived without my help, and he said he would always be grateful to me. Letters like that made it all the more worthwhile.

As for me, another new chapter in my life was about to begin. I was a free agent and spoilt for choice. It was like having the keys to a Porsche and a Bugatti at the same time – which do you choose? I had the two biggest clubs in France after my signature. Half of me was attracted to Paris Saint Germain and the other half to Marseille. They both have totally different characters but are both phenomenal football clubs. All I knew for certain was that I wanted to get back to the top level as quickly as possible, to prove I could perform on the highest stage. It was almost an incredibly difficult choice, but in the end I plumped for Paris.

CHAPTER NINE

Paris match

*'Paris Saint Germain was where all the dreams I had
had as a child came true'*

With the two biggest clubs in France chasing me, I was in a
privileged position. Part of me wanted to go to Paris Saint
Germain, while the other half found the possibility of a move to
Olympique Marseille more attractive. In the end I decided to
go and help PSG's drive for honours. For the first time in my
life my decision was strongly motivated by money. I hadn't
been paid for the last three months at Brest and I was financially strapped, to the extent that I had my bank manager on
the phone almost every day. I had bills to pay like any normal
person. The other things that appealed to me about Paris were
that I knew the manager Artur Jorge really wanted me, I felt
relaxed with the people at the club and I liked the atmosphere,
whereas at Marseille it was Bernard Tapie, the President, who
was keen to have me there, rather than the manager. But the

renumeration package Tapie was proposing was insufficient. He was offering me a low basic salary but with lots of bonuses if the club was successful. I couldn't afford to take the gamble of hoping that we would win things so I could earn my bonus. At Paris, the contract they were offering included high wages, with bonuses for winning trophies on top – that was what I wanted. When I didn't join Marseille, I understand that Tapie called his PSG counterpart Michel Denisot and said: 'You've stolen my player, but let me tell you something: David will finish his career at Marseille!'

I also felt that if I went to Marseille my lifestyle would be more pressurised, because there would be so many people around me from home. We were just about to have a baby and I didn't need all the added pressure of these other demands on my time. Although I had had doubts about life in the capital city when I joined Matra, this time I was really looking forward to the experience. I had friends and favourite haunts and I knew my way around Paris.

Everybody from the South wanted me to go to Marseille and I was now considered a traitor in their eyes. The problem is that a permanent war exists between Marseille and PSG, fuelled by the difference in mentality between the people of Paris and those who live in the South. The rivalry between the clubs is what I would call intense and it is greater than anything I have seen anywhere else in the world – it makes Spurs and Arsenal look tame by comparison. There is real hatred there, and unless you are French you cannot understand it. The rivalry is a tale of two cities, not just a tale of two football teams. It stems from many years ago when Paris was made the capital and Marseille was cast in its shadow. Ever since then there has been competition, with each city wanting to show it is the best. There is also a difference in the accent. In Marseille the accent of the people is more down-to-earth, typical of the countryside, and like the Italians they use their hands a lot when they speak. But in Paris I suppose the style of speech may be considered more refined.

Soon after I joined PSG in January 1992, we had a game at Martigues, which is a town close to Marseille, and a lot of Marseille supporters went to the game to give me abuse. Someone thought it would be a good idea to throw a corkscrew at me, which fortunately did not result in a serious injury. It was a terrible experience, though, and a couple of years later my manager decided not to pick me for a game at Martigues because he feared that feelings of hatred still might be directed towards me.

It was while I was at PSG that I had my one and only experience of hate mail – and to be honest it affected me for a while. When you receive hundreds of nice letters every day, all from fans, you open them and enjoy reading them. You don't expect to read anything nasty. But one day when I was opening a pile of letters, I came across one that really shocked me. It was a picture depicting a body hanging from the gallows in a noose, with blood dripping from it. It had obviously come from someone who was really crazy and one never knows what such people are capable of. I didn't report the matter to the police however because I didn't want to make a big fuss about it. Fortunately, I heard nothing more after that, but it was still a worrying incident.

In the end, it was absolutely the right decision to go to PSG. My best footballing years were spent there – the number of medals I collected was proof positive of that. It was where all the dreams I had had as a child came true. When I arrived, PSG was definitely on the up; it had made remarkable progress considering it was still a relatively young club. It was only formed in 1970 and struggled to make a big impact until the television station Canal Plus took the club over in 1991 and gradually began to build a financially secure business structure to enable the club to flourish. Now it's a sporting institution, with its magnificent Parc des Princes hosting rugby, basketball, boxing and volleyball teams as well as football.

When the trophies began arriving one after another, it was a wonderful feeling. There was a great team spirit at that time. For three-and-a-half years we shared some incredible experiences and even for those players who didn't have much in common there was an unshakeable bond which helped carry us through the difficult matches.

Apart from the success I enjoyed, there was also relief at missing out on the bribery scandal that engulfed Marseille in the early nineties. They were banned from European competition by UEFA and demoted by the French Football Federation from the First Division after being found guilty of trying to fix a match against Valenciennes by bribing three opposing players. The idea was that Marseille would have an easy fixture the week before the European Cup final. There were massive repercussions for the club. They were stripped of the 1993 European Cup (they had beaten AC Milan 1–0 in France's only 'success' in this prestigious competition) and the league title. In addition, their president Bernard Tapie was jailed for two years. On top of that, in their first year in exile, Marseille won the Second Division but the authorities wouldn't let them back into the top flight because of the club's shady financial situation.

The harm all this inflicted on the region was immense. If you are from the South, you inevitably love Olympique Marseille. It's all you hear about and all you read, the club is a legend and the fans are the most passionate in France. Had I joined them,

I would have felt the same disillusionment as all the other players. At that time, Marseille were at the pinnacle of French football, winning the French championship and French Cup and, surpassing all that, had just been crowned champions of Europe. The whole bribery scandal was a disaster for the club and the region.

Joining PSG also gave me the pleasure of being reunited with Artur Jorge. He had been my coach at Matra for one season and was someone I respected a great deal. While I was at Matra he had lost his wife and left the club to try and cope with his personal tragedy. When it was time for him to get on with his life again, he went to PSG and tried to sign me for the club as soon as he could. In the years since I had last worked with him, I had developed far more physically, and his first words on seeing me this time around were: 'You are a grown man now, eh?'

It would be hard to imagine a more different character to Kevin Keegan. Yet like my former Newcastle boss Artur had the knack of being able to handle players in the right way. Unmistakable with that thick moustache, he didn't speak very much but when he did, you listened. Sometimes the way he looked at you said more than words. When I did something that impressed him he would just look at his assistant and puff his cheeks out in acknowledgement. Sometimes, all it needs is a pat on the back or for the manager to ruffle your hair. It can be more effective than a thousand words.

My PSG experience was highly rewarding in so many ways. I learned a lot there in terms of approaching everything with the right mentality. I gained a great deal of experience because we played against some big teams. I found maturity. Best of all, I managed to win things and it was a fantastic feeling, after so many years of striving hard yet winning nothing, to hold aloft my first trophy in 1993, the French Cup, returning to the Parc des Princes as a winner – and beating my old friend Frank Leboeuf, then playing for FC Nantes, in the final! It was another reminder that if you continue to believe in yourself and keep working hard and never give up, then you can achieve all that you desire.

The following season we won the French championship for only the second time in the club's history. What a party we had that night! We headed off for the Champs Elysees which the police had blocked off for us and our supporters. We had a big celebration in a famous restaurant, Le Fouquets, and hung out of the first floor windows to acknowledge all our supporters who were going mad in the streets outside. I remember Bernard Lama hoisted me on to his shoulders, beamed up at me and shouted: 'You are the star. It's your title!' Whenever I think back to that night, it gives me a warm glow inside. Some of the scenes were just incredible.

In Europe we were beaten in the semi-finals of the major club competitions in three successive years, 1993-95, losing to Juventus, Arsenal and AC Milan, who all went on to lift the silverware, which was a minor consolation for us. There were some great memories, none more so than our 1993 UEFA Cup victories over first Real Madrid, and then Barcelona in the quarter-final stage. There is nothing more enthralling than to win a big game, on a big stage, with all the attendant excitement.

One of my best memories concerns the UEFA Cup tie with Real Madrid because that really established us as a European force. We lost the first leg in Spain 3–1 but I scored the away goal which gave us a chance for the return. It was a strike that sent shockwaves through Madrid and I was christened 'El Magnifico' in the Spanish newspapers. However, there was still much for us to do and we were rank outsiders going into the second leg. Thankfully, it all fell into place and we came through 4–1 winners at the Parc des Princes. I scored one of the goals as did George Weah. We were elated and what made it so special was that we had come back from a seemingly impossible position. It was one of the most amazing matches I have been involved in.

Two years later we were up against Barcelona in the Champions' League quarter-final. They were managed by Johan Cruyff, one of my boyhood heroes and someone who inspired in me an image of football as poetry in motion. I was sad when Holland lost the World Cup final to West Germany in 1974 because Cruyff had been inspirational throughout the tournament and now, 20 years on, I wanted him to admire me as I had admired him. It was another tough test for us because Barcelona were packed with stars like Gheorge Hagi, Ronald Koeman and Hristo Stoichkov, but we were full of confidence because we had won every game in our Champions' League group which consisted of Bayern Munich, Dinamo Kiev and Spartak Moscow. We gained a 1–1 draw at the Nou Camp thanks to a brilliant effort from George Weah. The second leg picked up at the same feverish pace, Barcelona scored a goal on the break but then we hit back to score through Rai before clinching the game with a late winner.

I had been at PSG for about a year when I noticed the change in the way people looked at me in the street. They would stare at me and I found it a little bit unnerving at first. The letters began to arrive, I started to appear on the television and the whole thing snowballed. Whereas before I could walk down the street and nobody would take the slightest bit of notice, now people were chasing me and trying to get close to me. I guess this recognition meant I had finally arrived.

The amount of publicity surrounding me was something

PSG had not encountered before. Before me there were only two players who had generated this kind of interest in terms of media coverage, Jean-Pierre Papin and Eric Cantona. The attention the three of us received was something that almost transcended the game of football. Wherever you went in France, even into the smallest villages, people had heard of Papin, Cantona and myself.

Papin was the focal point of the Marseille team that won four consecutive championships, and he was at his peak before footballers became commercially valuable, whereas Eric and I have had great marketing forces behind us. Football became so glamorous in the nineties that companies queued up to have their products endorsed by the best players. Company directors might earn fabulously large salaries but they can walk down the street and no one gives them a second glance because they are unknown to the wider public. I can imagine them feeling that their own achievements may be as great as ours and wondering why they never receive the same attention. Ironically, we footballers would sometimes like to be in their shoes and to walk down the street without people always stopping us and asking for autographs. I didn't become a football star to be pointed at in the street, but there's nothing that can be done about it. It comes with the territory. However it's important not to lose sight of the fact that the fame comes only from my footballing talent, and nothing else.

Of course the attention can sometimes get too much. For instance, I couldn't believe the reaction when my house in Newcastle was burgled at the end of my first season on Tyneside. The news of the break-in was everywhere, newspapers, television, even on teletext, but to me it had limited value in terms of real news. Reporters from England even came over to France to track me down to the house where I was staying. It

FAME & FASHION

On the catwalk with rugby stars Emile N'Tamack and Laurant Cabannes when we modelled for Nino Cerruti.

Coraline and I attend the Cannes Film Festival, which is always an enjoyable and star-studded occasion.

A cheesy grin as I help promote a cheese festival with some fair maidens.

Above: Time on my hands, a moment in reflective mood.

Left: Making a lasting impression as I have prints of my hands made for L'Oreal.

Right: Meeting Prince Albert, with Catherine Deneuve (left) and Ornella Muti at the opening of a health spa in Monaco.

Left: Rubbing shoulders with supermodel Kate Moss at the Cannes Film Festival.

Right: Man from Atlantis, eat your heart out!

Left. Making an exhibition of myself again at the Monet show in London.

Right: Anything to declare? I joined forces with Gary Lineker for a customs and excise anti-drugs campaign ahead of Euro 2000.

A chance to indulge in my passion for art at the Ingres exhibition at the National Gallery.

FRANCE

Above: Happier days. This was when I was part of the France team (*back row, third from left*) managed by Gerard Houllier.

Right: Winning my second international cap, against Brazil in August 1992.

A crucial 2–3 loss at home to Israel during a World Cup qualifier for USA 94, with Eric Cantona in the background. Despite scoring and being the best player on the pitch, I was substituted with five minutes to go.

NEWCASTLE

Talk of the Toon. Here I am signing for Newcastle flanked by assistant manager Terry McDermott (*left*) and chairman Sir John Hall.

A double honour for the club as I am named Carling Player of the Month and Kevin Keegan is Manager of the Month as things start well at Newcastle.

Dashing down the wing during one of my first matches for Newcastle.

Running out at St James' Park alongside Dion Dublin, for my Newcastle debut versus Coventry City, 19 August 1995.

The Toon army give me a warm welcome on my arrival at St James' Park. I will never forget the warmth and devotion of the Newcastle fans.

The 1996 FA Charity Shield with Newcastle team-mates (*from left*) John Beresford, Alan Shearer and Rob Lee.

Grounded following a hard challenge. I still insist that I am no diver.

I had to ponder my future at Newcastle once Keegan left.

was all too much, but I appreciate that I must put up with this kind of hassle. I am of interest to the news organisations because my footballing talent makes me of interest to the public. It did annoy me though when the newspapers reported that I was ready to leave Newcastle and join Barcelona after my first season in England because my house had been burgled. That was rubbish. Of course I wasn't happy to have been robbed, but it had no bearing on my wish to move to Spain. My house in Paris was burgled when I was on my holidays with PSG. It happens in life – I have to concede that fame and wealth make me an obvious target.

I am under no illusions that being a star will always work in my favour. You could say I experienced the downside with the coverage over the burglary, and also with all the attention that surrounded my relationship with George Graham and the comments that it provoked in the newspapers every time he decided to substitute me. I know that the day the media don't want me anymore they will drop me as quickly as they first picked me up. That won't bother me too much, because I started off as a nobody and it's no hardship to return to relative obscurity.

Another source of irritation for me was the media's obsession with my relationship with Eric Cantona. They tried to make out there was a rift between us but it was purely a ruse to sell more papers. Just because we are both French and were both playing in England at that time, that does not mean there was a problem between us. Of course not, no more than it means we are bosom buddies either. The fact that Cantona's team pipped mine to the title in 1995 made no difference to my feelings. It could have been Manchester United, it could have been Bolton, that part of it was irrelevant. The only thing that mattered to me was that it wasn't Newcastle.

As I became more famous with PSG and the demands from the media increased, I was forced to find someone who could deal with things on my behalf. Every French player has an agent but generally all they do is negotiate for them with their particular club. I needed someone who could handle the influx of requests that were coming my way. Dominique Rocheteau, known once as St Etienne's 'Green Angel', had been looking after me and he suggested that I should talk to a guy called Olivier Godalier because he didn't have any marketing expertise himself. I was, and still have been, very selective about the type of commercial work I take on. Apart from anything else there is a commitment to the club you are at. It wouldn't do your career any good if you were here and there honouring contracts and engagements when your club wants you to rest. Not all exposure is good exposure and younger players must take care not to accept any old thing just to get their face on television.

Having said that, it's fun to get involved in another world outside of football. It's an education – and if you can earn a bit of money from it, so much the better! If someone is willing to pay you lots of money just for wearing their sunglasses, you'd be mad to say no. It's not as if they are asking me to do anything outrageous for my money.

When I'm in the public eye, I always try and remember that there are young people watching and listening to me who will try and copy my actions. I am aware of the attention I attract. They are going to take what I say as gospel. Young people are naive, just as I was in my youth. I always preach: 'When I started out as a footballer, nobody wanted me. But I kept on fighting for what I wanted and I got there.' It is a positive message to convey to young people because life is not easy, especially when you are growing up, and it's an important example to set. I didn't have an easy time of it but I managed to climb the mountain through sheer determination. My greatest strength is that I will never be beaten by anyone. Whenever I face a difficult situation I find something in my mind and my body to push the problems away. In football, it is important to have mental strength because there are many situations that are easier to back away from with determination. If someone is faced with problems and remembers that message, and remembers that I didn't find it easy but I got there and so can they, then that's great.

The attempt to destroy my character after the doomed World Cup tie with Bulgaria and the abuse I had to deal with from fans and media alike, which I will deal with later, were just a few of the problems I had to deal with in the 1993/94 season. Manager Artur Jorge was coming under pressure that season. It was another of those perplexing situations which doesn't stand up to rational analysis yet which happens anyway. Consider these facts: PSG were moving with purpose towards the championship. The team was full of quality and the spirit in the dressing-room was first-class – if it wasn't, how would we have been able to achieve such good results? Yet the talk from the so-called experts was that PSG was a rocky ship and Jorge had to take the flak for it. It was grossly unfair and to try and unravel the reasons behind it is to confront some unpleasant home truths. Could it possibly have been because he was a foreigner enjoying success in France at the expense of Frenchmen? Surely no one could be that small-minded, and yet alternative explanations are hard to find.

Jorge had to go and that was a personal blow to me because I warmed to the man and I respected his knowledge of the game. He was good for French football but when the spectre of xenophobia rears it's ugly head, it is a battle that is hard to win. He left with the minimum of fuss and with his dignity intact. It was typical of the gentleman he was. I loved him for what he did for my game and I missed him when he was not around. His replacement was Luis Fernandez, a former team-mate of mine at Matra Racing. At least the press were happy: they had a French international who conformed more to their ideal of what a manager working in France should be like. That wish list did not include a reserved Portuguese manager, even if that person spoke with a lot of intelligence. As for me, let's just say that it was a difficult working relationship from day one. I wanted to like and respect Fernandez in the way I had Jorge, and so discouraged myself from having any preconceptions based on my knowledge of Fernandez at Matra. Sadly, it just didn't happen between us.

Yet, surprisingly, the new manager made me captain. Even now I find it hard to understand his decision because it certainly didn't help to make the relationship between us any sweeter. For a start it was difficult for me because the captaincy was being taken away from a friend, Paul Le Guen, for whom I had a great deal of time and respect. I went to Paul and explained that it was nothing to do with me and that I felt things should have been left as they were. Indeed, I didn't consider myself captaincy material. Fernandez's view was that it would add an extra dimension to my game and make me a better player.

Yet if I thought that by his handing me the captain's armband the manager was giving me his fulsome support, then events were to prove somewhat different. The manager made a habit of substituting me, usually with about three minutes or so to go. It is something I became used to at White Hart Lane under George Graham. But this was different. Obviously the captain should be treated no differently to anyone else if he is injured or off form, but it has to be remembered that he is the team leader and his presence is needed on the pitch. The fact that my withdrawals always came in the latter stages of games shows that it was not due to loss of form or because of injury. In my opinion, the manager was determined to make his point (whatever that point was) and I could only accept it.

Matters came to a head when I was taken off near the end of a 1995 Champions' League tie with Spartak Moscow. This was particularly humiliating for me because millions of television viewers were following the game. It had happened a few times before, but this time I couldn't deal with it. It just seemed to make no sense at all and my frustration boiled over. When I reached the bench, I called the manager every name I could think of. I got a lot of things off my chest that night and the time was well overdue when I eventually had my say. I was captain of the team and I was not prepared to suffer such public humiliation. His response was to order me to go and train on my own; he said I wouldn't be picked for the first team again. It seemed he had got his own way.

However, Fernandez knew he could not get along without me. Even though I say it myself, I was an important player to the team and the manager knew it. He continued to pick me but that is not to say there was any thaw in our relationship. Most days he would make some remark or do something that strengthened my resolve to leave the club in the summer. There was no way I could have been expected to stay on with things the way they were.

There were several reasons that I can point to now which explain the antagonism between us. Our philosophies were poles apart. To me football is a beautiful game, an art form to be cherished and admired for its beauty as well as the drama and emotion that surround match-days. Fernandez takes a different view. To him football is a war, a conflict and he left his players in no doubt of the consequences if we didn't join in with his fighting games. There was a pressure on us and it was not designed to bring the best out of us. On the contrary – pressure applied in this way can only yield a negative response. It seems logical that some of our problems hailed back to the time when we were team-mates. He was eight years older than me and he scarcely played during the season we were both at Matra. He seemed to resent that and at PSG he also seemed to resent all the things I was doing off the field. It cannot have been easy; unlike England where most top players get involved with endorsements and that kind of thing, in France that was more rare.

It's an easy assumption to make: player 'x' is doing this and that off the field, so he cannot be giving his best between three o'clock and a quarter to five. Yet it's a charge that I could never be accused of. For me, it is not difficult to keep them completely separate. I never lose sight of the fact that we only get the chance to do the other things, to get involved in commercial matters, because of what we have achieved in football. To forget that is to lose everything. Playing the game comes first, second and last; everything else, the nice big contracts, the fame and the attention, comes after that.

Sometimes the attention I attracted proved an embarrassment. It was inevitable that certain people would react jealously. The journalists milling around at training would always be seeking some comment from me, they didn't seem bothered with talking to the other players and sometimes they preferred to talk to me rather than the manager. What could I do? I couldn't tell them to go away, the journalists were only doing their job and I've always tried to make sure not to leave others out but to try and include everyone. It wasn't me trying to make out that I was something special.

The situation became uncomfortable, people were stirring things up behind the scenes. Nobody said anything to my face, only behind my back. I had a couple of close friends giving me support and their friendship was invaluable. They were the black players Bernard Lama and Antoine Kombouare and they had a really cool attitude to everything. It didn't matter to them that there was another article somewhere about David Ginola. Our friendship was based on solid principles – media reports and petty jealousies could never threaten that and it was important to me. We'd go out for drinks together and generally chill out. It was great to escape the suffocating pressures that were all around the PSG scene at that time.

I had made up my mind I would have to leave Paris and that meant leaving France as well. There was nowhere else for me to go. There were no other peaks in France to scale. Marseille were another big club but I had been down that route and, besides, they were still in Second Division exile, paying the price for the bribery scandal of a few years before. I had won everything there was to win in France with the exception of a European trophy. It was ironic, after three successive semi-finals, that PSG should enjoy their first European success, the Cup Winners' Cup, in 1996, the year after I had left. That gave me mixed feelings: delight on the one hand for my former team-mates and the supporters, but also a twinge of regret that I wasn't there to share in that success after all we had been through. It wasn't to be. My fall-out with Fernandez had put paid to that.

It was a strange situation because sometimes he would tell me that I reminded him of Garrincha – I recall as a youngster watching video clips of the great winger winning the World

Cup with Brazil in 1962. After beating Barcelona to reach the European Cup semi-finals he even whispered to me that he loved me. But it was much more common for him to put me down with little comments here and there and I knew well before the end of the season that PSG and I were about to divorce. My life, my career, were about to enter a new and exciting phase.

Having reached the decision to leave PSG and France, the pressing issue was to choose my next location. There was interest from clubs all over Europe and it made me feel proud that some of the biggest names wanted me on their books. Real Madrid, Inter Milan, Bayern Munich, Arsenal . . . I was like a hungry schoolboy given his pick in the tuck shop. Celtic and, of course, Newcastle were also keen but for a long time it seemed that my next home would be Barcelona. If I was hoping for a long rest in that summer of 1995, I was mistaken because a lot of time was spent flying here, there and everywhere. 'Where would I end up next?' was the million dollar question.

CHAPTER TEN

Faith, phobias and the French

*'I would see a faith healer myself if I really needed to,
so does that make me a crackpot too?'*

I have a lot of sympathy for Glenn Hoddle over the way he was treated for using a faith healer when he was England coach. I believe in everything that is helpful. I am prepared to try different methods if the conventional ones do not work. I know that in Brazil, for example, if you do not want to see a doctor then you can see a faith healer, someone who will treat your pain in a different way to a doctor. It is accepted there, unlike in this country. I would never say something is rubbish without trying it. If I was a manager I would say to a faith healer: 'If you can prove to me that what you do works for my players, then you can be part of my team. If a player is ruled out with an injury, and you can get him back on the training pitch and playing again, then I will believe you, so come and prove it to me and you are in.' Hoddle was labelled a crackpot for suggesting his players should visit faith healer Eileen Drewery, but I believe that's because people associated with football are intrinsically old fashioned, and are not prepared to open their mind to unorthodox methods – methods Hoddle had seen for himself and which he believed in. I would see a faith healer myself if I really needed to, so does that make me a crackpot too?

I believe in the power of faith healers because I have seen one at work with my own eyes. I have a friend in the south of France, Irene, who is absolutely brilliant – she is like a witch, with magical powers. A couple of years ago my daughter developed a very bad case of eczema, she had a rash all over her body. We had tried all the creams and medicines recommended by the specialist doctors, but nothing made a difference. It was difficult for Carla to explain her pain, because she was so young, and we were having trouble knowing what we could do to help her. At that time I didn't have a great deal of 'faith' in faith healers – if you'll pardon the pun – but I knew this woman was treating a friend of mine for a thyroid problem and was doing a good job for him, and he suggested I went to see her. Coraline and I decided to take a chance, and the moment we walked into her house and Irene saw Carla she smiled, as if she knew exactly what the problem was.

'Mr Ginola – can I call you David? Don't worry, this is nothing, I can make it go away within three or four days.'

I looked at her and said: 'Yeah, yeah, it is all very well saying that, let me see it.'

I thought I was wasting my time there, but she made Carla lay down and then put her hand on her stomach. After a couple of minutes she invited me to touch the skin, and I could feel a burning sensation. She was extracting all the pain from Carla's body into her own. I still didn't believe it, but then the top of Irene's hand developed a big bump, as if all the eczema had gathered there, and suddenly she couldn't move any more. Irene said: 'I have taken all the pain from your daughter, it is in me now and I will release it, don't worry.' Then she started shaking her other hand to throw away everything she had extracted from Carla. Within three days, Carla's condition had completely cleared up – it was amazing. Since then she has never had any more eczema anywhere on her body. We had seen every dermatologist and tried every cream, all to no avail, yet this woman had cured her simply by placing her hand over her stomach. I remember looking at Coraline after three days and saying: 'It works. I can't believe it, but it does.'

Irene's magical powers didn't stop there. I went to a skiing resort in France recently because I wanted to buy an apartment there. I met the builders and saw the plans, and I liked what I saw. I went away to consider paying a deposit, but two days later I received a phone call from Irene.

'David, I had a dream about you going to buy an apartment for when you go skiing.'

I couldn't believe she could know this, but she even told me the first name of the builder I had spoken to.

'This man has had many problems in the past. He starts building a complex, takes people's deposits and then runs off with the money before completing the work.'

I did some checking on this man, and everything she had told me turned out to be true, so she saved me from getting caught out and, needless to say, I didn't buy the apartment. Now, if I have an important decision to make, I call her and ask if she has seen any problem relating to me which I should be wary of. But she tells me not to worry, she will call me if ever she sees a problem ahead for me. Another friend of mine has cancer, and she has surprised all the doctors by working with him and improving his condition. So I would certainly be prepared to add a faith healer, such as Irene, to my medical team if I was in charge of a football club. I am sure she could help my players. I don't care if people call me a crackpot, I know this woman cured my daughter in three days, which is more than the doctors were able to do in months. I feel like a crackpot for NOT believing in her in the first place.

To witness something with your own eyes, no matter how strange or amazing it may seem, carries far more weight than anything you may have been told or heard. When I was a teenager my friends and I created our own séance, and it was a fascinating and spooky experience because we actually made contact with the spirit of someone's grandmother. It was the summer time and my friends and I used to go to a club in St Maxime where there was a huge outdoor swimming pool. In the evening we went to the clubhouse for parties, and one night we stayed behind after closing time, because we knew the people who looked after the place. One of the boys knew how to hold a séance, so we decided to try and contact the spiritual world. We sat down around a table and we all put our hands on the top of it. It was hard to concentrate at first because nobody believed in what we were doing and we were all laughing and joking, but after a while we got more serious . . . and suddenly we felt the table moving! We asked a few questions and then my friend said: 'Grandma, if you are there, knock twice.' Amazingly, the table lifted a couple of inches off the ground and banged down again twice, and this continued as the spirit of his grandmother talked to us. I wondered if it was a trick, but it couldn't have been as all our hands were on top of the table. Also, it would have been impossible for someone to raise the heavy table with their legs and bang it down without us noticing. It was really scary and I almost got straight on my bicycle and rode home. I thought about this for a long time afterwards, because I hadn't believed in it and then saw the proof with my own eyes. We were always doing things to scare ourselves, such as going to a friend's house to watch a horror movie like *Halloween*, or *Friday The 13th*, and then going into the garden in the dark – they were just things you do as a kid. We were a crowd of all boys, because we didn't think too much about girls at this time, we were more interested in boys' stuff such as playing football and having a laugh.

I am not religious, but there is something about religion that attracts me. I like going into a church, and spending some time just sitting there, the atmosphere makes me feel good. I know it is the house of Jesus and it gives me a feeling of peace. I don't think I could ever be a religious devotee, because the problems that arise from religion trouble me.

Although I would agree to see a faith healer myself, I do not think I would visit one as my first port of call. I would try an osteopath because if I have a problem in my calf, for example, I know it is not coming from the calf, but maybe from my back. If I have ankle trouble, the problem may stem from my knee. I learned in France that the body is connected in a certain way and that's how pains in the lower body can even come from a problem with my teeth. I know the osteopath can check every part of my body to find where the pain is coming from, then treat the right area. Just think of reflexology: by massaging the feet you can clear a blockage higher up in the body. Sadly, I think we are still rather in the dark ages when it comes to how footballers are treated. I know that manager Arsene Wenger tries to do things the right way at Arsenal. I'm told he has an osteopath who visits Highbury on a weekly basis just to check out the players. When you are playing 60 games a season, you have to provide the right treatments for the players. It is like servicing a car, it is vital. In the year 2000

I am surprised not to see every big club with a diverse medical team.

These days professional footballers not only have to be 100 per cent physically fit, but mentally fit, too. To this end, sports psychologists are becoming more important in the game. In Toulon I worked with a coach named Paul Orsatti and he was very big on using psychology to motivate players. I was very young at the time, but when I think back I can see he was really clever, and his approach was excellent – you don't come across many coaches or managers like him. He was using the brain more, helping the players to deal with emotions. Many other sports use psychologists, such as tennis and Formula One, and I think this is a good idea. They are part of the staff and they help the players attain the amount of effort needing in training. They are widely used everywhere around the world, except in football, where they could for example help you sustain the level of fitness you need to play games on Saturday–Wednesday–Saturday without being mentally tired. I think we are too old fashioned in football to accept new ideas like this. Footballers are expected to deal with all the mental pressures themselves, but it is important to be surrounded by good medical staff, as that can help you be more successful.

Even footballers who have conquered their mental frailties on the pitch might need some help to get over their phobias off it. At some point in my life I am determined to confront the one phobia I have. It frustrates me because I love water, I love swimming, and I love the underwater world – but I am obsessed by one thing. Sharks. I wake up in the night sometimes, sweating, after dreaming I'm being eaten by a shark. It all stems from when I was 12 and I went to see the film *Les Dents de la Mer*, or *Jaws*. I wasn't allowed to go, but I crept out of the house without my parents' permission and went to the cinema with some friends. It was just before the summer and the film really had a deep affect on my mind. Now fear of sharks has become a phobia that I cannot shift. Every time I went to the beach after that, I couldn't go swimming in the sea without looking behind me all the time. The film portrays a type of death which I find totally obsessive. If I was on a boat, stranded on the open sea, and you told me I had to swim back to shore I would do it, but I would be absolutely petrified that there was a shark behind me, out to get me. The death I fear most is not being drowned, but being eaten by a shark. If you are eaten by a shark you die before you have the chance to drown.

I think the only way for me to deal with my fear would be to confront a Great White shark from the safety of a diver's cage – although it may even make it worse, who knows! Last year in Mauritius my wife dived with sharks, 20 metres under the sea, and got a diploma for it. She was laying on the bottom of the sea with other people and the instructor pointed out the sharks. She said it was beautiful and I should go with her, but where there are sharks I won't put one toe in the water!

Isn't it strange how we French are obsessed with animals? Remember my fellow Frenchman Eric Cantona's famous quote about the trawlers and the seagulls? I don't think there are many football fans in this country who could forget Eric's colourful career in the Premiership. Personally, I think mental pressure was something which Eric found difficult to handle. I'm convinced he resented me coming to play in England. Until I arrived at Newcastle in 1995 he had been the only French star in the English game. But I stole his limelight. Football came between our friendship. Football drove us apart. Eric was idolised at Manchester United and always wanted to be the king in England – but I wanted the same, so there was an inevitable clash. But our friendship has not really been the same since a bust-up before a World Cup qualifier against Bulgaria in 1993. I will go into more detail about that later, but following that we never spoke again and that made me sad. I remember playing against Eric when both our clubs were fighting for the title in my first season. French television covered the match and the whole focus was on whether or not we would shake hands at the end of the game. The cameras followed our every move to see what would happen. In the event, we avoided each other.

Eric was quite simply one of, if not the best players ever to play in English football and he helped turn Manchester United into the world power they are today. But he didn't get the recognition he deserved in France, because people were scared of his character and he is sometimes difficult to understand. I think people either love him or are scared of him. But we are similar in many ways – he, like me, is from the South of France and both of us are proud of our roots. We share similar views on life and on things such as nature. Eric is a simple person who has different values. He once told me that when he looked to the future he saw himself living in a cabin somewhere deep in the forest with a gun for hunting. He would certainly be clever enough to live like that. He described to me how he could see himself living near a stream and going fishing or shooting birds to get food for his family. He is a very expressive person, though he has a tendency to exaggerate things.

We are not in touch with each other now, but I want us to meet up when I am no longer playing football, and I know Eric feels the same way. I met Eric's brother, Joel, at Disneyland Paris a couple of years ago and said to him: 'I want you to send my regards to Eric. Tell him we will have a 'pastis' together when I stop playing football. [A 'pastis' is a typical French drink, which is aniseed based, and a stronger version of Greek ouzo.] We will go to a nice place, have a meal together and talk about everything. I think at the moment we are surrounded by people who are not always looking for the best in us, so it is better to meet after our football lives are finished.' Joel told me: 'I am sure Eric feels the same.'

Our international careers were similar in that they were both cut short because of things we said and did. He was wasted by the French team. He upset the French Football Federation, by calling the manager of France, Ari Michel, a 'bag of shit'. Obviously they didn't appreciate that, but he was speaking from his heart and I can understand that. He was a pioneer for French footballers in what he did by establishing himself in English football, and if it wasn't for Eric I don't think so many French people would be involved in the game in England. English clubs had some bad opinions about French players, but Eric changed all that with his success and made them keen to have French players in their team in the hope they would be like him. I admit I was surprised that he was allowed to carry on in English football after his infamous kung-fu assault on a Crystal Palace fan at Selhurst Park. If you allow things like that, then you open the door to all kinds of trouble. Sometimes you do things on the spur of the moment, but he surprised me.

The fact that he was overlooked for the French national team competing in Euro 96 in England was, in my opinion, not fair. I am sure he would have been a great asset to France, playing on the grounds where he plied his trade week in, week out. Maybe that snub is what pushed him into making the decision to retire from the game altogether; he'd had enough and he was fed up with football's mentality. But I think he can be just as prolific in his new chosen career in films. I have seen his work at the movies and every time I look at him, I can see he is really the guy from the South of France. He is an actor as a person, so I believe he can go far on the silver screen.

During his time in England, Eric had a cult following at Old Trafford. He was back in England in the summer playing beach football and said he would love to manage United when Alex Ferguson retires. I am sure he would be a popular choice with the Reds' supporters. But he was also hated and despised by rival fans. I don't think this was an anti-French feeling, just an example of jealousy, that he was not working wonders in their own team. I have suffered similar taunts and abuse from opposition fans who try and upset me. But I take this as a back-handed compliment and I rise above it. I have never experienced racism and I don't think English fans are being racist when they pick on the French footballers playing here. All French players are different. If Arsenal's Thierry Henry says something, for example, then it doesn't mean that all French players in the Premier League feel and think the same way. Just because I am French doesn't mean I necessarily agree with what the others say – for example, I didn't agree with the reasoning behind Nicolas Anelka's £23 million move from Arsenal to Real Madrid or the way it was handled; and I didn't agree with some of the negative things about English football that Frank Leboeuf said at Chelsea. I just think we are foreigners playing in the Premier League, and when we play well the crowd try to put us off our game, that is their target. And after France won the last World Cup it became even worse for the guys who were in the national team. But you have to take it as a compliment, and I know most opposition fans appreciate me. They also see me take things in the right spirit, because if I hear their comments I give them the thumbs-up, and they laugh with me, not at me, because I don't take it seriously – which is the opposite way they want me to react.

Anelka came to England for a lot of reasons – the football, the financial rewards, a whole new way of life. The fans loved him and if I was him I would have stayed at Arsenal for a few more years and stuck with English football. He should have taken on board any advice he was given and then made his own decision. I have good people around me and I always listen to what they have to say, but in the end I decide what I want to do. If I don't like something on my plate and someone says to me 'David, this is very good,' I still won't eat it if I don't like it, simple as that. Anelka was too young to handle all the attention, which is why having the right people to look after you is so important. As a 20-year-old you are not capable of accepting all that responsibility, so I don't put all the blame on him. It was a shame for Arsenal fans, but I hope he is able to get on with his football because I believe he is the typical striker of the future, and in the next ten years he can become the number one striker in the world – and hopefully he will help the French national team.

CHAPTER ELEVEN

Branded a murderer

'It was as if he [Houllier] had flicked the switch on the guillotine – with my head on the block'

I have been taught by some of the best coaches in the world that football is a team game. I know it may sound like I am stating the obvious, but you win as 11 players and you lose as 11 players. You score a goal and there are ten other players out there with you to share the success; or you make a mistake and there are ten players who can help you.

So I would like to know this: how can one man be blamed for a nation's failure to qualify for the finals of a World Cup? Yet that is exactly what happened to me when France suffered the huge disappointment of failing to reach the 1994 finals in the USA – and I became Public Enemy Number One in my homeland.

The man responsible for my public execution was the manager of the French national team at the time, Gerard Houllier, who, like me, is now working in England, as the manager of Liverpool. It is something I can never forgive him for, as it was a cruel attempt to wreck my life, and my family and I have been paying the price ever since. His vicious verbal assault had my family in tears . . . and very nearly killed my grandfather.

Houllier blamed me for 'murdering' France's bid to qualify for the finals. My 'crime' was to over-hit a cross aimed for Eric Cantona during our last qualifying match against Bulgaria, in Paris on 17 November 1993. We needed just a point to book our tickets to the USA and were drawing 1–1 as I attempted the cross. Unfortunately, the ball fell to the Bulgarians, who went up the other end and scored with almost the last kick of the game to end our dreams. Yet the punishment handed out to me so far out-weighed the crime that it was to have a dramatic affect on my life and on the lives of the people closest to me – and I feel that it is something which will haunt me for the rest of my days.

I believe that a weaker person would have been destroyed by what I was forced to go through. Indeed, it would have been easy for me to simply retreat into a shell, give up on football – and to some extent on life – and gradually disappear from the game altogether. But nobody will ever be able to dictate my life for me, least of all someone like Houllier.

To set the scene properly, I need to go back to the previous qualifying games, culminating a month before the Bulgaria debacle, when we played at home to Israel and lost 3–2.

The first World Cup qualifier saw us lose 2–0 against Bulgaria in Sofia in September 1992, but we were to put that right in Tel Aviv the following February when we beat Israel 4–0. From a team point of view it was a very good performance, and I remember that we made it easy for ourselves against a team who were not the hardest of opponents. I

remember that we preferred to travel and always found it difficult to play in Paris, at the Parc des Princes. There was more
pressure in Paris because of the high expectation of the fans
and the press. We didn't seem to get such good results on
home territory when there was such a great focus on us.

From my own point of view, I never found it a problem.
That was because, as a Paris Saint Germain player, I was playing on my home ground, so I felt very much a part of the place.
A lot of the fans who came to watch France were PSG fans, and
I even had my own section in the stadium which was a kind of
David Ginola fan club. I was playing for PSG in the Parc des
Princes on Saturday, then for France in the same stadium
the next Wednesday, so I was never fazed by it, whereas some
players may have been affected by coming from other parts
of France to the home of football where there was so much
expectation. In fact I felt comfortable playing international
football, especially as I was also having a very good year playing
for my club.

We did win in Paris in our next game against Sweden, 2–1,
although I was substituted a minute into the second half, but
then came the two crucial games starting with Israel in
October 1993. I played in this game from the start and created
the first goal and scored the second, putting us 2–1 up with 20
minutes to go. I can remember my goal well, it was a typical
David Ginola effort. It was raining a lot and the pitch was very
heavy. I received the ball on the left wing, controlled it in an
instant, turned and ran at the defender. Then I cut inside and
curled the ball from 25 yards into the far corner of the goal – it
was a great effort, especially if you see it from all the different
camera angles. It was one of my best performances for my
country because I had never been involved quite as much as in
this game, and I really thought this was going to be the start of

a long and successful international career. If you could refer to one match as the turning point in your career, where you could say 'That's it, I am not scared any more,' then this for me was it, in the sixth game of my international career.

So I was having a great game, regarded by many as by far the best player on the pitch, but with 20 minutes to go Houllier took me off. I didn't understand why, but I was substituted. Israel then scored two goals in those last 20 minutes and we lost the game.

If we had beaten Israel it was all over, we would have qualified for the World Cup finals. But now, all attention had to be turned to our last match of the Group against Bulgaria, from which we needed to gain a point to still make it through.

The inquest into the game against Israel naturally asked the question of why we failed to book our place against a country we were expected to beat comfortably. All the journalists said David Ginola was tremendous, he had a fantastic game, but Gerard Houllier started to say things like 'we have to go back to a traditional 4-4-2'. Looking back at it now, and reading between the lines, I can see that he was already preparing to drop me for the game against Bulgaria. Against Israel we had played a 4-3-3 formation with me on the left, Jean-Pierre Papin in the centre and Eric Cantona on the right; but I was the newest member of the team out of the three of us, so I figured I would be the one to be sacrificed in a more traditional 4-4-2 line-up. Houllier never thought I was capable of playing as a midfield player, he saw me as a forward, and he wanted the team to be more compact. The reaction to my substitution in the press was one of surprise. In France, in the following day's newspapers, you always have reports on how the players performed and I was given the top marks and made the star player, although the headlines were not so good because we

176

had lost the game. There was never any expectation or suggestion from the press that I would be dropped for the next game.

In France, we say we have 60 million national coaches, because every member of public has a different opinion of what the French team should be, just like in England and most other countries, I suppose. I never put myself in the position of the manager – maybe one day I will wear the skin of a manager but in the meantime I am happy to retain a player's perspective. I never judge other players, although some judge me. We had some very good individuals in the team. In front of goal Jean-Pierre Papin was amazing and Eric Cantona was a brilliant player. Defensively we were strong too, with players like Laurent Blanc, Marcel Desailly and Bernard Lama in goal, and Didier Deschamps in midfield. We were intrinsically very good, there was a good balance, but the key was to make us more compact and work as a team. In terms of results we were inconsistent, gaining one good one followed by one average one. We just couldn't put a good run of form together.

This is where I think Houllier failed us, as it is the manager's job to get the best out of his players and build the right spirit. I look at how England performed during Euro '96 and I think a lot of that was down to the man in charge, Terry Venables, as he commanded tremendous respect from his players and they went out and gave their best. It is hard to become a great manager because it is not only about the training every day, it is having the ability to build the strength and spirit of the team. In my view, I don't think Houllier commanded that respect in the dressing room. He was a pleasant enough guy and the training routines devised by him and his assistant Aime Jacquet were actually very interesting when the national squad assembled for four or five days, and we enjoyed ourselves. But in terms of inspiring the team, I don't feel he was the best at doing that.

In the intervening month prior to the final game against Bulgaria, I did not receive one phone call from Houllier. There was a big build-up in the press leading up to such an important occasion, and anything I learned about the forthcoming game was from reading it in the newspapers. I do not think Houllier showed good man-management skills in the way he handled my situation and I would like to think that if I had been the manager, I would have handled it differently. If I wanted to drop a player who had played very well in the previous game, I would talk to him and explain the thinking behind the decision, just to put his mind at rest. Especially as I am a sensitive person, I would have understood 100 per cent if it had been explained properly to me. Some journalists came to me and said: 'David, what do you think of that, you were tremendous in the last game, and no matter how well you play, you still receive criticism.' This is where I don't think Houllier really took the trouble to understand me, although I must admit that in today's game there are such big squads that it is very difficult for a manager to get to know all his players, learning what makes them tick. I think he assumed I would just accept his decision to drop me without the need to talk to me beforehand, but that shows he didn't understand me or take the trouble to get to know me as an individual.

I know that, as football players, we are all different – physically, mentally and technically. Some are able to do certain things and others can't. If I look at a player who is left-footed, for example, and if he always strikes the ball with his left foot, then I would have a training session where he was allowed to use only his right foot, as that way it would improve him as a footballer. It is all about taking the time and trouble to know your players, and also a matter of commonsense. If when a player receives a ball he can only receive it with his right foot, then he creates a problem for himself as he can only shape his body in a certain position. But if he can receive it with either foot he opens up his game and gives himself more options. I have a weakness, which is heading, so every day I work on heading the ball, in every single training session. I worked hard last season on learning when to jump so that I can meet the trajectory of the ball – and it began to pay off as even George Graham said he had never seen me win so many headers! To work on something you are weak on and to improve is a good feeling.

I shall never forget the goal I scored for France against Slovakia in one of my last appearances in April 1995, when we won 4–0 in Nantes. It was our second goal, after 42 minutes. The ball was launched from the halfway line into the 18-yard box and I jumped with the defender and sent a bullet header into the corner – it was amazing! Everyone was looking at me and pointing at their head, because it was unusual for me to score such a goal.

Anyway, I started to wonder what I could possibly do to be an accepted member of the French national team. My colleagues are always surprised to learn that I have earned so few caps – my career total is 17 – but the only explanation as to why I had won only two caps before playing in the World Cup qualifiers was that I was a bit of a late starter in the game in terms of establishing myself at the highest level. Until I played for PSG, I was not playing in European competition on a regular basis, and so not in the spotlight.

It was when I arrived at Clairefontaine on the Sunday to prepare for the Bulgaria game on the following Wednesday that I made my first mistake. Every morning at 11.00 am there was a press conference for the manager and players. On the Tuesday morning Houllier announced his team to the press and I wasn't in it. That was the only change from the previous game. Until that point I did not have any strong feelings that I was going to be dropped, because he hadn't made it look that way on the training ground. The only hint I had was that the press had suggested in the run-up to the game that we would revert to a 4-4-2 formation. But by dropping only me from the team which lost to Israel, it was as if Houllier was implying the defeat was all my fault – even though I had been our best player, according to many observers. In my mind I believed it was my fault, even though we were winning while I was still on the pitch. However, I don't believe it was just a coincidence that Israel came back against us after I was taken off. The Israeli team had a lot of respect, even fear, for me, and always had two players marking me. So when I was substituted they recovered their shape in the last 25 minutes and started to believe they had a chance without me on the pitch.

I was young and naïve but the journalists were very clever and I got a call in my room from the French press officer to say that some of the press wanted to talk to me. I didn't want to go and talk to the journalists, I wanted to stay in my room and focus on the game, but he insisted and I agreed to make a brief appearance. I sat in the corner with just one journalist and he asked me how I felt about the fact I was not playing. It was a surprise to me, as it made me realise I was always hearing things from the media rather than from the manager, which is not the way it should be done. Nobody from the management team had called me after the Israel game to say: 'David, you played well in the previous match but we need to try something different for the last game, and don't worry.' I would have understood this and been prepared, but instead I couldn't believe I had to wait until I arrived at the training camp to hear for the first time that I was not going to be in the team, because

Houllier must have known well in advance of the Tuesday announcement that I would not be in his starting line-up, yet he made no attempts at communicating with me.

The more I started to speak, the bigger the crowd of journalists around me grew. I became more and more angry and frustrated, and I was asked what I thought about some of the players in the team. I did not mention any names, but said I felt that some of the players were being picked on the strength of their personality which had maybe influenced the manager's decision. In other words, he wanted to keep them happy. The journalists mentioned some names, but I refused to be drawn and did not speak about any one particular player. Then I finished the interview and returned to my room.

I was sitting on my bed when all of a sudden Eric Cantona burst in and hovered menacingly at the doorway.

'What have you said about me and Jean-Pierre Papin?' he demanded.

'What are you talking about?'

'You accused us of affecting the team.'

'No,' I said calmly. 'I was talking to the press and I was upset and said that some players with their personalities were affecting the decisions of the manager – that is the only thing I said.'

He hit back: 'The press told me you mentioned our names.'

'Listen Eric, if you don't trust me, then go away. You know me and you should know that the press are just trying to divide us – don't fall into the trap.'

He stormed out just as suddenly and dramatically as he had arrived. I had a lot of respect for Cantona as a player, and the same went for Papin, so I would never have bad-mouthed them. Papin had this great ability in front of goal. He could strike the ball from any position. He didn't think about controlling the ball, he thought only about putting it in the net. He was tremendously dedicated and would always stay for an hour after training – even with the national team – to practice his shooting and volleying. He is a good example to youngsters because he wasn't the best player when he started in the game but he worked extremely hard to reach the top.

I realised I had stayed too long talking to the press that morning, and in the dressing room at that afternoon's training session the mood of the players was very down as they thought I had been talking about them. As I looked around the dressing room nobody was saying anything, but I could feel the tension and there was so much pressure ahead of the game. Houllier came in with Aime Jacquet, and made a speech.

'If anyone has any doubts about me or my personality, then now is the time to speak.'

So I stood up and said: 'I suppose you are talking about me.'

I defended myself to the team, explaining it was a misunderstanding and that I was frustrated after being dropped and I was unhappy at the way I had been treated. I didn't think I deserved that. The mood in training was sombre, and that continued into the next day, the day of the game.

I started on the bench, but I came on with ten minutes to go for Papin, when the score was 1–1 which would have been enough for us to qualify. Houllier gave me instructions to go out and attack, and even try to score us the goal which would have put the result beyond doubt. I was on fire even in such a short time; I was unlucky not to score when I cut in from the left and the goalkeeper saved my shot. I was everywhere on the pitch and I was excited because we were on the verge of qualifying for the World Cup finals. I went on a run and was barged to the floor by a defender, which gave us a free-kick on the right flank, a few yards from the corner flag. The free-kick was tapped short to me and I crossed the ball for Cantona who was unmarked in the 18-yard box. But the ball went just over his head and Bulgaria regained possession on the far side. Five passes later they were in our box and Emil Kostadinov superbly struck the ball under our crossbar and it was 2–1. Thirty seconds later the referee blew the final whistle.

The scene and the mood in the dressing room was one of total devastation. It was so quiet and I can honestly say that throughout my entire career I have never been in a dressing room where it was so full of people, yet so quiet – you could have heard a pin drop. Everyone just sat there with their heads down, looking at the floor and avoiding eye contact with one another. It was like a church during a silent prayer. It did not really sink in that we had been eliminated from the World Cup qualifiers. I sat there certain it was a nightmare. 'Surely this is a dream,' I told myself. 'Soon I will wake up in my bed the day before the game thinking about what was still to come.' A party had already been planned at a restaurant in Paris – supposedly to celebrate our qualification – but that was the last thing we wanted to do, so we all put in a brief appearance before going our separate ways.

At this time, I had no thoughts whatsoever that I might be blamed for what had happened. I assumed we would be blamed as a team, not me as an individual. But then on the way home Coraline said something to me.

'David, I don't know why but I have a feeling they will put this on you.'

'No way, everything will be fine.'

The next day I got a call at home from a journalist who told me I should switch on the television immediately. I switched between channels but no matter which one I chose, I saw Houllier's face. I couldn't believe what I was hearing. He was saying things like 'The fact that one player cracked up was like a drop of acid . . . David Ginola is the murderer of the team . . . he sent an Exocet missile through the heart of French football . . . David Ginola committed a crime against the team, I repeat, a crime against the team.'

It was as if he had flicked the switch on the guillotine – with my head on the block.

My father Rene telephoned me to ask what was going on. Everyone around me was crying, my wife, my mother and father, even my friends. I was not concerned for myself, only for those close to me, and I knew I needed to put on a brave face. But inside, I was thinking: 'How can I possibly go on after this?' That night I lay awake with all these thoughts going through my head: 'How can I play the next game on Saturday? What will be the reaction of the crowd? What will be my future in football?' If I didn't have a strong character it would have destroyed me – and I can think of many players I have known whose careers would have been finished by this experience because they would not have been emotionally strong enough.

My family were distraught for me. They knew I was putting so much into my job and they couldn't understand how not one person in football stood up for me. I was on my own and everybody was hiding behind me because they were relieved that I was getting the blame instead of them. My mum and dad are very sensitive too and this affected my father so badly that he lost all his passion for the game of football, saying that if this was the way the game could treat someone then he did not want to see any more football for the rest of his life. Houllier chose bad words in saying I had murdered the team. They particularly affected my grandfather – he nearly died from the pain of seeing how they hurt his family. He was 85 years of age and very passionate about football, having followed my career since I was very young, so when he heard Houllier's outburst on the television he said: 'No, that is not my David.'

It wasn't just me who suffered. My parents were snubbed wherever they went, and they were also both verbally abused at work. My father was working in the factory and my mother was now a secretary for France Telecom, and both of them were treated badly by their work colleagues who jumped on the Houllier bandwagon and blamed their son for France's failure to qualify for USA '94. They were treated like outcasts. In the end they were hiding from people, and they certainly weren't able to sleep at night. My parents describe this as a 'black hole' in their lives, and they are still badly scarred by it to this day – I don't think they will ever get over it. My mother worries now whenever the phone rings, in case I am calling with bad news. It is only when she hears that my voice is happy that she can relax and not worry that something is wrong – it must be terrible for her.

Although my parents had no doubts I had a strong enough character to bounce back, their initial reaction was that they wanted me to stop playing football. They feared for my safety, and I know my father was hoping I might leave France and find a club abroad to play for, so that I would be out of the spotlight in my home country. Mum and Dad were worried that I might be attacked by fans at rival grounds in France. If the fans believed Houllier and blamed me for their national team's downfall, then who knew what lengths they might go to in order to take revenge on me? That is why, when I eventually moved to Newcastle, my parents were very happy for me. They saw it as a new beginning for me, and a chance to heal the wounds because they could see I was loved by the Geordie fans rather than hated by the followers of French football.

I was so angry with Houllier, because he had tried to destroy me with his very personal attack. Really, he was the one who should have taken the blame. Even the journalists who were at his press conference were surprised by what he was saying, but they could not resist the chance to jump on such a sensational story. To highlight how much of a hypocrite he was, Houllier even said: 'I'm sure this will not harm David's international career.' What a joke!

I said nothing in response to the attack on me. I knew the only answer I could give was to perform well on the pitch – my football would have to be my answer to all the criticism. I thought: 'Fair enough Mr Houllier, you tried to kill my career and destroy me as a person, but I will prove to you in my own way that I am stronger than that.'

My next game for PSG was only four days after the Bulgaria match, away to Toulouse. I was in the tunnel outside the dressing rooms and the Toulouse players were coming up to me and telling me not to worry, that I was a great player, which was comforting. My own team-mates were also very support- ive and told me not to listen to Houllier because I was better than that. Along with George Weah I was one of the most respected players in the club. The chairman of PSG, Michel Denisot, always said I was the symbol of the club. I wanted to show my team-mates I was strong enough to come through this; I didn't want to put any doubts in their heads about me.

My Paris team went out on to the pitch together before the game to inspect the pitch, and I was practically the last man out of the tunnel. All of a sudden it hit me. It was as if everyone inside the stadium was booing and whistling at me. I began to realise the full impact of Houllier's words. They all thought I had murdered the French team. I went back to the dressing room and I was very down, and the manager Artur Jorge asked me if I felt okay to play. 'I will understand if you do not feel like it,' he said. 'No, no, no,' I replied. ' I want to play. This is my job, this is what I love doing and I want to show everyone that I can overcome this.' I owed it to my club, my team-mates, the fans and, of course, my family.

After ten minutes I scored a goal, a header, and I just cried like a baby. All the pent-up emotion came flooding out. There were my team-mates congratulating me – George Weah, Alain Roche, Antoine Kombouare and the Brazilians Ricardo Gomes and Valdo – with cries of 'You are the best!' and I just stood there in tears, looking all around the stadium as the crowd were still booing me and whistling. I was showing them fantastic skill, yet every time I got the ball they were booing me. When I scored a goal and still got the same reaction, I knew it was going to be very difficult from then on. Anyone listening to the French manager talking the day after the Bulgaria game – even if they knew nothing about football – would believe him when he said David Ginola was a criminal. The booing would continue in every game until the end of the season.

A few things kept me going. Firstly, I had a manager in Artur Jorge who trusted me very much. He told me I was a great player and that the club counted on me. The club chairman Michel Denisot also telephoned me to offer me support. But it was difficult because they were not suffering the daily hell like I was. Secondly, wherever I went, people were not so bad to me once they had met me and spoken to me, which reassured me.

I never know when I am beaten, and the only way I knew how to respond was to come out fighting and play the best football of my life. It obviously worked, because I ended the season by being voted France's Footballer of the Year. I didn't care that the media thought I had lots of skill and scored spectacular goals – more important for me was for them to realise that here was a man who was almost destroyed by the manager of the French national team, but battled back to be the best player in the league that same season. By voting for me, it proved that the journalists who had been deprived of the chance of going to America for the World Cup were not blaming me after all.

It also proved to me that I had been justified in carrying on after what had happened. But I was not the same person, and I am still not the same person. This man, Gerard Houllier, has ensured that I have to carry this stigma around with me for the rest of my life. I still cannot believe he did that.

I suppose Houllier's hypocritical attitude should not have surprised me. In France, he used to talk about English football with a little smirk on his face, not treating it very seriously. So it shocked me a little when he came to England to be manager of Liverpool, as I couldn't understand what made him want to work in a country whose football he did not really respect. Maybe he has changed his mind now, I don't know.

Houllier quit as national coach after the Bulgaria game – jumping before he was pushed, having deflected the blame away from himself and on to me – but things were not about to get any better for me in international terms because he was replaced by Aime Jacquet, who had been his right-hand man. You can imagine how close they were at this time, having worked together, and when Jacquet took over they were still in close contact. I played in the next game the following February, which was a friendly against Italy in Naples. It was the first match after the disaster against Bulgaria, but we beat a strong Italian team 1–0, with me setting up the goal for Youri Djorkaeff. But these internationals were meaningless for us, because we were not involved in USA '94.

I went to play in England in the summer of 1995 and, in a way, that made it easier for Jacquet and France to disregard me, a case of 'out of sight, out of mind'. But I was playing so well for Newcastle that, after a while, Jacquet found that he couldn't avoid picking me for his squad. It turned out to be the end of my international career when I gained my 17th cap for my country on 6 September 1995.

I was called up for the European Championship qualifier against Azerbaijan, which was being played in Auxerre, but I was named as a substitute. On the bench with me was a guy called Christophe Cocard, who is playing now for Kilmarnock in Scotland, but who, at the time, was a local favourite playing for Auxerre. The French team were winning 7–0 with 25 minutes to go and all the substitutes were warming up behind the goal. The crowd were shouting '*Cocard, Cocard*' for their hero, and I thought the obvious thing would be for Jacquet to put him on to please the crowd as, after all, the match was already won by this stage. But suddenly Henri Emile, one of Jacquet's assistants, came running over to us and told me to get ready as I was going on. I told him to go and tell Aime to put Cocard on first as the crowd were all shouting for him, but he told me Aime wanted me.

I got stripped off and the moment the crowd saw me step on to the pitch they started screaming even louder, '*Cocard, Cocard*'. I couldn't believe that Jacquet hadn't listened to me, and because he had put me on ahead of the local hero, I immediately had the crowd on my back. We went on to win 10–0, but the only guy who wasn't happy was me. I said to Jacquet afterwards: 'I have come all the way from the north-east of England where they love me at my new club, to be booed by my home fans. Why did you make such a bad decision? A bit of commonsense would tell you that at 7–0 up with 30,000 fans shouting for Cocard it is obvious which substitute you should use first – I am hardly likely to complain.' To this day, I do not know if Jacquet did that deliberately to antagonise me but could he really have been that naïve? That experience simply added to my international heartache.

I missed the next game for France because of a calf injury but after recovering from that I was soon on fire again for Newcastle. There was another international coming up in Paris and I felt sure I must have a chance of being included. I decided to fly back to France with my family on the Wednesday so that when I was named in the squad that afternoon, I could spend three days with my family in Disneyland Paris, and then join the team on Saturday at Clairefontaine. But on the Wednesday afternoon when Jacquet named his squad, I wasn't included. Nobody had the courtesy to call me, so I made a phone call to ask Jacquet why. He had a weak excuse about me being injured for the previous game, while the players who came in did well which meant I was not in the squad this time. It didn't matter that I was doing very well with my club, he had his excuse to drop me and that was it for my international career. I was not being arrogant, I felt I'd had good reason to fly to Paris expecting to be included.

As far as I was concerned, it wasn't just a gamble. Previously I'd had a visit at Newcastle from one of the French technical staff, Roger Lemerre, whose job it was to check the progress of the French players who were playing at clubs outside of France. He came into the dressing room at St James' Park and told me how well he thought I'd played. Therefore, it was only natural for me to assume he would write a favourable report on me. How wrong I was.

The final nail in the coffin came a few years later, in December 1997. I was now at Tottenham and playing some of the best football of my career, and was hoping I would figure in Jacquet's plans for the World Cup finals which France were hosting the following summer. But I wasn't even included in a squad of 40 players who were chosen to go to a training camp in Tignes. The people in charge of the national team were saying that I was not among the best 40 French players, and that hurt me because I still had ambitions of playing in the World Cup finals.

France '98 was to prove another nightmare for me in my turbulent international career.

CHAPTER TWELVE

Shattered dreams

*'I should have been on a desert island, unable
to hear anything about the World Cup finals'*

One of the greatest regrets in my football career is missing out
on the chance to win the World Cup with France in 1998. The
fact that I was snubbed from the squad is a bitter pill to
swallow and, believe me, the pain of it is something I shall have
to live with every day of my life. My son Andrea provides a
constant reminder to me because he often goes around the
house singing a song which was adopted after the final, which
goes: *'One, Two, Three, Zero'* (a Un, a Deux, a Trois, Zero) in
memory of the victorious 3–0 scoreline against Brazil.

Many people have told me they thought France played well
during the tournament but felt there was still something missing on the left and they wanted to see me there. All I can think
of is how proud I would have been to have won the World Cup
for my son and for my daughter Carla – to have given them

that would have been so special, or I think of giving it to my grandparents, my father Rene, my mother Mireille, brother Sebastien and my wife Coraline. I wanted so much to give this to the people close to me, they deserve it. It hurts me so much that they never had the chance to experience the happiness they deserved, especially my father, yet they were deprived of it because of the people running the French national team. I am really upset for all of them, and the opportunity has gone for good now. Whenever my son watches the French team he asks me: 'Daddy, why are you not playing?' So how do you explain that to an innocent eight-year-old child?

When I think about it I ask myself what more I could have done to have been there. Maybe I should have made a telephone call to Aime Jacquet, the French national team coach, to try and heal the rift, but never in my life have I called a manager and tried to push my opinions on him. Once when I was in Paris and captain of PSG, the manager, who had been my team-mate, called me and said: 'David, come to my house and we shall have a coffee together and talk about what you think of the team.' I said: 'No, I will never do that. I am the captain, okay, but I will never talk about the other players to you.' Some people can be hypocritical. They can talk about a manager behind his back and then call him up and pretend they are his best friend, so that they make sure they are in the team. But I could never do that. Some people did advise me to call Jacquet, and I will always have this question in my mind, always wondering if it would have made a difference if I had been hypocritical enough to make that call. One day I want people to explain to me why I was excluded from the best event in French sporting history.

One of the things which made it worse for me was actually being present at the whole tournament. With all due respect to the two television stations, BBC in England and TFI in France, I made a mistake by agreeing to work for them during the tournament as a guest analyser. I should have been on a desert island, unable to hear anything about the World Cup finals. I didn't want to be there in France, watching the games. I was there physically and gave my best in all the work I did for television, but I was not there mentally. I was watching games but at the same time thinking: 'What am I doing here?' I was there during my holidays, watching more games than I had ever done in my life, avoiding my family and the people I loved most. The best thing I can say about it all is that I had a tremendous experience with the BBC, and I was pleased to be associated with so many professionals. I would wake up every day and think about what I should be saying, and what I really wanted to be saying, especially when I had to commentate on France games. I wanted to say: 'This is hell, it is ridiculous, I should be out there playing, helping my country.' I have always fought hard to be successful in life, but here I was passive, sitting quietly drinking my Coca-Cola and talking about football like a true pundit. I had such mixed emotions and feelings. I remember the day of the final so well. I was in the Stade de France with my BBC colleagues Gary Lineker and Ally McCoist, and a car came to take us back to our hotel after the game. They were talking very loudly and very excitedly, understandably on a high after commentating on the World Cup final, and looking forward to the celebrations that were planned for the rest of the night. But I was sitting there very quietly, thinking only one thing: 'Get me out of here, get me back to my hotel room where I can lock myself away from all this.' When I did arrive back at the hotel I stayed in my room all night while, outside, I could hear thousands of people enjoying themselves. At least the atmosphere in my hotel matched my mood, because it was mostly occupied by Brazilians. I was very proud for the French people, and I was pleased to see everyone cheering the fantastic achievement of the nation's football team lifting the world's greatest trophy, but I was hurting inside. My head was divided. One half was saying how proud I was and the other half was saying: 'They stole my dream.'

Many French celebrities came to the final, from politicians like the French Prime Minister to actors such as Gerard Depardieu, but I didn't mix with them on the Sunday because I was working for the BBC and so surrounded mainly by English people. A car took me to the Stade de France on the afternoon of the final and we drove into an underground car park so I did not mix with the fans either when I arrived. I was taken straight up to the gantry overlooking the pitch, from where we would broadcast the game. I can remember the fantastic mix of colours all around; the blue, white and red of France alongside the green and yellow of Brazil. I have never seen so much attention given to a football game in France. The Stade de France is a great stadium, and I have never played in it during my career, although that is the venue where I recorded my first L'Oreal advert. I also noticed the amount of women who were attending the match, proving that the final had captured the imagination of the whole population, not just the men who usually watch football. The women had been fed up with the evenings they spent alone in the past while their men watched football matches, so this was their opportunity to join in and I was amazed by their numbers. Their faces were painted in team colours and they were carrying flags and wearing scarves, and it was a great sight. It was a dream come true for France to have the final of the number one sport in their home country, with their own team contesting it. I talked to lots of people around me, and their reaction was: 'David, you should be out there with the lads.' But it didn't give me any real consolation.

I was already hurting inside, but my heart really sank when the players came out to warm up and the crowd cheered them. It is such a shame for me to have to say that this was a sad moment for me on such a happy occasion for France. I mean no disrespect to my country because, as a Frenchman, I am proud for my country to be world champions, but I cannot hide the sadness I felt on a personal level. It frustrated me because I wanted to be out there playing. My mind was taken off the situation briefly because we had plenty to talk about in the commentary box, as there was the controversy and confusion over whether or not Ronaldo was going to play for Brazil, and we were speculating about that. I just sat there and stared out the window watching the magnificent celebrations that my fellow countrymen were enjoying.

I was a little disappointed that nobody in the team mentioned me when they were interviewed on the television after the game. I thought maybe one of them might have said: 'This is for David, as well.' I wasn't really expecting it in my heart of hearts, but it would have been nice to hear, and I know that I would have done that had the roles been reversed.

I hope people can understand that my dream was stolen from me, and so that is why it was hard for me to celebrate as the three goals went in, and then as France captain Didier Deschamps lifted the fabulous golden trophy. I watched every single moment and I can understand why for so many French people it was one of their best ever memories. I am sorry, but I cannot share that feeling. I think it still shows how passionate a person I am, because I cared that France won the World Cup but had such mixed emotions. Later, when I was back in my hotel room, my closest friends called me, and they knew exactly what I was going through. They were disappointed for me because they knew I was devastated.

I always try to do my job to the best of my ability and to always do the right thing, but after what happened to me with Gerard Houllier and the Bulgaria game I wondered what I had done to deserve this pain again four-and-a-half years on. It was really bad. What a big mistake it was to watch France lift the World Cup but not be part of the team. It was not as if I didn't deserve to be there on merit, as that season I had played some of the best football of my life, which was confirmed when I was voted Footballer of the Year in England, both by my fellow professionals and by the football writers. I know my children look up to me and try to copy me, and I remember when I won the Worthington Cup with Tottenham in 1999. I was running around Wembley celebrating and I looked up and saw my children in the stand on my father's shoulders. I was blowing them kisses and they were almost crying and sending me kisses back – it was funny because some girls sitting in front of them thought I was blowing kisses to them! But at this moment all I could think about was the World Cup final and my children. 'I wish I could have given you that as well.'

I have always been so proud to represent my country. Playing for your national team is your target and motivation even in everyday training with your club. Whenever I have been overlooked for an international fixture in my time at both Newcastle and Tottenham, it has been a strange feeling to see all my international colleagues going off to join up with their respective countries while I was left behind. George Graham even had to bring in apprentices to train with us one time because there weren't enough players left to play five-a-side! I would arrive for training at Spurs during an international week and find that Sol Campbell, Darren Anderton and Ian Walker were with England, Allan Nielsen with Denmark, Steffen Iversen and Espen Baardsen with Norway, and so on.

You know, it is quite hard when you think about it to always be in a good mood. But I made sure I was always smiling because I didn't want to show the apprentices and the rest of the players who were left that it had affected me and hurt me – I owed it to them out of respect and I cared about their feelings. Many times, however, I was thinking: 'What am I doing here? I am supposed to be training with my national squad and playing for my country.' These are feelings and emotions that I didn't share with anyone. I always try to put myself in the position of someone who is looking at me and I try to imagine what it is they expect to see when they look at David Ginola. The apprentices were there and were looking up to me, so I could not let them down. I have read articles in which these young players have said they would like to have some of the skills that I have, so if they think that about me and come training with me then I want to portray the right image. But that is difficult when, maybe, I didn't really want to be there. I was very upset inside, but I kept it hidden from everyone, even from my wife. I questioned why I was made to suffer and I wondered if, maybe, I was a bad person and had done something in my past which wasn't right, and for which I was now paying.

I am totally dedicated in whatever I do and I believe you must be motivated in the same way for every game, whether it is against Manchester United or Macclesfield. Every game must be taken with the same approach and with the same focus. If you are not focussed for a lesser game then you risk being injured, and these are the kind of things about which I can advise the apprentices. Sometimes I wish I was not so caring and more like people who think freely and live their life as they wish without a care in the world. Their attitude is: 'Tomorrow is another day.' The problem in my life is that people always have some kind of strong feeling towards me – they either love me or they hate me. I always have a very high level of expectation to live up to, and, maybe, I should be more arrogant, more the way people perceive me, but I cannot, because that would not be the real me. I will never change.

To add to the hurt of missing out on France '98, I was enjoying some of the best form of my career. Yet even though I was honoured with both the PFA and Football Writer's Footballer of the Year awards in London, I never received a letter or a telephone call from the French Football Federation to congratulate me, or to say I was a good ambassador for French football. I wasn't expecting anything, but a gesture of some sort would have meant a lot to me.

I think I was resented because I was doing so much work outside of football, yet I was still a top professional. I showed them that, despite all the blame they put on me and their accusations that I would not succeed, I did. They said I couldn't combine football with my advertising and charity work. They said I would not be a success in England. They said I would not be able to concentrate fully on my main occupation of playing football. How wrong they were. After France won the World Cup, several of the players picked up lucrative advertising contracts and there was not a murmur of discontent from the football authorities because they were the world champions. Yet the real pioneers – some years earlier – were me, Eric Cantona and Jean-Pierre Papin. But we found people were jealous of our success and the fact that we were earning more money than other players.

CHAPTER THIRTEEN

Following in famous footsteps

'Yet still the children looked into my eyes, as if to say:
"Is this a good guy, or a bad guy?"'

I can never forgive the *Express* newspaper for turning around the meaning of one of my comments – which I made in reference to the Red Cross Anti-Landmines Campaign and the late Princess Diana – and making it seem as if I said I was a more important figurehead for the Red Cross than the Princess of Wales. The headline they used, which really hurt me, was: 'To most Africans a blonde means nothing . . . I am a much greater ambassador than she [Diana] ever was.'

What I said was, of course it was nice for the black children of Africa to see a white, blonde woman among them, someone special who knew how to make them smile and lit up their lives. When I visited Angola I took a football with me and played with the kids, and kicking a ball around with a professional player was something they could really enjoy. In reference to

201

this, all I said was that I thought some of the kids, from seven to 14, were happier playing a 35-minute game of football with me than speaking to the Princess. But the *Express* article implied that I thought I was more of an ambassador than Diana, and more important than her. That is, of course, rubbish. I would never dare say I was more important than the Princess of Wales – she made headlines all around the world because of her work for the anti-landmines campaign, and because of her these kids have been given a chance.

My agent Chantal made a request to the editor of the *Express*, Rosie Boycott, to retract the story, but that was ignored. I was so frustrated because it felt like I had taken one step forward and then been dragged ten steps back.

When I first arrived in the small African villages I expected to see a lot of children waiting to greet me, so I was surprised when there weren't that many. But how could they have known who I was? They do not buy or read newspapers every day, or watch the news on television, and they probably didn't know who I was, any more than they knew who Princess Diana was when she first arrived there. What did appeal to these kids was the fact that a man had arrived carrying a football, and their eyes lit up at the prospect of being able to kick around a proper ball, rather than an old tin can. Yet still the children looked into my eyes, as if to say: "Is this a good guy or a bad guy?" That was all part of the fear they had been living under during years of civil war, so it was up to me to make them feel at ease, and in that sense football became a universal language.

My association with the Red Cross began in 1998. I was approached by somebody in France who informed me that the Red Cross would be very keen to have me on board as one of their ambassadors in France, helping to raise awareness of their anti-personnel landmines campaign. I was delighted to be able to help out and said I would try my best for them and represented them at a few engagements in France. There was a limited amount I could do for them because I was living in England and it was difficult to find time with my commitment to training and playing matches. But then I was approached by a Red Cross representative in England who asked me to help them out in this country as well, so I attended a few of their functions. After a few months they asked me if I could find time in my schedule to make a trip, which I thought was a good idea. We decided that I should go to Angola, because that was the country whose problems had been highlighted by Princess Diana, and we felt it would be good for me to try and continue her good work. I was aware of the problems out there, the fact that the country had just been through many years of civil war, that the recovery of its people was being hampered by the number of landmines laid during the war which were being accidentally set off, killing or maiming innocent civilians, young and old. So it was an incredible experience for me to see, first-hand, what the problems were in my capacity as a United Nations ambassador.

There are a total of 66 countries throughout the world that are infested with landmines, and Angola is the one which has the most. A total of 24,000 people are killed or injured by landmines every year, which works out at a staggering rate of one person every 20 minutes. To give you an idea of the kind of money involved in the campaign, I shall reveal some other interesting statistics. Since 1979 the International Committee of the Red Cross has manufactured more than 120,000 prostheses, with each one costing US$125. A child's artificial limb has to be replaced every six months as he or she grows, while an adult's limb is replaced every three to five years depending on wear and tear. As for the mines, an anti-personnel landmine costs anything from US$3 to US$30 to manufacture, but up to US$1,000 to clear. I am happy to say that our campaign is making progress, and by March 2000 there were 136 countries that had signed the Ottawa Treaty, which bans the use, production, stockpiling and export of mines. You can find out all you need to know about the whole situation by logging on to my website* which I launched this year, and which I shall explain in more detail later.

My trip to Angola took place during the 1997/98 football season, but as it was a week of international fixtures I was given permission by my manager Christian Gross to visit for five days. I know that Tottenham were concerned for my safety and didn't want me to contract any kind of disease, but as the chairman Alan Sugar does a lot of work himself for charity I know he would have found it hard to stand in my way.

We flew into Angola and I was bursting to visit the toilet after drinking a lot of water on the flight, so I started to hurry along the tarmac to get inside the small terminal building to find the Gents. But suddenly there was a shriek of 'No!' from the Head of Mission of the International Committee of the Red Cross, Edmond Corthesy. I stopped in my tracks and he came up to me and said: 'David, it is very important that you do not stray from the tarmac, as there are 20,000 landmines buried at this airport.' After getting over the initial shock, I realised that airports are always important military targets, so it made sense for this one to be so heavily mined. I looked around and could see a few red posts in the ground, which signified where mines had been discovered. I later heard that the very next day two mines were discovered just off the tarmac along which I had been walking.

---

* www.walkwithoutfear.com

As we drove away from the airport, the first thing that struck me was the poverty. But then I saw some smiling kids, some who still believed in life even though they didn't have too many things around them to believe in.

Although I was unknown in the smaller villages, when I visited Luanda, the capital, a lot of children seemed to know who I was. I met some of the wonderful volunteers who work for nothing to educate the children about the problems. I also visited a school and witnessed a little play they put on to help the kids learn about the landmines. The thing that really amazed me were the clothes the children were wearing. I didn't see once a clean colour, like white, red, green, or blue. Instead it was a dirty, off-white, or red or whatever. So when we arrived with brand new T-shirts, which were brilliant white, the children loved them. I handed out colour action pictures of me playing football, which I signed, and the children were looking at them in amazement. We also took with us proper footballs, which brought out shrieks of excitement.

I visited Quito-Humbo, a village surrounded by landmines. You could see the terrible legacies of the war on the buildings because people were shooting at each other from opposite sides of the street, and the bullets lodged in the walls of the houses. I was staying at the Swiss Embassy, but I couldn't sleep at night because all I could hear were guns going off, rat-tat-tat. Someone came in and told me not to worry, but then I heard later how a person who was just walking in the street one day was killed by a sniper. Just like that.

When I visited the main hospital the next day, the problems were there for all to see. There were no pipes in the toilets to get rid of the waste, and the stench was just awful. Everywhere there were children, amputees, lying on army blankets. There were no sheets, no pillows, nothing. I spoke to one of the doctors who said: 'Mr Ginola, our problem is very simple. We are not paid by the Government so we have no money to feed our families. When we receive tablets, drugs, medicines, and all the other supplies, we sell them to get some money to feed our loved ones. The medicines and drugs never get to the patients who need them.' To make matters worse, the Government has knowledge of the situation, but doesn't seem to care. It was a horrible sight to see the patients being operated on without anaesthetic, and the bandages on their wounds dripping with blood and surrounded with flies.

I spoke to the army captain who was responsible for clearing the landmines from the area and he explained another problem to me.

'Mr Ginola, you see this area here, we cleared it of hundreds of landmines over a few weeks so it would be safe for the people. We went to work in another area and when we came back it was covered in new landmines which had been put in overnight.'

I had a shock because we were in a field, wearing special protective body armour and face shields and carefully trying to detect landmines, when all of a sudden I saw a woman 100 metres away walking across the field with her children. I turned in amazement to the captain and he explained that the path she was taking was okay, because they had cleared it first so the people could cross the field to go to work every day. I didn't know this, and my reaction was: 'My God, what is this woman doing? She will be blown up.' But I did hear a story of how someone was blown up on the path, because some evil people had come in the night and hidden fresh landmines there. I later met a girl, no more than seven or eight, who had trodden on a landmine whilst walking with her mother down a path they used every day to collect water from a pond. I was lost for words and simply held her hand. But I could see in her eyes that she was thinking: 'You, white man, what are you doing here and can you explain why this has happened to me?'

There were times I felt my life was in danger and I was always asking the captain: 'Are you 100 per cent sure this field is clear of landmines?' He told me it was safe, but in the back of my mind I always had the worry that someone had come in the night and laid fresh mines.

I learned that by us bringing gifts for the children we had created a problem, although we were just trying to bring some pleasure into their lives. We brought a large number of footballs, photographs and T-shirts, but it was still not enough for everyone. If you have 50 kids around you and you hand out presents, this attracts even more kids. When you run out of presents you end up with the kids chasing each other, fighting to get a ball off one another. So the question that must be asked is: is it right to bring presents when it results in children fighting amongst themselves? You cannot win.

In Quito-Humbo a small boy of about seven came to the Red Cross headquarters asking for a football. I told him we had run out, but he just sat there in the hall and started crying. 'I don't have a ball, I don't have a ball,' he was inconsolable. I told him we had given out every last present we had brought with us, but he just sat there in tears. I gave him my Nike cap and put it on his head, but that was no good and he kept saying: 'I want a ball, I want a ball.' We tried everything and, in the end, one of the Red Cross workers went to his house and found a ball which we gave the boy to keep him happy.

I also played a game of football with the amputees. It was frustrating for me to see the kids around me, trying to do well – and they did very well – but when they wanted to accelerate they couldn't because they didn't have the manoeuvrability. It must have been so frustrating for them too, not being able to run after the ball. It was remarkable, though, because they were playing great football, and they train every day using both the prosthesis and the other leg to kick the ball. A member of our team scored two goals, one with his normal leg and one with the prosthesis. Sometimes the players forget they have lost a leg. They put on a brand new pair of training shoes provided by the Red Cross and they are quite happy. We try and instil in them the attitude that although they might have had their leg blown off by a mine, life isn't finished for them yet.

Every single moment was a sad moment, but you have to try and put on a brave face all the time, smiling for them, looking into their eyes and showing them that you understand their problems. It is important that you show them no feelings of shame, or embarrassment. While I was out in Angola, I thought about my own kids, and the times when they are not happy with the soup in their bowl, or the pasta on their plate. After a trip like that, you come home and you are more strict with your children because you realise how lucky you are, and when they turn their noses up at their food I tell them about the starving children I have seen. It is important to make them understand, without frightening them, so I encourage them to watch the reports on the news when they show the famine in Africa. My son is that bit older, and he understands. It is all about getting them to appreciate that some people in the world live in bad conditions, so they must be happy with what they have.

When I came home I was a guest on a BBC radio programme in London which linked up directly with Radio Africa. I was in the BBC studio talking about the problems, and I was being given a really hard time by two African women in the African studio who doubted my motives for getting involved in the anti-landmines campaign. They thought I had just gone to attract publicity for myself, and accused me of not wanting to pick up the sick babies, or when I did they said I washed my hands with antiseptic, once the cameras had switched off, which of course wasn't true. I was surprised and hurt by this personal attack, although I could understand their suspicions to some extent. I told them how I was afraid to pick up some babies because they were so skinny and fragile that I was frightened I might hurt them with my big hands. It must have been hard for them to accept that it could take them two weeks to get their message across, while here was this white man who would be heard immediately. I managed to convince them that my heart was really in it. I told them I knew I wasn't going to change the world, but I was at least making more people aware of the problems.

At the end of the programme, the two women told me they believed my motives, which was very satisfying because it meant they accepted I was genuine. I could even hear them kiss the microphone at the end of the interview, which I guess was their way of showing approval of me.

I am disappointed that I never got the chance to meet Princess Diana. She was someone who gave so much to so many people. She had such an aura around her that when she did her work for the Red Cross she carried the world's press everywhere she went. People complained that the Princess was hounded by the press, and in many aspects of her life this was sadly too true. But she knew that where the anti-landmines campaign was concerned, the idea was to attract as much media attention as she could, because this was the best way to increase awareness of the problem. What would have been the point of her going to Angola otherwise? Anybody can go to Angola, but the point of asking Diana to go was that her very presence there created such a major focus on the campaign.

I remember when I was there that television reporters were fighting to get their two-minute slot included in that evening's news bulletin. I never went there to get myself on television – I went there because I knew it meant I would bring the campaign on to prime-time television.

I would never say I took over from Princess Diana as the figurehead for the anti-landmines campaign. I am simply following in her footsteps. Diana was such a huge personality that nobody could ever take her place. I often wonder why I was chosen to follow her, because I honestly do not see myself as someone special. My aim is to raise awareness of the problems in these countries and, of course, to raise money. It is important for me to do something for charity. If I can achieve just one per cent of what Diana achieved, then I will be satisfied.

When Princess Diana died so tragically it affected me, because I was an admirer of hers, like most people in the world. I appreciate that she couldn't have her life to herself because of who she was, and I find this an incredible shame. Before marrying Prince Charles she had a normal life, with tranquillity. But she could never have that once she became the Princess of Wales and no matter where she went in the world she could not hide from the photographers and the paparazzi. After her death, I never saw so many sad people before in my life, and the scenes at her funeral were very moving. Everywhere in London that day was so silent, it was almost like the Queen had died, yet she was simply the Princess of Wales.

It was the same in France, where everything came to a standstill. The people of France were upset that she died in their country as they felt somehow responsible and embarrassed, especially because of the circumstances of her death. French people would do anything they could to change the fact that she died in their country. It was a big shock and people couldn't understand why it happened. The French loved her as much as the English, in fact I think she was loved by the whole world – America, China, everyone – because she was not just English, she was part of the whole world.

To me she was a legend and her fate was similar to that of James Dean, or Marilyn Monroe, or even John F Kennedy – legends who have died suddenly and tragically. Diana was one of the greatest people in the world and she shouldn't have died when she did. She deserved to live longer, especially for her boys who needed their mother throughout their lives. But at least she showed them the way by the kind of person she was.

Before the anti-landmines campaign I always was attracted to smaller charities, the ones who don't have the same resources as major organisations such as Cancer Research. I realised they would not get the recognition, help and money they needed from the Government, so I needed to help them raise their profile. One of the early charities I got involved in was called Giant Navus Congenital, for people whose bodies are covered by birthmarks, sometimes as much as 80 per cent of the body. I helped raise money to help sufferers have these marks cut away and replaced by other skin. This doesn't get the recognition from the Government because only one child in a million is born like this – but it is still one child too many.

The fact that I got involved meant the charity was mentioned on television and radio. I also attended a go-kart event, which raised £50,000. Just think, if everyone famous on the planet did something for charity every year, there would be fewer problems in the world today. On another occasion last season I went to Barnet Football Club to auction one of my signed shirts for charity, and was amazed when someone paid £7,000 for it. Last year the *Mail* newspaper helped to run a fund-raising campaign, and at the end of it I was proud to hand over a cheque for £2.5 million to the Red Cross. Needless to say, they were very happy.

When I finish football I shall devote more of my time to charity work. It's the least I can do to use my fame to help less fortunate people in the world. I owe it to myself, and I owe it to them.

CHAPTER FOURTEEN

So near, yet so far

'Keegan talked the players' language, thought the players'
thoughts and at the same time was able to operate at
another level to enable him to have an influence
elsewhere in the club'

When the time came for me to leave Paris Saint Germain, I would have joined Barcelona if only Barca had got their act together. Negotiations over my proposed transfer during that summer of 1995 went on for a month and even after that we had to overcome the problem of the restrictions limiting the number of non-Spanish players at the Nou Camp. Barcelona already had six on their books and to include me in their collection would mean off-loading at least a couple of them. They told me to be patient, that everything would be okay once they had sold two players, but nothing tangible seemed to be happening and, even though it was an honour to be wanted by them, and it would have been a thrilling prospect to work under Johan Cruyff, my patience was wearing thin.

When Newcastle United stepped up their interest my thoughts began to turn away from the Nou Camp for the first time. Nobody had shown as much interest in me as the Geordie club. I was attracted by the drive and enthusiasm of their manager Kevin Keegan, but I also had the feeling that everyone at the club wanted me there. It was also important to me that everything was tied up quickly. The process took just three days – some contrast to the never-ending discussions with Barcelona.

There was, however, a last-ditch attempt to sign me by Arsenal, somewhat ironic when you consider that I went on to play for their arch-rivals! My agent in Paris told me that another agent in Amsterdam – football can be complicated with all these agents who get involved – had a deal for me with Arsenal. We had almost agreed the move to Newcastle when at 1.30 am my agent had a call from Arsenal vice-chairman David Dein. I spoke to him and he said he wanted me to join the Gunners. It was the second time Arsenal had tried to sign me, as a year before George Graham had wanted to take me from PSG. But we were playing in the semi-finals of the Champions' League against AC Milan and the PSG chairman Michel Denisot did not want me to leave at that stage, but said he might let me go in the summer. Arsenal still wanted me and made their approach this time, but their offer was not as good as Newcastle's, so I went to Tyneside.

In France the reaction to my move was one of shock. You couldn't blame the sceptics, I suppose. Newcastle may have had many years of success way back in the 1970s but from a French viewpoint they were virtually unknown and the city had a reputation somewhat below Paris in cultural terms!

Manchester United, Liverpool and Arsenal were the famous names but here I was staking my faith not with one of the giants in the English game but in a club only recently experiencing a revival, who were stuck far away in the north-east. It didn't make sense to the people in my homeland but that didn't worry me at all. There's nothing I like more than a challenge and I knew that under Keegan, Newcastle were going places. They were spending £2.5 million on me but that deal was dwarfed by the £6 million they splashed out a short time later to sign Les Ferdinand from QPR.

I also knew I was joining a team who would conform to my beliefs in an attacking game. For many years the English had been dogged by a reputation for an overly-physical approach, with skill submerged by the crunching tackles, but the Premiership was changing and in one of my first conversations with Keegan he assured me that Newcastle would always try to play attractive football. I am proud that I played my part in a team who strove to entertain the fans as well as to provide winning football. It was an exciting time to be joining Newcastle United.

Obviously I knew of Kevin Keegan as a player, and also his assistant Terry McDermott, both of whom played a big part in that successful Liverpool era of the seventies and eighties. I was also aware of the tremendous following that Newcastle enjoyed. Apart from that I knew little about what I was walking into, but that is all part of the fun and the learning process. I had only been to England twice before, once for a shopping expedition with my wife and the other time for PSG's Cup Winners' Cup tie with Arsenal two years before. I had talked over the prospect of coming to England with Eric Cantona when we met up for international games and he was full of enthusiasm for what I would find if I ever decided to take the plunge. He had stressed that the quality of football had improved and that life away from the game was very enjoyable. I could also not fail to notice that Ruud Gullit and Dennis Bergkamp had decided to leave Italy for England at the same time. It seemed the right place to be at the right time.

Not that people back home agreed with me. After so much talk that I was heading for Barcelona, they were surprised that I was going to Newcastle. They couldn't understand it and I had to preach caution. I had to tell them to give me time to make the move a success. It annoys me when others rush to make judgement. Of course, when Newcastle got off to a flying start they started singing a different tune and were now fully understanding of why I wanted to go to St James' Park. It is not my style to say 'I told you so' but I had to smile to myself at how quickly their opinion changed.

I didn't meet Kevin Keegan until we reported for pre-season training. He had been on holiday when the deal was struck and I had only a brief conversation with him on the telephone. When we met for the first time he was everything I had imagined, friendly and welcoming. He even used some French words as we shook hands, saying 'Comment ca va?' and 'Allez les Verts!' which was a reference to St Etienne, who he had faced while playing for Liverpool in the European Cup in the seventies. I liked Keegan's style, he was very positive and always encouraging me, even when I wasn't at my best.

At that time Sir John Hall was the driving force behind Newcastle. It was his money and vision for the football team and the area it served that had been responsible for enticing Keegan to leave his sun-kissed retirement by the golf course. Sir John wanted to create a vast sporting club with football at the centre of it. He was quite clearly the main man and it is so much better when there is just one person in overall charge of

RED CROSS

Above: A poignant moment amid the horror and carnage created by landmines.

Below: This young lad had his leg blown off by a landmine, but with the aid of the Red Cross in Cambodia he is trying to rebuild his life.

Time to reflect during my trip to Cambodia in my capacity as an ambassador for the Red Cross anti-personnel landmine campaign.

Above: Treading very carefully, I am shown how Mine Awareness Group workers detect the landmines. This was one of the most harrowing experiences that I have been through in my life.

Below: I come in peace. Visiting the monks who live in a Cambodian village infested with mines.

One of the highlights of my trip to Cambodia was playing football with young men who have lost limbs as a result of landmines. As you can see, it hasn't dampened their enthusiasm for the beautiful game.

Staff at a components factory in Phnom Penh explain the workings of an artificial limb.

David Ginola – footballer and ambassador for the Red Cross 'Walk Without Fear' campaign.

A lighter moment as I share a laugh with my journalist friend Neil Silver – as we enjoy a boat trip on the Mekong River.

SPURS ... AND BEYOND

A proud occasion for me as I receive my trophy for being voted Footballer of the Year by the English football writers in 1999. I also won the PFA trophy that same season.

We won the Cup! Celebrating Tottenham's triumph in the 1999 Worthington Cup final with skipper Sol Campbell (*right*) and striker Steffen Iversen.

The men in charge. Key figures at Tottenham (*from left*) director Martin Peters, manager George Graham, chairman Alan Sugar and director of football David Pleat.

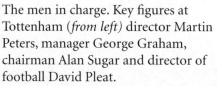

Pitting my wits against Manchester United and England star Paul Scholes.

Above: I just manage to slip away from Robbie Savage's sliding tackle during Tottenham's 1999 Worthington Cup final victory over Leicester at Wembley.

Below: That Worthington Cup success was a special occasion for me, as I acknowledge with the fans. It was certainly one of the highlights of my Tottenham career.

Left: Ouch! Erik Bakke sends me crashing to the ground during an FA Premiership match versus Leeds United at Elland Road in February 2000.

Below: Taking the applause of the crowd after being substituted by George Graham (yet again) during a Tottenham game.

Below: Meeting the fans at Villa Park after signing for the club in August 2000. I really appreciated the warm welcome they gave me.

the club and its finances. In France the finances can be pooled together from the town hall, the municipality and the region itself and in my opinion diversification leads to loose and woolly management. When it's not your own money involved it's inevitable that your interest and attention to detail is not as great. And that can lead to disaster. Marseille were an example of that but small clubs in France were also being run as if they had lots of money in the bank when that was far from the case.

Newcastle is not Paris. That might be stating the obvious but after a couple of months or so in my new surroundings, it hit me that for all the warmth of the reception that was afforded me and my family by the wonderful people of the north-east, it was not going to be easy to settle. At first there was nothing I missed because there was so many new things to discover. I threw myself into the task of learning about my new team and team-mates as well as finding out everything I could about the city itself. I should have known that difficulties lay ahead for us from our very first day in Newcastle, however. Coraline and I went for a drive to familiarise ourselves with our new environment, when suddenly she burst out crying in my arms. She was finding it so different from Paris. She was concerned at leaving behind everything we had created in Paris and concerned about what the future held for us in this remote corner of England. It was not as if we had come to London, with all the excitement that would have been involved in living in another capital city. Newcastle was a long, long way away and it was natural for her to worry. It was easier for me because there was a lot to occupy me both physically and mentally but for the family, who spend more time at home and don't have the excuse of meeting new people, it can be tough. Fortunately Coraline is a strong person, and she trusted me when I told her that everything would be fine.

Coraline did get used to living in the north east of England and gradually made a new life and new friends for herself. She was taken around the area by the chairman's chauffeur to look at houses, and she found us a place to live. We also had to consider Andrea's schooling and the difficulties for him leaving behind his pals and uprooting to go and live in a different country and learning a new language.

After a couple of months in Newcastle, it hit me just how much I was missing my family and friends, and my lifestyle in France. Kevin Keegan was a big help at this time. He said I was free to take some time off and go back home and I really appreciated his concern. He was speaking from experience because when he went to Germany to play for SV Hamburg he had his own low moments. He hadn't forgotten how difficult it was to live in a foreign country. That's why he was good for me. Other managers would not be so sensitive or understanding about their players' needs. To be a good manager you have to know how the players are thinking, what makes them respond in a positive way, what will make them more determined. The best managers are those who are able to see the whole picture.

Keegan talked the players' language, thought the players' thoughts and at the same time was able to operate at another level to enable him to have an influence elsewhere in the club. He is a special man and he always finds time for people. He is loved by everyone and that is almost an impossibility for a manager because if he's not picking you for the team, then you don't want to like him. Somehow with Keegan, it was different.

One of the things that I really miss about France is the sea. In Paris, there are so many things to occupy your time after training. There are all the museums, shops and parks, whereas in Newcastle it used to be a case of 'What am I going to do now?' We used to take a drive and perhaps go to the seaside but it was not the same. How could it be? But I had to keep reminding myself that I was in England to play football, to further my career. I wasn't a tourist out to see the sights. I didn't really do a lot outside the game but I didn't need to. I don't have to have a lot of friends and to be invited out here there and everywhere. It's not even important for my team-mates to be close friends. As long as you get on well with them and share a mutual respect and a camaraderie that enables you to pull together on the pitch, that is sufficient. You don't have to be bosom pals.

If nothing else, it is a good education to go and sample life in a different country. Despite all the hardships you have to put up with and the homesickness in the early days, it is an experience that can only improve you as a human being. It is amazing just how different England is from France considering the two countries are only separated by a small stretch of water. Take food for instance. I must say that living in England has made me appreciate French food even more! Back home, eating is an experience to be savoured, but in England, eating is often no more than a means to an end. There is not the joy in food that you find back home and my friends assume it must be hard to live in England because of that. Nevertheless, I was happy to try and adapt to everything English and that included getting stuck into English food. However, I did miss my baby artichokes, a Provençal speciality, which are quite delicious.

Before I came to England I had never seen a bottle of brown ale because in France most people drink wine and spirits. And there is a different culture here surrounding drink. You see people falling over, being sick in the streets, that kind of thing. In France, even if someone has had too much to drink, that would never happen. There is also a difference in how women react to me here. In England if a girl likes you she will make her intentions pretty clear, she will touch you and act quite suggestively. The French women might think the same but they go about it with a good deal more discretion. They might look you up and down provocatively, but their approach is more cool and reserved. Perhaps it also derives from the different drinking cultures. In England you see groups of women going around together, and having a good time. That really struck me because in France they would never act as openly as that. They are far more worried about what people will think.

Footballers do seem to be a magnet for attention and if my daughter Carla brought home a footballer, I would advise her to always keep both eyes open. Even when she is asleep she should keep one eye open! English people in particular go on a lot about the image of the French 'Romeo' and I heard this many times in the early months of my arrival in England. My experience is that some Englishmen are equally sentimental as Frenchmen, it's just that they go about it in a slightly less romantic way, because of cultural differences. I am a typical Mediterranean – a bit of a male chauvinist. To my mind, there is nothing wrong with the man going out while the woman stays at home and does the work! It's the Italian mentality and it applies to those in southern France as well. Walk into any restaurant in southern Europe and you'll find groups of men sitting around and chatting and basically doing nothing while the wife is slaving away. It's tradition, and tradition is something I am keen to keep alive. We all have to remember where we come from and the principles that have served our forefathers down the years.

I had a good feeling about my first season with Newcastle. The management team of Kevin Keegan and Terry McDermott were obviously excited about the new signings they had made and this positive vibe transferred itself to the team. We couldn't wait to get started and see how the players, both old and new, gelled. For me there was the obvious excitement and challenge of getting to grips with a new style of football and a new league. Our first game was at home to Coventry. I was especially nervous but when I emerged from the tunnel to be greeted by the acclaim of 36,000 Geordies, the adrenaline rush was incredible. If I wasn't motivated before, I certainly was now, and everything went really well. We won 3–0, it was a great experience and you could sense afterwards that if there were any doubts among the supporters about the season ahead, the performance and the result had swept them all away. Everybody said such nice things about me and I knew I had made the right choice to come to St James' Park.

Things continued to go really well and after the first few weeks I was voted the Carling Player of the Month – something no other foreigner had achieved in his first month in England. It was so important for me as a foreigner to make a good start and I could not have wished for anything better. It was easy for me to give of my best because the people were so encouraging. The team was playing well, the fans responded and we were all carried forward. On that first day of the season we went to the top of the table and suffered defeat only once in the first 20 games. We won all our home matches up until March. From an early stage, people were writing about us as champions-elect.

I scored my first Newcastle goal in our third match at Sheffield Wednesday and it came in front of a television audience in France. That made it all the more special for me because I was still sensitive to the scepticism back home surrounding my summer transfer. My team-mates were delighted for me: they all ran over to offer their congratulations. The

221

next game was a local derby against Middlesbrough and I earned more plaudits for a piece of trickery on the edge of our area that bamboozled their defender, Neil Cox. It was replayed time and again on television. Then I found room to execute the cross from which Les Ferdinand scored the only goal of the game. I could not have wished for a better start to my Newcastle career.

One of my first impressions about the English league was that there were no easy matches. That's a cliché that those involved in the game here like to trot out, but for a foreign newcomer it was still something that caught me by surprise. It was borne out in our second game of the season which brought us face to face with Bolton, who had just been promoted from the first division. Even when there is a wide disparity in the skill levels of two competing teams in the Premiership, you can bank on the underdog always giving their all and putting up a hell of a fight. At the end of the season, even when there's a team that is looking near-certainties for relegation, they will still be battling away until it's mathematically impossible for them to save themselves. In France, the team's attitude would be one of resignation; they would concede the game almost before they had stepped out on to the pitch.

After Christmas the pace of the game here caught up with me. There was no winter break, whereas I was used to having two weeks off over Christmas. In England, the Christmas holiday period is one of the most intensive periods in the fixture calendar. It cannot remain that way. The players will demand a mid-winter break because their bodies will tell them they can't put up with it anymore. The requirement to turn out Saturday, then Wednesday, and then Saturday again, then to go away on international duty and then to take part in the big tournaments like the World Cup and the European Championships instead of taking a decent summer break, is bound to take an exacting toll. You need a rest from the mental strain apart from anything else. You need to get away from the club scene and switch off because it is such a long haul from July, when pre-season training begins, to the end of the campaign in May. Of course, clubs want to play over Christmas and New Year because holiday crowds bring in extra revenue, but the welfare of the players cannot be ignored indefinitely. Sometimes, if you pack too many fixtures into a short period, the quality of the football suffers, because the players are exhausted, so the fans suffer as well.

I can't pretend that I find it easy to play football when there's snow and ice on the ground. I need to be able to feel what I am doing, to feel the ground beneath my feet. If I am not sure of my footing because the conditions have made the surface slippery, then I am not comfortable and my game is affected. It's different for an attacker because he is the one who has to do something with the ball, to create, whereas the defender's job is simply to destroy. He can do that a lot easier when the conditions are in his favour.

The turn of the year brought the first disappointments of my first season in England and the first indications that it might not end in the glorious finale predicted. We went out of the FA Cup at the hands of Chelsea, and, to add insult to injury, in a penalty shoot-out in front of our own supporters. Around the same time I was also sent-off in a Coca Cola Cup-tie at Arsenal, a decision that brought me a lot of personal anguish. It came about because of the belief, gathering momentum at the time, that I cheated and took dives to win penalties and free-kicks. Because of what was being written, the opposition fans were quick to boo me and an unhappy situation got worse. At Stoke in an earlier round of the Coca-Cola competition their manager Lou Macari had accused me of diving to get one of their players sent off, but I have never tried to get another player sent off in my career. It's not within the spirit of the game and it's something I would never do.

Against Arsenal I had a real personal battle with Lee Dixon and I was being constantly fouled. At one time he tackled me and his boot went straight through my shin guard. Then, when Nigel Winterburn tripped me as I was in the throes of a run from midfield to the penalty area, it was me who was shown the yellow card. I couldn't believe it, I just did not understand what was going on. Why would I take a dive if I was already in a position from where I could score?

My frustration escalated and I admit I thrust out an arm which struck Dixon. I didn't set out to elbow him or to make contact with his head; he was holding my shirt and I just wanted to shake him off, so I was waving my arm behind me trying to get him off me, but the referee saw it as vindictive and ordered me off. I was the victim of an injustice and I was not at all happy with the referee. Obviously I respect the man who is out in the middle to keep law and order and I would never let my anger with him get out of control (even though in this instance there were many things I wanted to do to him). But at the same time, you expect the referee to be fair. He must not have any preconceptions about any of the players or who he wants to win.

I felt harshly treated at Highbury. I was the one trying to play football and make a show for the fans and yet I was the one shown the red card. I am not after preferential treatment but I do think that referees should bear in mind that supporters pay good money to see entertaining players. When they go home after a match they talk about a wonderful piece of skill from one of the attacking players that brought a goal or a near-miss. In the main, they do not talk about a tackle. The entertainers deserve to win some protection and I believe it is the referee's job to encourage those spectacular moments that get the crowd out of their seats. If some defenders are too aggressive in their desperation to stop the flair players, then the referee should warn them that it won't be tolerated.

I could certainly understand what overtook Eric Cantona on that fateful night at Selhurst Park when he launched himself at a supporter after he was sent-off for kicking out at an opponent. He was not happy with all the things that surrounded the incident and boiled over. In his opinion the referee had not given him sufficient protection and the red mist came down. Having said that, you have to try and exercise self-control and some restraint. There is a big difference between feeling like doing something and actually doing it, and Eric crossed that line of no return. When you are a professional, and particularly when you are a professional of the stature that Eric was at the time, there is a certain code of behaviour to observe. You owe it to the profession which has given you so many privileges and good times. You also owe it to the youngsters who will be following your every move because in their eyes you're a hero.

I was banned for three games after the sending-off at Highbury. It doesn't sound too bad but bearing in mind that I considered I was the injured party, I was greatly aggrieved. I felt it was a significant turning point in my season because I never really recaptured my best form after it. Because of the way the fixtures fell I was actually out of the team for six weeks. I lost my competitive edge and also my rhythm, because I am the sort of player who doesn't respond well to an interruption. I went back to France for a rest and to get away from it all. It was some compensation for what had happened, because

225

February in the south of France is one of the most delightful times of the year. The days are starting to warm up and it's also carnival season. For a time I could lose myself and forget all about my problems in England.

When I returned to Newcastle I trained very hard to stay in peak condition, but with no game at the end of the week there wasn't a competitive edge to my work and it was easy to get depressed. It was the first time I had been out of the game for such a long period: with injuries or suspension I had not encountered a six-week break before. If you are a competitor it is never enough just to train, you need a game at the end of the week to focus your attention and give a point to your work. It used to hurt me to see the lads preparing for the next game while I remained out on the training field.

While I was serving my sentence Newcastle went and signed Faustino Asprilla, a player I knew to be an exciting performer with Parma and Colombia. There were lots of stories about his colourful life away from football and of course the inevitable suggestions that he would not be able to fit in. We welcomed him to Newcastle – it would have been silly to respond any other way because it benefits all of us if the squad get on well together – but in any case he quickly won us over. He's a good lad and his impact in his first game made everyone sit up and take notice. After coming on as a substitute he set up the equaliser against Middlesbrough with his special brand of trickery.

By the time I was back in the side our hold on the championship had loosened somewhat. We were losing too many away games and it did not augur well for our prospects. Away from home we were missing chances and there was a price to be paid. We were 12 points ahead of the second-placed club at one time and I was confident that everything would be okay.

So were most people. The television and newspaper experts said the race was as good as over and we were all taken in. The crunch came in March, when we faced our closest rivals, Manchester United, at St James' Park. Naturally it was billed as a championship decider even though there were games to come. We dominated possession but again failed to take our chances, whereas late in the game they had one chance and scored. It had been said before the start that if Manchester United didn't win, then the gap would have been too big to make up. The effect of them winning was much greater than the three points. It was a huge psychological boost for them to beat us on our own ground.

It was a crucial defeat and one that defied understanding because we did everything but put the ball in the net. It was the first time we had lost at St James' Park that season and undoubtedly it damaged our spirit. Although we won our next game, another home fixture, this time against West Ham, we then travelled to Arsenal, went down 2–0 and were knocked off our leader's perch which we had occupied since the first weekend of the season. This was a different game to the Manchester United one because we didn't play well and all we could do afterwards was hold our hands up and admit the better team had won.

There was more psychological damage to come in the defeats at Liverpool and Blackburn which both followed a similar pattern. They were cruel setbacks for a team who always sought to put on a show for the fans and deserved a lucky break. Instead, the fates seemed to have it in for us because at Anfield we lost to two goals in the last ten minutes. This was despite leading 2–1 and then 3–2. Some of the football we played that night was scintillating but then Liverpool hit us late on with a double whammy and took the honours in a seven-goal thriller. When the game finished I refused to acknowledge what had happened. I thought: 'This is impossible.' At that time it was no consolation to have taken part in a spectacle that would have people all over the world clamouring to buy the video recording of the match, but later, when the pain had eased, it was possible to reflect on what an occasion it had been. Once again it taught me that in English football nothing is certain until the final whistle has gone.

We had now lost three games in four and at the same time Manchester United were winning. A similar story was to unfold at Blackburn where we were 1–0 up until five minutes from time. Incredibly Blackburn hit back twice and we were losers once again. It is the worst possible period in a game to concede goals; there is not enough time left to hit back. During this second half of the season there were too many gaps between games. After my six-week break I came back, played a game, and then straight away there was another break of two weeks. I found it impossible to slip back into the groove and at one stage Keegan said to me: 'What's happening with you David?' I was used to playing 60 games a season but all this stop-start was no good to me at all, the Christmas break apart.

In my last four years with PSG it was common to have a game every three days from November up until May. Competing for the championship, French Cup, League cup and trying to win a place in the national team at the same time kept me on my toes, but I preferred it that way. At Newcastle I seemed to be training more than playing and I had not experienced that before. It was especially difficult when we were losing games, because what you want more than anything is to get out onto the pitch straight away and put matters right. If you haven't got a game for two weeks then the disappointment and frustration is allowed to fester. It's no different to having a car accident, if you don't get back behind the wheel fairly soon you will become afraid and won't be able to go through with it.

Manchester United had the distraction of the FA Cup which I think was to their benefit. Often people will put forward the counter-argument, that it was to our advantage to have a clear run at the title because we could rest on Cup weekends after Chelsea had knocked us out in the third round. But I think that mentally it favoured United because it enabled them to put Premiership pressures aside for a while. For us the pressure was all around, there was no escape. With nothing else for us to think about it became something even bigger than it really was and the tension got greater and greater. To try and relax I would spend time listening to music. I could lose myself in the blues because the sounds allow me to enter a world far, far away, to my holidays or back to St Maxime where I was social-ising with friends. To be able to play music is something I would like to do when my career is over. I would love to play the piano or the guitar – to me, nothing can compare with what you feel when you play an instrument and make a sound with your mouth or your fingers.

By now the wonderful free-flowing football that we were producing week in, week out, earlier in the season existed only in the memory. Then we seemed to collect victories even when we were not playing well. Now we were playing well and find-ing it hard to win. Teams were raising their games against us, motivated by what we had done to them earlier in the cam-paign, and at one stage we won three consecutive games by 1–0. It was important only that we took all three points. Entertainment value now came a very poor second to the need to keep pressure on United. Unfortunately for us, they were proving very strong. Every time we left the pitch, having given everything in pursuit of victory, it was to learn that United had also won. They were indomitable and it broke our hearts.

With one week remaining we had three games left to play. We needed United to slip up and realistically you couldn't see that happening. Kevin Keegan talked up our possibilities at every opportunity and tried to keep our spirits high but even for him this was a tough task. He had a memorable public spat with Alex Ferguson who had annoyed us by trying to provoke a response from our opponents, reminding them of their duty to try as hard as they could against us. As if they needed telling! It was a sign of the tension and the steps people will take to try and obtain the slightest advantage.

The final week began with Manchester United in action at Nottingham Forest. I watched the game on television and after 25 minutes it was 0–0 which was good for us. It seemed to lull me into a false sense of security because I nodded off to sleep. When I woke with 15 minutes to go United were 4–0 to the good: another disappointment for Newcastle. We had to beat Leeds the next day to stay alive in the race and travelled down later in the afternoon to our hotel. I was suspended but I wanted to be with the lads to offer moral support. It was important at this stage that we all stuck together. If it was not going to happen for us, we didn't want anyone pointing an accusing finger at our lack of team-spirit, but to be truthful that was never a problem. We trained in the morning and rested in the afternoon. At the game I sat on the bench along-side Kevin Keegan and shouted a great deal. It was an eye-opening experience, you like to think you can influence events from there but in reality it's hard to make yourself heard.

I didn't play because I had reached 21 disciplinary points and was serving a one-match ban. I had been booked more times in that season than at any time in France, yet I don't consider that I was any more dirty. Certainly the refereeing was a lot more strict and some of them adopted a disciplinarian approach. At times it was like they saw themselves as the headmaster and we were the naughty schoolboys. It was ridiculous and what used to make me really angry was that they seemed to enjoy handing out yellow cards. With the card would come a sardonic smile. It was like they were saying, 'You French so-and-so.' Certainly the official who sent me off at Arsenal seemed happy with himself as he made that decision. He looked pleased to give me the first yellow card. He didn't warn me, he talked to Lee Dixon and then turned to show me the yellow.

Funnily enough the referee we had for the match that followed Leeds, a match which came three days later at Nottingham Forest, was great. He had a passion for the game but also a sense of humour and had a nice way of handling situations. Back in the team after suspension, I was doubly determined and went slightly over the top with one or two challenges. He didn't punish me but instead pulled me aside to say: 'Be careful, I can't accept this.' It was all he needed to say and I respected his approach. I got the message well enough and calmed down after that. The referee can't be over-friendly but at the same time he shouldn't think that he is above us. The best referees are those who show the players respect. After all, the supporters have come to see us, not him. As long as the referee shows me respect, I will treat him the same.

We needed to win at Forest because a draw was not much better than a defeat. Yet that was all we got after Peter Beardsley had struck an early goal and Forest later found an equaliser. It was wake-up time because it was a result that meant we were no longer going to win the league. We travelled home in silence, a beaten army, both defeated and shell-shocked. It was difficult to find anything positive to say but we didn't lose the championship on this particular game. And if we had only got a draw in those games we had lost, then things would have been so different. A draw at home against Manchester United for instance or a point at Liverpool and Blackburn might have made the difference. It was so frustrating.

The only way we could now finish as champions was for Manchester United to lose at Middlesbrough. If they drew we had to score seven times against Tottenham at St James' Park. It did not leave us with much hope and on the Friday I went about arranging to return to France, paying the bills and things like that, in a mood of disappointment. For the last month of the season I had been living alone, Coraline and the children having gone back to France, and although that made it quiet for me it was best for them to be at home. I missed them and it goes without saying that the telephone bill was pretty large!

The last game of a season that had promised so much, but which had now gone flat, took place on the Sunday. Kevin Keegan was remarkably upbeat in his team talk. Once again it amazed me how resilient the English are. Tottenham made it difficult for us because they were still chasing a place in Europe and the game finished 1–1. It was irrelevant in the end because United won 3–0. We were runners-up and with nothing to show for a season which contained some magnificent football.

We went on a lap of honour. It was important because there was no way we should feel ashamed at missing out even though our lead had been as big as 12 points at one stage. It was also important to show our appreciation to the magnificent Geordie fans. From my own perspective they had made things so much easier by the warm way they had responded to me. So intent was I on saying thanks that I hadn't realised I was suddenly on my own out on the pitch. The other lads had gone back into the dressing-room and left me all alone!

The fans are so important to a team's success and the Newcastle fans are more important than most. They will probably never realise just how much we appreciated their support during that incredible 1995/96 season. It really is a shared experience – they can set the mood for us and help to drive us on just by cheering that bit louder. The Newcastle fans were always around us, the numbers that used to come and watch us train dwarfed anything we used to see at PSG. They are desperate for success and that pushes you on to a higher level. They are so passionate about Newcastle Football Club that they love it before they love their wife. You want to succeed for them as well as for yourself and I was sorry that we couldn't give them the success they deserved. They had waited so long to be able to parade a trophy and I pray that under Bobby Robson, a man of the people if ever there was one, they can achieve that very soon.

I also felt for the Geordie boys in the team, for Peter Beardsley, Lee Clark and Steve Watson. Peter was an example to everyone at Newcastle but especially the youngsters. He was a 35-year-old playing like a 20-something and a marvellous professional who would give his all in training every single day. Even at that age he was still working hard, still seeking to improve, and I know I can go on for a few years yet just like he did.

It was also heartbreaking to see Kevin Keegan as we left the field after the Tottenham game. He was so upset and although he told us we should be proud of what we had achieved, you could tell in his voice that he was desperately sad. His face was a big give-away and I was more upset for him than I was for myself. Kevin is a great manager but he is also a great person and I am sure the England team will benefit under his leadership. He has so many qualities and a lovely personal touch when dealing with people, no matter from what walk of life they hail, or how important they are. He is a good guy to be around because you can learn so much from him both as a footballing man and as a human being. If ever I become a manager I would like to try and imitate Keegan. I would also model myself on Artur Jorge, and take the positive things I have learned from George Graham.

As our 12-point lead began to slip away it became fashionable in the press to attack Keegan. They were obviously just after a story, trying to create a situation to sell papers, but they were so far off the mark it wasn't true. The journalists should try and look at things a bit more rationally and with intelligence instead of going bang, bang, bang, and shooting at every easy target in sight. Some of these so-called experts attempted to shift some of the blame on to Faustino Asprilla for our demise in the title race. The results might seem to support that because after Tino arrived we lost more games, but there's no way that one player can shoulder the blame for a defeat – as I know only too well. Football will never be a matter of statistics, it is the sum total of all the little things that go on in a football match and which contribute to a win or a loss. If the team had concentrated better and not conceded late goals then no one would have been criticising Tino.

I had some friends over for the final game and we all went back to my house. On the doorstep there was a present waiting for me. The message attached to it read: 'To David, you are the best. You have given your best all the way through the season. I give you some French beer and one packet of cigarettes for your party tonight.' It cheered me up no end and after three or four beers my depression lifted. Later, some young fans wearing black and white shirts came to the house to speak to me. There was no aggression or blame but instead a nice discussion about the season. In France if you have lost, the supporters only want to argue with you, but the Newcastle fans seemed more upset than we were. We ended up with a night-time game of football in the garden. The season was over – roll on the holidays!

I wasn't in England for Euro '96 and I couldn't be bothered to watch France play. Apart from the semi-finals when they lost to the Czech Republic in a penalty shoot-out, I couldn't even bear to watch it. The thought of France playing at St James' Park did depress me. I couldn't bring myself to watch it because it only made my exclusion from the national team that much harder to bear. That was my stadium and my country and it cut right through me. Really though, I was happy to put some distance between myself and football and to throw myself into my holidays at the end of a gruelling season. I am so lucky to have somewhere like St Maxime to return to. To my mind there is no place better in the world and it is so comfortable for me there, with an absence of pressure and insecurity. I have a good friend, Fabien, who owns a beach bar there. He has travelled all over the world and when he returns he regales us with his stories of all the wonderful places he has visited. But he agrees with me: we live in the most beautiful place of all.

When I'm on holiday I wake up nice and early so I can enjoy the whole day. I might play golf in the morning, have lunch with the family and go to the beach in the afternoon. How bad is that? Then with my day filled with excitement, I can crash into bed. It's always a relaxing time but an enriching one as well. Sometimes we go fishing or take a drive into the country to visit some nice villages. I have a scooter to get me around in St Maxime and it's better than driving because in the high season the road from St Tropez to St Maxime is no different to the M25 – one long traffic jam.

There was a lot of time for me to reflect on the season. To my mind it's no bad thing to have regrets, because it then makes you more passionate and content when success finally comes your way. I had the bonus of being named third in both the Footballer of the Year award and the Players' Player of the Year. For the following season I vowed to return a better and stronger player but that summer there then emerged the distraction of a possible transfer to Barcelona – yes, again! A year after they tried and failed to sign me from PSG, they approached Newcastle for my signature. Joining Barcelona had always been a dream and I couldn't believe they were in for me again. I didn't want to leave Newcastle but when a club as big as Barcelona comes in you have to give it serious consideration. Alongside Real Madrid, AC Milan, Manchester United and Juventus they are among a handful of clubs known and revered around the world. It was a fabulous opportunity for me and another consideration was that with the 1998 World Cup to be held in France it would have improved my chances of getting back into the national squad.

At that time I didn't want to leave the marvellous Geordie fans for another English outfit and when Newcastle were approached by a few other clubs neither the board nor myself encouraged the interest. I would only abandon what I had started at Newcastle for a big, much bigger institution. Barcelona fitted that particular bill – they had won all three European trophies, countless Spanish championships and regularly filled the Nou Camp with 100,000 supporters. In the end, the bid failed because the two clubs couldn't agree a fee. I suppose Newcastle were looking after their interests in the way

I was looking after mine in wanting to go to Barcelona. But once again, it left a bitter taste in my mouth.

Newcastle tried to scare off Barcelona by pricing me out of the market. When an official approach was made, Newcastle quoted the ridiculous sum of £12 million for me. The Spaniards told them to be realistic, because that was too expensive, and instead offered £4 million. This was rejected by Newcastle but after a while they went back to Barcelona and told them I could go for £7.5 million. Barcelona then climbed up to £6 million for me, but the two clubs were still £1.5 million apart. Unfortunately for me, they could not find any common ground and agree to meet in the middle. I was upset to think that my dream move fell apart over a relatively small amount in the end, but I knew Newcastle were not prepared to let me go at that time. If Keegan had gone to see the board and told them to sell David Ginola for £6 million to Barcelona straight away, they would have done it. He had that power, but he never utilised it.

It was a terrible shame for me because Barcelona were always successful, in Spain and Europe, and had a very good image around the world, as they still do today. I knew all about the club and their magnificent Nou Camp stadium, having played against Johan Cruyff's team there for PSG in the European Cup. We were in a group with Barcelona, Bayern Munich and Spartak Moscow, and we won six out of six games, beating each of the three other teams home and away.

Spain is a fascinating country for its football, and I remember an incredible experience when I played for PSG at a ground which I thought was even better than the Nou Camp – Real Madrid's Bernabeau stadium. At the end of the players' tunnel, just before you go out on to the pitch, is a chapel, where the players can go and pray. We were lining up in the tunnel before a match there and as I glanced across I could see through the open doorway a crypt, candles and a bench. I thought: 'God, these people must be serious believers.' Seeing that was just one of the interesting experiences you get when you travel around Europe, it gives you a whole new education.

So when Keegan left Newcastle six months later I was very disappointed; and when Kenny Dalglish was announced as his successor I wasn't very happy with the situation. I am sure it affected my form that season. In my head I was already at Barcelona, and it took a long time for me to come to terms with the fact that another one of my dreams had been taken away from me.

The Geordies will never understand this. But for me, I am French, I am from the south of France, so to go and play for Barcelona would have been the perfect mix of everything about my roots – my life and my football – and I would have felt more like I belonged there than in Newcastle. Barcelona is a great place to chill out, and the people seem to really enjoy themselves there. There are lots of parties, and people standing outside bars on the pavement, drinking and eating tapas. Life goes on late into the night and I would have enjoyed living there.

I was naturally upset and a little bit angry when Keegan left Newcastle, because I signed for him. He stopped me joining Barcelona in the summer and then six months later he left the club – what was I supposed to think?

I felt like I had been stabbed in the back.

CHAPTER FIFTEEN

Success is the Spurs

*'I am the man in possession. You can try everything
you want, but you are not going to replace me because
I make things happen'*

The first words Alan Sugar uttered when I met him on his yacht were plain enough: 'David,' he said, 'You have to help me. You have to help Spurs get into Europe.' Yet at the end of the season we were fighting against relegation – something I obviously had not envisaged when I first joined the club.

After signing my contract, the following day I flew straight out to Norway to meet up with my new team-mates. Co-incidentally, I travelled out with the then Wimbledon chairman Sam Hammam and captain Robbie Earle, as they too were on their way to Oslo to play a game there, and they welcomed me to the London soccer scene.

I was looking forward to moving to London. I had visited the capital quite a few times during my stay at Newcastle and I realised life was good there. At first, when I decided to leave Newcastle I thought I would go to another country, some-where warmer or more like the place I came from. But I felt London would be a nice place to live – it is the centre of Europe, very cosmopolitan, and I thought it would be a good choice for the family, which is always my number one concern. The kids could carry on with their English, and it was also easier for them to travel back to Nice when they wanted to. The whole package seemed right. The fact that being based in London might help my work outside of football was not really a main consideration, as I always put my football before any advertising contracts and never let them interfere with my game. But I was aware that being in London might help. I had been wanted by Arsenal just before I joined Newcastle two years earlier, so here I was coming to London second time around.

When I arrived at the Tottenham team's hotel in Norway the other players were at a gym across the road, so I got changed and was introduced to everybody by Roger Cross, who was Gerry Francis' assistant. The atmosphere and spirit in the camp was very good in anticipation of the new season ahead and I was looking forward to a fresh start, and felt this was going to be a good club to play for. Obviously I didn't expect to have such a disappointing first season.

I got on very well with Gerry Francis, he was a good tactician and he allowed me to express myself on the pitch without any real restrictions. He was strong on defending and on fitness, and one of his famed training routines was dubbed 'Terror Tuesday' because it was a gruelling session of box-to-box run-ning. But to be honest, I had experienced harder training in France, so I never really found it a problem. Footballers in general don't like running routines on their own because they are a bit boring, but we know in the back of our minds that we have to do them to be fit.

During pre-season we played Fiorentina in a testimonial match for David Howells. Their side included Rui Costa and Gabriel Batistuta, and we couldn't match them. That was the first time I felt things might be difficult in the season ahead as we didn't seem to gel very well as a team on the pitch. We started the season badly and that hit confidence immediately. When you are winning, you enjoy training and you are impatient for Saturday to come so you can play another game, but if you start with a couple of defeats then everyone is low. The press immediately started criticising Gerry Francis, Alan Sugar and the players, and they began speculating about the futures of certain people at the club, which made it even harder for the players to concentrate on the job at hand.

Gerry Francis survived only until November 1997, and it wasn't really a surprise for the players to hear he was leaving the club, considering all the negative publicity. There was something in the air in the weeks leading up to his departure, and we saw Alan Sugar making more frequent visits to the training ground, which we took as a bad sign for the manager. Even Gerry was frustrated by the lack of results at the end and he saw no point in staying around and taking all the stick from the fans. He was desperately unlucky that he had so many key players missing through injury at crucial times. He loved the club and did not want to see it suffering, so as the team slipped into the bottom half of the table he decided the best thing to do was to resign. I think Alan Sugar tried to persuade him to stay on, but Gerry is a very honest guy and once he made up his mind, he was determined to move on. I believe we tried hard for him on the pitch. I felt bad for him because he had signed me, and I did my best for him because I did not want to see him go.

I have to admit that I had never heard of Christian Gross, the man chosen by Alan Sugar to replace Francis. I was surprised when I heard about his appointment, as I really thought Sugar would be bringing in a big name as manager, not somebody from Grasshoppers Zurich. But I was prepared to wait and see for myself what he was like, rather than jump to any wrong conclusions, because everyone deserves a chance.

Before Gross even arrived the press started writing that he was a very tough manager, and the first player out of the door would be David Ginola 'because Tottenham could not afford to have a luxury like him'. It was such utter nonsense. How can these people write these things about me when they have never been to one of our training sessions to watch how hard I work? They assumed that Gross' first decision would be to get rid of me, without even giving me a chance. I had been playing football for 12 years, under some tough managers, and not one of them had complained about my lack of effort. If you speak to every manager I have played under, the first thing they will tell you is how surprised they were about how hard I trained.

When Gross arrived, he called me into his office and told me that he expected me to be one of the most important members of his team, and to help him turn the club around and save them from relegation. I responded to him and gave him what he wanted, and in his first game in charge I scored the second goal in a 2–0 win at Everton. Some players respond to a new manager coming in and it gives them a boost to play better, but I never need that kind of motivation as I try to give my best in every game I play. My job was always to do my best for Spurs.

Gross took a lot of stick in the media when he first arrived at the club because he chose to travel from Heathrow to Tottenham on the tube, to be like a regular fan. The players didn't respond to this, but we were able to laugh with Gross for a different reason. When he spoke, he often got his English wrong. The best example I can give you came during one pre-match team talk. I recall the manager saying in his strong Swiss-German accent: 'I want a white sheet from you today boys!' Of course, he meant he wanted a clean sheet, for the team not to concede a goal, and we understood him, but the players fell about laughing. Gross asked what he had said wrong, and Chris Hughton, who was assisting him, had to explain it to him, but at least he saw the funny side.

It didn't help when Gross' fitness coach was refused a work permit and couldn't join the club from Switzerland. Gross wanted him as his right-hand man and was very disappointed at not getting him, because he was on his own after that. I am not sure Gross was helped too much either by the return of Jurgen Klinsmann. Jurgen is a great player, but he had left the club the first time around in bitter circumstances, and I think there was some unresolved baggage remaining when he arrived at the club for a second time. He wanted to dictate to the manager how he felt the team should play tactically. For example, at one stage Jurgen complained about me. He wanted to stick me on the left to supply him, whereas Gross wanted me to play through the middle, and that caused a bit of tension. But Jurgen did his bit towards the end of the season when he scored four goals in a 6–2 win over Wimbledon at Selhurst Park, a result that ensured our survival.

Klinsmann had a far worse reputation for diving than I did the first time he arrived at Spurs. But he was quite clever the way he played on the stick he got from the fans in the very first game. This was before my time at Tottenham and when he scored on his debut he celebrated with his famous spreadea-gled dive on the ground, with all his team-mates joining in. I mention this because I don't like elaborate goal celebrations.

Some of them are really over the top, and I look at them and laugh. Scoring a goal is always a fantastic feeling, but when I watch goal highlights on television I can't believe some of the celebrations. As far as I am concerned, it is okay for the goalscorer to go wild, but I have to laugh when the whole team joins in and performs a dance of some kind – it makes them look like they are doing the Hokey Cokey!

I learned something from Gross during the summer about how to get the squad to bond together, and if ever I become a manager it is something I would like to do. The spirit was good when we came back from our holidays because we had avoided relegation and were still in the Premiership, where the club belongs. But he took us all to St Moritz for some pre-season training – where he used to go with Grasshoppers – and after a hard week's work he gave us the weekend off. But rather than have us sitting around doing nothing, he organised several enjoyable activities for all the players and staff. On the Saturday morning we went for a tour in a helicopter over the Swiss Alps, which was beautiful, then in the afternoon we rented mountain bikes. We started at the bottom of the mountains then followed a lovely trail through the forest, along the river, climbing our way towards a restaurant at the top. The scenery was tremendous, with snow-capped peaks, waterfalls, and cows in the fields, so it took our minds off the 10 km uphill ride. It was also done at a leisurely pace, with us stopping to eat raspberries and to swim in the river. I was with Ramon Vega and Jose Dominguez, and we had a great time. Once we reached the top we went to a waterfall, stripped naked and jumped in, which was fantastic.

In the evening it was all downhill, and it was a great race back to the resort. We had a special dinner with Swiss food, then on the Sunday morning we went over the border to Italy and then abseiled down a canyon. It was very exciting, like riding the rapids but without any boats. We wore wet-suits and helmets and used ropes to climb down the rocks before sliding along in the water with the rapids. Then after lunch at an Italian restaurant we spent the afternoon at a go-kart track. It was a brilliant weekend and we came back with a lot of happy stories and memories, and it gave us a great boost going into the next week and left us feeling fresh. The training had been tough, with three sessions a day, but everyone enjoyed it and we were never bored at all. Every morning when we woke at 7.30 am and opened the curtains we saw the mountains and the pine trees, and could take in the fresh smell of the mountain air.

Life was okay for me. The family had settled in London and we had found a nice house and school for the children. But the start to the new 1998/99 season failed to live up to people's expectations and by the first week of September Gross had been axed.

I liked Gross, but he never really got the full support of the players, the fans or everybody behind the scenes at the club. He was an unknown, unproven in the English game, and that worked against him. In the end our results suffered. The pressure must have told on Alan Sugar, because he didn't hang around and one Saturday he issued a simple statement to the Press Association announcing Christian's departure from the club. That was it, he was gone, just like that, and it was time to seek out a new manager.

David Pleat took charge temporarily and he seemed to like putting on his tracksuit again and being more involved in the football side. This meant we had our fourth boss in less than a year – Gerry Francis, Chris Hughton temporarily, Christian Gross and now Pleat. Results improved, but I think the team just felt we had to do better. I don't think it had anything to do with the removal of Gross and if the chairman had waited a bit longer then he may have been the manager who enjoyed a change in fortunes.

It didn't take too long for Alan Sugar to find his next manager, and it was announced that George Graham would be joining us from Leeds. For me, it was a case of 'here we go again' because the newspapers immediately started suggesting that David Ginola would be the first casualty of the George Graham regime. I had proved myself once by doing the opposite everyone had expected of me under Christian Gross, and here I was again, being put under the microscope by the media, who expected me to fall foul of George Graham instead. I began to wonder if the journalists knew something, that they had spoken to Graham and been told that he wasn't sure if he was going to keep me, because there is no smoke without fire. But again, I knew I had to wait for the new manager to arrive and prove myself all over again.

I went to see Graham in his office as soon as he arrived, to speak to him about the future.

'I read a lot of things in the paper and I would like to know what you want to do with me,' I said.

'Quite frankly,' he replied, 'I intend to wait and see – not just with you, but with the other players as well – and then I will make up my mind what I am going to do with the team. Just let me have a look for two or three months.'

I worked hard for him and I think he was surprised, because I gave him the opposite of what he had expected – or at least what he had been led to believe. I gave him sincerity on the pitch, and I was really sweating for the club and I think he was pleased with that. I felt that I was on trial more than all the others, but I am never better than when I am in a situation like that.

It is unbelievable the strength of mind I have, to be able to achieve something if I really want to do it – there is nobody who can stop me. When I was with PSG, a coupled of left-sided players were being signed and people were saying 'maybe it will be difficult for David to keep his place'. But I was playing 50 games a season and my so-called 'replacement' was sitting for 50 games on the bench, coming on before the end to give me a break. Every time I see a bit of a threat I say: 'I am the man in possession. You can try everything you want, but you are not going to replace me because I make things happen.' The players who came in were feeling very down after a few months because they could see they were not going to be able to give the team what I was providing.

So as soon as George Graham came in and I felt maybe there was a bit of pressure on my shoulders, and I realised I had to do more to give him a good first impression. I like surprising people by letting them see for themselves how good I can be. It is always hard for me because people have high expectations of me. I understand that, because you always ask for more from a player who has talent. If a new manager comes in and doesn't expect much from someone, then he is pleasantly surprised by a player who tries hard and does well. But I am expected to perform to a certain level anyway, so I have to be doing some special things to earn any credit, otherwise people will pick on me if I am below 100 per cent. It is a team effort, but someone like George Graham would still come to me in the dressing room and whisper: 'Give me some magic today.' You know the manager expects it from you because he knows you are the one player who can turn a match. Some players will hold on to the draw for you, and others will win you the game. I fall into the latter category and the expectation is on my shoulders, both from the manager and from the fans. Also, if we are a couple of goals up, I know the manager enjoys seeing me try a clever back-heel or some fancy trick as much as the fans – and why not?

The arrival of Graham boosted the team because everyone saw it as a fresh start, even the players who were out of favour under the previous regime, and everyone wanted to make a good impression and play in the team. After three months I knew he was satisfied with me – we didn't need to talk again.

I know this will sound a bit strange, but sometimes when I score a special goal, I have an 'out-of-body experience'. It is as if time freezes for a couple of seconds and I step out of my body and watch myself scoring the goal. For example, a goal of mine that is often talked about in England is the one I scored for Newcastle in the UEFA Cup against Ferencvaros. I knew I was going to score that goal before I controlled the ball. When it came towards me it was as if there was a voice in my head saying: 'Don't worry, because this is going in the back of the net,' although I couldn't actually hear the voice. I knew what was going to happen a second before it did. Everything around me stopped, the ball came across from the right, I controlled it on my thigh, brought it inside and volleyed it into the goal. When the ball hit the back of the net there was silence, and slow motion, and then it was as if someone clapped their hands to re-start time and I heard the tremendous roar of the crowd. The first time I had this experience I was playing in the third division with Toulon, in Chamberry. I thought to myself: 'What on earth is going on?' I received the ball, time stood still while I hit it towards the goal, then it was like a film director shouting 'action' and I heard the roar of the crowd as the ball hit the back of the net. I don't know what happens to me when I have this experience, but time stands still. It doesn't happen every time I score a goal – only for the special ones.

People still ask me about the FA Cup goal I scored for Spurs at Barnsley in the quarter-finals in 1998 when I cut in from the left flank, beat a trail of defenders and tucked the ball home. But I remember only the moment I struck the ball past the goalkeeper, I don't remember the first touch, or the dribble – it was like I was stepping aside and watching myself doing it. I can only remember the end of the action and can't tell you how I started it. It is like a blackout. Another goal like that was a spectacular volley against Leeds, a month before the Barnsley game.

I don't know why, but I have tended to do well against Barnsley. They are good opposition for me. They are the only team against whom I have scored two goals in one game for Spurs, and also the team I scored some of my most memorable goals against. I have places where I enjoy going to play, and others which are bogey grounds – such as Chelsea and Leeds, two places where I have had unhappy times and bad results.

The highlight of George Graham's first season at White Hart Lane was our Worthington Cup triumph at Wembley, when we beat Leicester 1-0 in the final to book our place in the following season's UEFA Cup. It was a remarkable turn-around of fortunes, and Graham himself said that the success came sooner than even he had really expected.

The road to Wembley started back in September 1998, with a two-legged second-round tie at London neighbours Brentford. This could have been a tricky tie, as we were the potential Premiership scalps, there to be shot down, and the Bees gave us a run for our money on their tight pitch. The first match was at their Griffin Park Stadium and we won 3–2. My main contribution was to supply the corner from which Ramon Vega headed home our third goal to ensure we took a slender advantage back to White Hart Lane for the second leg. It was also significant for Stephen Carr, as he scored his first goal for the club.

The second leg also finished 3–2, to give us a 6–4 aggregate win and set up an away trip to Northampton in the third round. I played my part against Brentford again as it was my shot that was saved by their goalkeeper, only for Sol Campbell to follow up and head the ball in to put us 2–1 up. I then released Allan Nielsen whose shot came back off the post, and Chris Armstrong tucked it away to put us 3–1 ahead and effectively seal the tie. At this stage of the competition I had no thoughts of Wembley, there was still a long way to go.

We headed off up the M1 to Northampton at the end of October and progressed after a professional performance and a 3–1 win. I took the corner from which Sol Campbell scored with his head to put us 2–1 up. Then in the 77th minute I had the chance to wrap up the game from the penalty spot. I enjoy the responsibility of taking a penalty. I see too many players shy away because they don't fancy it, whereas I want to take them. My first goal for Tottenham was from the penalty spot, in a Cup game against Carlisle, because I just grabbed the ball and took it. But it was a wet night at Northampton and the pitch was very muddy. I didn't hit the ball cleanly or hard enough and it lost pace on the muddy surface and the goalkeeper guessed the right way and made a good save. I made up for it in some way by feeding Darren Anderton and he set up Chris Armstrong to score the third.

In round four we claimed the scalp of Liverpool at Anfield with a fine 3–1 win. It was not such a great night for me, however, as I didn't have a particularly good 45 minutes and was substituted at the end of the first half.

The quarter-final saw us land the plum draw at home to Manchester United. Even though Alex Ferguson did not field his strongest line-up there was still plenty of quality in their team. But we were beginning to believe in ourselves and rose to the occasion to record another fine 3–1 win, keeping up our record of scoring three goals in every tie up until then. I made up for my disappointing performance at Anfield with one of my better games at White Hart Lane. I made the run and supplied the cross from which Chris Armstrong put us 2–1 up, then I cracked home the third goal myself from just outside the box. For the first time, I began to dream about Wembley, as we were now only two matches away from the final. When you start to beat teams like Liverpool and Manchester United, two of the best sides in the country, you start to think 'maybe we can go all the way'. All that stood between us and a place at Wembley were our rivals Wimbledon in the two-legged semi-final.

Those two games were never going to be loaded with pretty football. At that stage it is all about winning and getting through. The first leg, at White Hart Lane, was very tight as expected and finished 0–0. It was another close game at Selhurst Park but Steffen Iversen scored the only goal of the tie to see us through 1–0 on aggregate, and earn a final clash with Leicester. It was a tremendous feeling at the final whistle, with all our fans rushing on to the pitch to celebrate with us. It meant a lot to me to be going back to Wembley. The last time I was there was with Newcastle in the Charity Shield, and we lost 4–0 to Manchester United, so I wanted to erase those memories and be a winner for Tottenham.

The day of the final didn't really register in my memory until we were on the coach and on the way to the famous stadium, when I saw the twin towers. I started to think 'this is it'. It wasn't important just to win the trophy, we knew this was also our route into Europe, which is a big thing for the club, the players and the fans. I wasn't nervous, but the palms of my hands were certainly sweating. George Graham treated it like any other normal game. He told us to think about what we had done in the previous rounds, and that we mustn't allow ourselves to be able to say we never gave 100 per cent in this game. We had come this far, we could walk away as winners. When we walked out on to the pitch the atmosphere was electric – I wish we could play in a stadium like that every week.

The final was tight, as you would expect, and I know I didn't have the best game of my career at Tottenham, but I was heavily marked because Leicester manager Martin O'Neill had singled me out as the danger man. I never once received the ball without one or two Leicester players snapping at my heels. It was very difficult for me, but at least it meant it created some space for other players on the field. The turning point was probably the sending off of our left back, Justin Edinburgh, following a clash with Robbie Savage. I felt sorry for Justin but that was the referee's decision. Instead of feeling deflated at going down to 10 men, we boosted ourselves up and doubled our determination to succeed. We knew we had to push ourselves more and that caused problems for Leicester as they could see we were not going to lie down and surrender.

When Allan Nielsen scored the winning goal in the dying moments, I was really pleased. I was happy for him because he is a nice guy and deserved the attention. The goal came late enough to secure the victory – Leicester never had time to hit back before the final whistle. When the ref's whistle blew for full-time, I said to myself: 'This is it, you have won your first trophy in England!' It may not have been the biggest trophy, but it was significant for a number of reasons, not least because we had booked our place in the UEFA Cup. I felt so pleased for our fans because they had waited a long time for a moment like this – eight years, in fact – and I saw that they were so happy. As a player, this is the feeling you want to give to your fans every year. It was quite a debut season for George Graham, guiding the club to a trophy and a place in Europe, and he was naturally very happy. The lap of honour was brilliant, I hadn't experienced that since my time in Paris. I had my family there and I was waving to my father, my brother and my children in the stand. The team had a party in the evening, then I went from there with all my family to a friend's restaurant for our own private celebration, with French music and French food.

David Ginola was back in Europe, and this was important for me because playing on that stage is the only way for you and the club to be seen around the world. It was almost two years since Alan Sugar had asked me to get Tottenham into Europe. Now the chairman had got his wish.

That summer, Alan Sugar signed me on a new three-year contract, something he knew was important to the club and the fans. The fact that I was on a new long-term deal meant he was able to block any chance I had of joining Manchester United when an opportunity seemed to present itself a few months later.

I think this shows that people who run football clubs have no compassion. They don't think about me and the fact that this would have been my last chance to play for a really top club. They don't look at the good service I've given them and send me on my way with their blessing, as maybe they should do. I have seen this happen to many players – they can spend ten years or more giving loyal service and then are treated badly at the end of it. People in charge think only about their own success – but their success depends on that of the team.

Although this would have been a dream move for me, I accept that Tottenham fans would not have seen it that way.

But to be presented with such an opportunity at my age, when I don't have a lot of time left at the very top, would have been fantastic. I feel I deserved such an opportunity. I've played for 16 years as a professional and when I think about my quality, my skills, what I am capable of doing on the pitch, surely I deserve to play in a really top team. I am not saying Newcastle, Tottenham, and Aston Villa are not big clubs, but they are not on the same scale as AC Milan, Barcelona and Manchester United.

Moving to Old Trafford would have been fantastic but I want to make it clear that I was not looking to leave White Hart Lane. I did not go out and seek such a move. I was perfectly happy with what I had at Spurs and this was something which suddenly came to me, rather than the other way round. I just hope people can see why it might have appealed to me. Also, I should point out that when I signed for Spurs I was promised that more top names would follow but these never materialised.

I am not a troublemaker. I never went to the press and made waves by saying Manchester United had contacted me and that I wished to leave the club. Maybe I wanted to protect Alan Sugar from a situation where he would be under fire if I'd said I wanted to leave. I want the club to realise I protected them over this and did the right thing. This is because I think Alan Sugar has good intentions and is trying to do the best for the club in his eyes. But, on the other hand, I know people at the top of football clubs will never have compassion for me or their other players.

CHAPTER SIXTEEN

Management and me

*'I would like to become a manager in three or four
years' time, because I think I have a lot to offer'*

I respect George Graham as a manager and as a person, but
sometimes he was very hard on me. Maybe that is because I
was the highest earner in the club. What frustrated me is that
sometimes he didn't appreciate how tightly I am marked in
every game. When I receive the ball I am so closely policed that
I have to shake off my marker before I can make something
happen. He didn't understand how difficult it was for me
sometimes. Last season I was so tightly marked in one away
game that he took me off at half-time because he was unhappy
with me. But I should have played in the second half because I
am the type of player who can always make something happen.
He has frustrated me before by criticising me in the press and I
had to ask myself why he does it. He was attracting controversy
because journalists would come to me and say: 'Have you

heard what George Graham has said about you? What is your reaction?' I didn't want the journalists coming to me, so he was stirring something up, and he shouldn't have said anything to provoke this situation. It is a shame that things like this happened, because I don't think we had a particularly bad relationship on a day-to-day basis. I tried my best for him, like I would for any manager, and there were some very good aspects about his management style, which I would use if ever I became a manager, such as his sound defensive knowledge.

Statistics do not lie, and I think there is one particular piece of data that tells an interesting story. In my period at Tottenham after Graham's arrival, I started 79 matches for him, and was substituted in 36 of them, up until the end of the 1999/2000 season. What hurt me is that I felt I was always able – even if I was having an average game – to produce something which might turn the match and help us convert a defeat into a draw or one point into three. So why take me off with 20 minutes to go when I might have my moment in the 89th minute? You have to understand that my game is all about creativity, and that it may take time for my creativity to get its chance – it is a flash, it is not something you build, but I always feel sure it will come at some point in a game. I knew somewhere in my mind that I was not George Graham's kind of player. No matter what I did, it never seemed to be enough for him. I could score a hat-trick, but he would probably be thinking that I didn't make many saving tackles in my own penalty area! I knew he would rather have players who defend more, but I am afraid he had to take me as I am, because I wasn't going to change.

I found him a hard man to read, and he surprised me at times, like last season when he gave an interview in the press in which he said I was one of the best players he had ever worked with – there were no 'buts'. I knew that for him I was an entertainer, rather than a team player, so sometimes I was a luxury for him when he wants to play a tight 4-4-2 system comprising hard work and no entertainment. It was a shame to think like that, because I was a potential matchwinner. One time George came into the dressing room after a game and said to everyone: 'Hey guys, most of the time I shout at David but today I take my hat off to him because he is working, doing what I asked him to do.' But I didn't want to be treated like this in front of the other players – I was just doing my job, so I preferred to be left in a corner to get on with it.

Tottenham fans always hope for a good run in either the FA Cup or the League Cup as a consolation for not challenging for the championship, but I am afraid they were let down in both those competitions in the 1999/2000 season. They love going to Wembley and I wish we could have given them the opportunity to go every season, because we loved that too. Our defence of the Worthington Cup was a big disappointment, losing at First Division Fulham in the fourth round, and it was even more humiliating to fall at the first hurdle in the FA Cup with a 6–1 thrashing at my old club Newcastle in a third-round replay. The fact of the matter is, we should have beaten Newcastle at White Hart Lane and avoided having to travel to the north-east. It was the story of our season that we did not show enough maturity on the pitch, and there were lots of games in which we should have finished off our opponents early on, but instead we allowed them to get back into the game and salvage a draw or even a win. We lost too many points like that, by not taking our clear chances to kill games.

These Cup defeats, coupled with another average season in the Premiership, made it a boring campaign really. I think the season ended for many players that night early in November when we lost in Kaiserslautern. At one stage we were sixth in the league, with a chance of pushing into the top five, but we had a bad run and lost some strange games, particularly at home.

If I am playing in a game and we are 2–0 or 3–0 up with 10 or 15 minutes to go, then I have no objections whatsoever if the manager wants to replace me with one of the younger players to give them experience. But if we are 1–0 down, then I'm sorry, I do not agree. Even if I am not having a very good game, my moment may still come. I need only look back to a month before the end of that season, at Leicester on 19 April, to prove my point. The score was 0–0, but in the 89th minute I scored the goal which won us the match.

My goal against Watford in the 4–0 home win on Boxing Day was probably my best goal of the season, as I cut in on a mazy run and scored, but that one at Leicester was probably the most important. We had not won in our last five matches, and I had never been victorious at Filbert Street since I had been playing in England, so it was a significant goal. It also came in the final minute – when I am often not on the pitch – and it lifted our spirits. The youngsters in our team came to me afterwards and said: 'Thanks David, instead of going to Brighton for our holidays we can go to Tenerife with that win bonus!'

It was well documented in our penultimate home game last season how I left the ground almost immediately after the match. We were losing 1–0 to Derby with 20 minutes to go and Stewart Houston substituted me. He was in charge of first-team affairs while George Graham was off work troubled by an arthritic condition. It was not like the week before. On that occasion we were 2–0 up against Wimbledon and the game was safe, so I had no complaints when I was brought off so that one of the younger players could have a run out and gain some first-team experience in the closing minutes. But against Derby we were losing, and I was one of the few players who might have been able to turn things around. If you know a bit about football, you know it is logical to keep an attacking player like me on the pitch in a situation like that. But even when we were losing, the management didn't want to lose the team's tight shape; so rather than risk taking off a defender and playing with an extra attacker so we could go for broke and try to rescue the result, they sacrificed an attacker. Surely you have to try, you have to take risks, and that means keeping your creativity. Especially as it was really a meaningless game at the end of the season for us – we couldn't finish high enough in the league to qualify for Europe and we couldn't be relegated, so where is the risk in taking off a defender rather than a forward?

I was frustrated that I was taken off in this game. I always feel I can influence a game at any stage – it is just a question of trusting me. I couldn't bring myself to shake Houston's hand and sit on the bench, I was too upset, so I went straight into the dressing room and I have never taken a shower as quickly as I did on that particular Saturday. I could hear the crowd chanting *Houston out!* so I knew they agreed with me, even though, on this occasion, Spurs did equalise in the last minute and Houston got away with it. I put on my suit, sat down and waited for the players to come into the dressing room so that I could congratulate them on salvaging a point from the game. I wanted to say 'well done' to goalscorer Stephen Clemence and the rest of the lads. The fact I was substituted had nothing to do with the players, it was not their fault, so I would never vent my anger on them. As soon as Houston finished his post-match speech, I left. On a typical match day I am usually one of the last out of the dressing room. Along with Sol Campbell I like to take my time, have a long shower, sit and relax, then go out and meet the fans and talk to the press. I never leave the ground in five minutes like I did on this occasion.

I dashed straight to my car and started to drive out of White Hart Lane. I could only inch my way along because the crowds were still pouring out of the ground. When the fans saw it was me in the car, I think they worried that I was so upset I would be leaving the club for good, because they all clamoured around the car shouting: 'Don't go, David!' But they needn't have worried. When I went into training on the following Monday, some of the staff tried to make light of the situation, and my friend Hans Segers – our goalkeeping coach – started singing '*Ginola, Ginola!*' when I arrived.

The thing which made matters worse for me was that an article I did for the *Observer* newspaper appeared on the day after the match, and the reporter had let me down badly by adding his own interpretation to something I had said. The whole point of the article was to publicise my forthcoming trip to Cambodia with the Red Cross. I was looking forward to talking to the *Observer* about this, and I think that part of it came out very well. But at the end the interviewer asked me some questions about football, and I told him that although I was very happy in England I felt it would have been nice in my career to have played for a really big club, like Manchester United, which is something I have already explained in this book. Unfortunately, the reporter put his own interpretation on my remark and claimed I 'felt I had wasted my time playing in England'. I was very angry and upset, because at no time did I say or imply that, and it is certainly not how I feel – I have enjoyed my time in England and do not regret coming here at all. The agreement I had with the *Observer* was for them to send me the article before it appeared, so I could read it through and approve it. But they never showed it to me – and now I can see why. If you cannot trust a newspaper like the *Observer*, then who can you trust? It left a bitter taste, because the following day there were headlines elsewhere claiming that David Ginola feels he has wasted his time in England. The reporter from the *Observer* must have realised his mistake, as a week later he sent me a letter of apology. The fact that this article appeared the day after I had made my swift departure from White Hart Lane was just unfortunate timing.

However, worse was to follow the following Saturday. I was axed for one of our biggest games of the season, the clash with Manchester United at Old Trafford, less than two hours before the kick-off. I was left wondering about my future after that game. I had to ask myself why the management were not picking me for the big games – why didn't they want me? The only other time I had been dropped all season was for our biggest game of them all, in Kaiserslautern in the UEFA Cup. I was bitterly disappointed. Playing against the best teams brings out the best in me, and we all know they don't come any bigger than Manchester United. I was relishing the chance to play in front of a record 61,600 fans at Old Trafford, and had trained hard all week for the game. I was upset for the Spurs fans as I could do nothing to help the team, who lost 3–1. I was offered the chance to sit on the bench but thought if I was being dropped to give one of the youngsters a chance, I may as well step aside and let another youngster have my place on the bench, along with any bonuses which might go with it, so I declined. If I was never going to figure in the team, then I cannot understand why I was taken on a four-hour coach journey and made to warm up, before being told I wasn't needed.

There was a lot of publicity about me in the week leading up to our final game of the season, at home to Sunderland. Two days before it, Graham gave an interview in the *Mail* in which he didn't mince his words. He said: 'David had better get used to the idea that no one is guaranteed to start every game. It is unlikely he will get as many starts next season. Let's not forget that of our 37 league matches so far this season he's started 34. That's a lot more than Kanu at Highbury or Solskjaer at Old Trafford, to name but two of many internationals in the Premiership, not to mention the revolving door at Chelsea.' It followed an interview on Radio Five Live with David Pleat in which our director of football described me as 'difficult for any manager to have among his flock'. I felt that I didn't deserve to be treated in such a disrespectful way by the management. In three years I had given so much to Tottenham and brightened up the club, helping them find success again by winning a trophy and getting into Europe, so I deserved more respect. When I was signed by Tottenham, the club promised me there would be more big signings, so I had a right to expect to be part of a successful squad. I loved the Tottenham fans and had a special relationship with them, but I needed to be motivated, so of course it hurt to hear my manager say these things.

The interview with Graham carried the headline: 'No Slacking. Ginola and Co warned as Graham starts phase two of his Spurs plan.' It upset me that anyone could suggest I was a slacker. I never missed a day's training, and I was one of the hardest workers – something Graham had gone on record as having said himself. I also did not see how he could compare my situation with other players such as Kanu or Solskjaer. At both Arsenal and Manchester United the bench contained world-class players. Kanu was competing for places with Henry, Bergkamp and Pires, while Solskjaer was up against Yorke, Cole and Sheringham. No disrespect to Tottenham, but they did not have that strength in depth. Graham was working

262

with a big squad of players at Spurs, yet his attacks seemed to be aimed at me personally. I am someone who prefers to be encouraged by the manager, rather than made the scapegoat. I also don't want people to think he had been giving me presents when he picked me, as I have always asked to be judged on my merits. I don't want to think I will be left on the bench when I am playing my best football, as it would be hard in that situation to see another player taking my place. I am 20 years old in my head, if not in my body, and I think it is good for me to show the young players that they can go on until they are 35. I never arrive for training without a smile on my face or in a bad mood because I know my role as one of the more experienced players is to bring a good spirit into the squad. I have never been a manager's favourite wherever I have played, I have always had to work harder to prove myself because of my talent and the way people see me. I had four managers at Spurs – Francis, Gross, Pleat and Graham – and I was never disrespectful to any of them. I respected my job and I always backed the club and did my best to promote it both on and off the pitch. I hate people saying I am just an entertainer – I am a winner too, and I have been proud to help bring success to Tottenham.

It is always difficult to speak about the future, because I am someone who is not planning things for a long time ahead. A football cliché is to say 'I take each game as it comes,' and now I take each day as it comes. A few years ago I was planning lots of things, but now I have a family and my outlook has changed. I want to enjoy today, I am nearer the end of my playing career than the beginning of it, so I don't want to wish away the last few years. If I start talking about what I will do afterwards then it means I am already planning for the time when I cannot play any more, which will be a very sad moment for me. I am not yet fed up with football and I honestly believe I will never ever be fed up with football. I am still very passionate and very ambitious, and if, as I am sure I will, I feel like this when I am 35, I shall want the opportunity to carry on until I am unable to perform on the pitch. My father played football until he was 38 and that could be my target as well – I would certainly like to try. The day I retire, I know I will not make any attempt at a comeback, so I want to play to the limit. Football is my life, and to be able to play for a further two years will be a bonus for me. Other players speak to me now and say: 'David, you can go on much longer because you will make a great playmaker in the middle of the pitch, with your quick feet, vision and skill.' Maybe I will even play as a sweeper! If I am still playing beyond the age of 35, I will need a manager who understands me, one who will let me decide what is good for my body. So if I want to finish training before the rest of the players and go in for a massage, he will know it is because I have pushed my body far enough and I need to recover, not because I want to go home early. A sensible manager will be able to get the best out of me. First and foremost, it will be nice to stay in England and play for Villa, but eventually I might enjoy going to a country like America or Japan to play for a couple of years. Or else I could travel around as an ambassador for football, making guest appearances in special matches.

If I was going to become a manager, then I would love to manage a big club. I have thought about becoming a manager, or maybe a coach who works with the kids, because I think I would be a good teacher and would get a lot of satisfaction from that. The only thing that might stop me from going into management is the fact that it would mean I had less time with my family, because if I was going to do it I would do it properly, travelling all over the world scouting for players and checking out opponents. I would not go into management thinking I will have time to go and play golf a few times a week – I never do anything without the spirit of winning. If I did become a manager, I would have to change the way I look, because I don't think the players would take me seriously with my long hair. Unfortunately, people form their first impression of you by the way you look, and a lot of people think I am arrogant just because of my appearance. Some people who I work with now look at me and think I shouldn't be playing football – they think I should be modelling for a glamour magazine, or appearing on the catwalk, or on television, and they don't take me as seriously as I would like, which upsets me. I pull them up and tell them: 'Hey, don't adopt that attitude with me, because I am working, just like you.' I would be tough as a manager, so the first thing I would do would be to shave my head, as that would make me look meaner and make people accept me. I would take the best bits of all the managers I have had in my career and blend them with my own qualities. If I make the team successful then the players will respect me, because I will be bringing them trophies – and how I look won't matter!

I am sure I would be good as a manager, because I am sensitive. I would introduce psychology to the players and develop relationships. Each member of a group of players is different, and to get the best out of them is to know each one as an individual. I would find out what I could say to this one, and that one, without hurting them, so as to boost their confidence. I would build my team around a very strong spine. That means bringing in the best goalkeeper, the best central defender, the best central midfielders, and the best striker. The holding midfielders are so important, and I would want a partnership such as Patrick Vieira and Emmanuel Petit formed at Arsenal. Two anchor men would allow the men on the flanks to go up and down and create a threat. When Franz Beckenbauer arrived at Marseille he said: 'The first thing I will do is build the defence,' and I would do the same, so I would have an imposing figure like Sol Campbell. The striker is very important, and I like players like Claudio Lopez, and they also don't come any better than Alan Shearer, a goalscorer who can hold the ball up front. When I played at PSG we had George Weah as the main striker with me playing off him. That is the way I wanted to play at Newcastle with Shearer, but it wasn't to be, and that is the way I would set up my team. I want players who work with the ball, who can keep it away from the opposition. The best managers in the world know that the idea of football is to build the team from a sound defensive base. I remember when I played in Paris for PSG under Artur Jorge that we got a lot of criticism because we didn't score many goals. But at the end of the season we won the title. If you keep a clean sheet then there is always the possibility of you scoring one goal and winning. So I would build from the back and have players like myself up front – that would be very nice! A few years ago I told journalists I did not want to become a manager because I didn't think I would be a good one. But it is more difficult for me to say that now. Footballers can become good managers because you work with so many managers in your life that if you are intelligent then you can take all the good things you have learnt from different people and mix them into the right formula. The other thing I believe in is to concentrate on the youth policy, bringing in the best young players who can make it to the top in the first team one day.

I would like to become a manager in three or four years' time, because I think I have a lot to offer. I would employ staff around me who are warm, respectful and approachable. I would make sure the players enjoy training. I would finish every session with a game of some kind, so they come back to the dressing room with a smile. They could play a five-a-side competition for ten minutes and the losers would have to buy lunch at a restaurant straight after training. The last memory of a session, especially a hard one, will be a happy one. I know from experience that, most of the time, the spirit of a team is built away from the pitch.

I know that what gives you strength is how you link the players, and the important thing is how you build team spirit. So I would have a family meeting every week, where the players could bring their wives and children. There would be a Christmas tree at the club every year, and family trips for the players, so they develop a good spirit and want to fight for me, for each other, for the club and for the fans. I would want to create a spirit like in an Italian family. If you don't know each other, how can you go on to the pitch on Saturday afternoon and fight for each other? It is easy to communicate with people who are happy, scoring goals and playing well; they will respond to you. I would also help a player if he was frustrated at not being able to get into the team. If he wanted to leave, then I would help him find another club, that is part of the deal as far as I am concerned – I won't leave them like an old pair of socks which have no use any more, I will be respectful. My door will always be open and I want the players to enjoy coming to play for my team.

I would probably need about £50 million to build a success-ful team, but I would get the chairman his money back by guiding the team into the Champions' League. If I can build a team who are playing in the major European competition year in, year out, then why shouldn't I be given the money? When I look at where football is going in the future I can see the formation of a European Super League, dominated by the tele-vision companies, and so you will have to be one of the top three teams in your country if you want to play in this league. If one day this Super League comes into existence and you are not in it, then you will be dead. You will receive no more money from television because the TV companies will all con-centrate on this new league instead. If you miss the boat now, you may never get the chance to get back, so you have to be clever now to protect your future.

If I was a manager I would place more importance on the psychological aspect of the game. I would get to know the players. Nowadays a manager is so busy that he doesn't have the time to get inside his players' heads. He doesn't know about them as an individual, as a human being, as a person, as a family man, they are just one of a big squad of players to work with. Every single player is different, each has a different way of life, a different view of life and a different view of foot-ball, and you can't work in the same way with a group of 30 players. You have to do things as a team but you also have to work players as individuals. For example, I am not so fantastic at heading the ball, so if I was the manager I would say: 'David, you do a special session and practise heading today.'

I would try to find out what makes the players tick. This is because I have learnt in football that when you train every day, the only thing which makes a difference is your mental state. If you are mentally prepared then you are 100 per cent and able to push all your qualities, but if you are not mentally prepared then come 3 o'clock on Saturday – even if you are a great player – you will just give 70 per cent instead of 100. The man-ager should know if you are the type of player who responds better to an arm around the shoulder or to a geeing-up with a clenched fist.

Whatever happens, I would like to take a year off when I hang up my boots, and do the simple things in life that I have missed, such as travelling with my family and going fishing with my father. During that year's sabbatical I shall take a step back from the action and think carefully about what I want to do, so that I don't make any rash decisions. There is only one day you have to worry about – today. Forget yesterday, because it has already gone, and don't fret about tomorrow, because it hasn't yet arrived. That says everything to me. I want to live well in the present, because if you don't live well in the present then you will not have a good future.

CHAPTER SEVENTEEN

Landmines and laughter

*'I am aware that as a UN ambassador I can play my
part, and am happy to do so, but it is also up to the
politicians to take responsibility'*

I race down the left flank. I beat one man, then another, and
finally a third, before sending a low cross into the penalty area.
Our centre forward balances on his good right leg and swings
at the ball first-time with his artificial one; it's a perfect strike
and he sends it crashing into the back of the net. Goal! It's 1–0
to Ginola's team and the crowd go wild.

This one moment of sporting pleasure was a real highlight
for me during a trip to Cambodia to increase awareness of the
Red Cross anti-personnel landmines campaign. It came when I
played a football match with two teams of amputees, and to see
the smiles on their faces when, in spite of their disability, they
participate in something they enjoy so much, is what makes
these kind of trips so worthwhile.

Let me take you back to May 2000. Another long, hard Premier League football season came to an end on Sunday 14th. Although it had been a disappointing campaign for Tottenham, at least we finished on a high note by beating Sunderland 3–1 at White Hart Lane. For a select few there was a very short break before joining up with their respective countries who they were hoping to represent in the European Championship the following month. For the rest, it meant the beginning of the summer holidays and I know that on Monday 15 May several of my team-mates were jetting off to the Caribbean or some other exotic location for a well-earned rest. But that was not the case for me. For the day after the football season ended I was on a 12-hour British Airways flight heading for Hong Kong and then on to Cambodia on an important charity mission for the International Committee of the Red Cross. I was tired and felt as if I needed a holiday with my family like everyone else, but it was for a good cause so I was happy to make the visit. When you get involved in these good causes you have to be 100 per cent committed, which I am. I was accompanied by my agent Chantal who had organised the trip, and my journalist friend Neil Silver.

First stop on a hectic, but worthwhile week-long tour, was the bustling city of Hong Kong, where I launched my own website*. It was set up by my American friend Steven Feuerstein and his company SportsNetGlobal Holdings Limited, and they have done an excellent job so I hope it is a success. Within the website is a link to my global internet campaign in which visitors to the site have the opportunity to interactively learn all about the Red Cross anti-personnel landmines campaign. The aim of my 'Walk Without Fear'

*www.ginola14.com

campaign is simple: to bury landmines forever, and also to graphically and emotionally raise the consciousness of the general public concerning the more than 24,000 killed or permanently maimed as a result of landmine explosions annually. We travelled through the night from London and as soon as we landed in Hong Kong we dropped off our bags at the Mandarin Oriental hotel before being driven to a press conference in the city centre. The launch of the website attracted a lot of interest, with several television stations and newspapers represented there.

Next stop was the Hong Kong Football Club, where I held a coaching session for local children, and also played in a football match with them, which was a lot of fun. The pitch is in the centre of the Happy Valley race track, so it is quite an amazing setting in which to play football. After a quick shower there was a dinner for about 40 guests, and these included some English businessmen who are based in Hong Kong. One of them held a question and answer session with me, and most of their questions were about my relationship with George Graham, so obviously the exiled fans were well in touch with what was going on at White Hart Lane. The Spurs fans in the group picked their favourite Tottenham team of all time, and they allowed me to just edge out Cliff Jones for the left-wing berth. It was an exciting team and I think it highlighted the kind of line-up Spurs fans dream about. The XI were: Pat Jennings; Steve Perryman, Dave McKay, Sol Campbell, Cyril Knowles; Ossie Ardiles, Glenn Hoddle, Paul Gascoigne, David Ginola; Jimmy Greaves, Gary Lineker. I signed a ball and my T-shirt and both items raised more than £4,000 in an impromptu auction in aid of my Walk Without Fear campaign – money which will provide new limbs for 20 people. My work for the day wasn't finished, however, as after the dinner I was taken to the BBC Radio offices in the city for a live interview. A late finish was followed by an early start the next morning, as I was live on American television station CNN talking about the campaign. Then it was off to the airport to fly to Cambodia for the second leg of the mission.

I had already visited Angola, which is the country infested with the most mines, and I felt it was important to go to Cambodia too, which has the next largest number of mines, somewhere in excess of three million. Most of the landmines in Cambodia were buried from 1975 when the rebel Khmer Rouge group seized control. The Khmers based themselves mainly in Battambang in the north and surrounded themselves with the mines by way of protection. But there were also mines planted by foreign troops who invaded the country, such as the Vietnamese in 1979. The warfare under the dictatorship of Pol Pot lasted until 1991 when the king came back from exile and the Paris Peace Agreement was signed to restore order. Now there is the job of clearing the mines, which is where I come in. In Angola, I found the poverty level was high, but this was not the case in Cambodia. Here, the people are much more content with what they have, and they live a happy and simple life, with better living conditions and a better quality of life. There is no famine, they cultivate the fields and utilise the forest – the only problem is the landmines. I particularly noticed how beautiful and healthy the small children were. The Government is trying to reduce the poverty that there is by introducing two main reforms. The first is land legislation, so that people can identify which piece of land they own, and the other is the demobilisation of 40,000 soldiers back into the community. I could see that the Cambodian Government cared about its people and was doing its bit to help those affected by the mines. It had also signed the Ottawa Treaty last year, which meant no more mines would be planted there and any components would be destroyed.

As soon as we touched down at Pochetong airport in the capital of Phnom Penh the massive contrast between Cambodia and Hong Kong was apparent. There was no grand terminal like the shiny silver building to greet you at Hong Kong International Airport, just a low-rise edifice, bustling with people trying to secure their entry visa, and it took no more than a few seconds to exit the airport after retrieving our luggage. Although we had our Red Cross escorts, you still have to be aware of safety issues, as I was told that six farmers were kidnapped by armed guerrillas the day we flew into Phnom Penh. It was straight down to the job in hand as we were driven from the airport to the Cambodian School of Prosthetics and Orthotics. This is where people who need artificial limbs are assessed, and they are measured and have the limbs cast to fit. Once they have had an artificial leg fitted, they are taught how to walk on all different types of terrain, such as gravel or steps. One man I met had his leg blown off when he was trying to defuse a mine himself. It may sound foolish but he wanted to recover the scrap metal to sell, and to use the explosives for fishing.

We moved on to our hotel and there I was briefed by the ICRC Head of Mission for Cambodia, Marianne Coradazzi. She coached me in how I should behave when I went around visiting people. For example, I was told not to pat a child on the head in a gesture of affection. This is because the children are the kings of the family and to touch them on the head as you would in a European country means you are trying to oppress them, so I was told to touch them on the arm instead. I was also told not to point my finger at anyone and not to raise my voice. Nor should I kiss anyone in public or even attempt to shake hands. Instead, I was told to clasp my hands together under my chin, Oriental style, and bow gently. Another tip I was given was not to try and talk to people about the atrocities of the past. The people are tired of war and want to forget about it, so instead they want to talk about the future. I was pleased to hear that progress is being made and people's awareness of the mines is increasing. In 1996 a total of 3,000 people were injured or killed by a mine, but last year the figure was down to 1,000, so the message appears to be getting across. The briefing was followed by a reception at which I met the British and French ambassadors, and then I was finally able to fall into bed and rest before the next day's visits.

The sun comes up very early in Cambodia and is very strong by 8.30 am, so we had to make an early start every day. We set off for the Kompong Speu Rehabilitation Centre, 45 km out-side the capital. The centre is operated by the American Red Cross, it has 32 staff and it takes in an average of 260 people per month. This is where people who have lost limbs go to be rehabilitated into the community. Here they are taught all about nutrition and how to grow their own vegetables. All ser-vices provided at the centre are free and since 1992 more than 4,600 patients have received help from the centre. The sleeping quarters have 14 beds to each small room, all laid side by side, but everyone mixes well together. Some of the sights you see are heart-breaking, such as the 10-year-old boy I met with no legs, but after having visited Angola I was more prepared for these sad images. The only thing I try to do is to be positive, to arrive with a smile on my face and show them that I care. All the victims put on a brave face as they prepare for their future, and their attitude is very positive – their life is not over just because they have lost a limb.

After looking around the rehabilitation centre it was one of the moments I had been waiting for, the football match with the amputees. The bumpy, barren pitch made Hackney Marshes look like Wembley, but nobody cared. There was a huge crowd and they loved every minute of it, as did the players. I was surprised how both the players and the crowd laughed whenever someone missed the ball completely, but it wasn't a question of making fun, just of people having a good time. Considering the players had one real leg and one false one, their ability was pretty good, and their enthusiasm was superb. I told them afterwards that I would have to take some of them back to England with me to play in the Premier League, and they loved the sound of that! My visits to these countries are for serious purposes, so it was nice to have a lighter moment like this. Some of the guys I spoke to told me they were training for the running events at the Paralympics, which again shows how they are looking to the future with a positive attitude.

We had a break for lunch and I enjoyed sampling the Cambodian food. We were taken to a restaurant alongside the road that the Red Cross workers favoured. It was the kind of place you pass right by unless you know it, and the food was good. Because of our early start it was still only 1 pm and we still had a busy afternoon ahead of us. Next stop was a Jesuit Service craft centre called the Bantey Prieb – or Centre of the Dove. The centre houses 90 people and it teaches victims who have been disabled by landmines how to find a career which will help them survive in life. There were a wide variety of skills being taught by the 20 teachers there. A group of young men were learning to become mechanics and were stripping down a motor cycle to understand its workings. In another hut people were learning sculpture and making beautiful wood carvings. There was also a classroom teaching electronics, one making wheelchairs, and another full of women weaving. This is another service provided free of charge to its residents, who stay for a year to learn their new skills, as well as social rehabilitation, so that they may be able to make a living for themselves when they return to the community. They have all their food, accommodation and education provided for and are allowed home three times a year for a holiday. The centre even loans money to people who want to open up a workshop when they leave, such is the faith they have in their students. I was presented with a beautiful red-and-white traditional Kema headscarf, which I wore throughout the rest of the trip. Also inside the centre is the Dancing Village of Prey Som Raong, and we were taken there to see a beautiful performance of a dance by the children of the village. It was a really colourful display and it is aimed at teaching awareness of the landmines through dance. The dance is divided into three acts: first, the landmines, played by young boys, are boastfully sitting on the land and scaring any living creatures who come near them; second, the butterflies, played by young girls, fly freely and happily in their own abode, and then innocently fly towards the danger zone; and third, the white doves, played by little girls, come to rescue the butterflies as they hear the cry for help. In the end, the doves and the butterflies escape the disaster together and help other living things to be free from danger. The dance shows that peace and happiness still prevail in their beloved nation. There is a song which goes with the dance, and the words are very poetic:

> *Holy holy dove of heaven,*
> *Such beautiful eyes and so is kind,*
> *She brings to the world for humankind.*
> *Holy holy white dove,*

She brings happiness to Cambodians,
Who try near and far,
Bring unity to the Kingdom of Cambodia.

After the performance I was asked to pose with the musicians for some photographs, and I ended up playing the drums for one number. This whole place was a fantastic cultural centre for the disabled and I was very impressed by the skills of the people living and training there. It was easy to be positive and complimentary when I spoke to the people, as I really admired all they were doing and enjoyed being attentive to them. The Father of the centre told me that those in rehabilitation would speak about my visit for months afterwards and he was very pleased that my trip to the school would raise the spirit to an even more positive level. This completed a memorable day, and it was early evening before we arrived back at our hotel, with just time for a massage and dinner before retiring to bed.

The following morning saw us make an even earlier start and embark on a journey I shall not forget in a hurry. Our destination was a village called Dei Sar, about 100 km from Phnom Penh. The population of Dei Sar fled the area in 1996 when fighting between Government forces and the Khmer Rouge intensified. The village was heavily fought over and used as a base by both sides. As a result, the whole area is now contaminated by landmines, unexploded mortar bombs and rockets. Sixty families who had been displaced by the fighting need to reclaim their village and rebuild their lives. As security in the area has improved over the past year, the villages have been slowly returning. Land is everything to the people of Cambodia, so these villagers are prepared to risk their lives by returning to their homes before the land is clear of mines. Up to the time of our visit, four people had already been killed, five injured and numerous cattle had been lost to landmines. We set off at 7.00 am, by which time it was already very hot, but at least our Land Rover had air conditioning. I travelled with Chantal and Neil, plus our Cambodian driver. The first part of our journey was long but straightforward, as we travelled along one of the modern roads built by the Americans. You place your life in the hands of your driver, as he overtakes bicycles, motor bikes and other vehicles along the way, but it is a common rule of the road out there. To pass the time, the three of us sang songs and told jokes, which was really good fun. I think that it was important we were in good spirits. We did not underestimate the seriousness of the visit ahead, but we did not want to arrive in a downbeat mood, as the whole point of visiting the village was to give the people there hope. After an hour-and-a-half on the straight, flat road, we turned on to what can only be described as a mud track. It felt like we were driving in a cross-country rally as our four-wheel drive vehicle bounced in and out of the large pot holes, most of them flooded with rain water. As we passed through the fields we could see the local children swimming in the dirty brown rivers, or playing happily outside their bamboo shacks which they called home. It was a simple life, a million miles away from the lifestyle of Europe, but I could see they were happy and innocent. Although we had to travel only about 10 km, it took almost an hour to make our way along the dirt track to the village.

As soon as we arrived at the village we were given a briefing on safety. We were told not to wander off, but to stay close to our guides, and under no circumstances were we to go beyond the barrier tapes. We were told that the day before a live mine had been discovered, and that they had waited for us to arrive so that we could see it being blown up – what's more, I was going to be the one to press the detonator. Our main host was a jolly Australian named Archie Law, who was the country programme manager for MAG, the Mines Advisory Group. This is an international non-governmental organisation dedicated to assisting poor communities faced with the legacy of conflict. MAG's primary focus is the eradication of landmines – making land safe to allow subsistence rural communities to live without fear of death and maiming and to rebuild their world after war. The MAG sent one of its 15-man teams to the Dei Sar area in March and their first task was to clear vitally needed priority areas for the community: to provide safe access to water, areas to build houses and access to the Pagoda, which is an important focus of life for the people. This is one of 10 areas they are currently clearing of mines and the team will be in the village until October 2000, which is how long it will take them to clear eight hectares in which the villagers can live, as that is all they have the funding for. Although we were inside barriers delineating the safe area – the MAG team assured me the area was '200 per cent safe from mines' – when I looked across the fence I could see children from the village playing in an adjacent field. I was horrified because there was no guarantee that area was safe from mines, but these were just innocent young children whose only thoughts were about playing in the sun. In the safe area we were shown all the different types of mine, and given a demonstration of how the mines are detected. It is a slow and a laborious task, but a vitally important one. The workers start by scanning a metal detector over every square inch of land; then, if their machine bleeps, they very carefully scrape away the surface of the earth to see what is below it. If they uncover a mine, they call a supervisor and then steps are taken to clear the area and the mine is blown up. All of us were kitted out with protective vests and helmets so that we could be shown around the village, and we were told to follow our leader very closely. Before we were taken to where the live mine had been uncovered the day before, I went to meet the villagers, who were being given mine awareness lessons by the workers with the aid of colourful posters, and again I was struck by the beauty of the small children. There was no fear on the faces of these innocent villagers, who simply want to live on their own land and grow their own crops, even if that meant living with the threat of landmines. I also met a group of monks who live in a temple next to the village. I learned that it was the chief of the monks who had discovered the very first mine there and I asked them how they felt about living in a place surrounded by mines. They just accepted it as a part of everyday life and did not let it interfere with their daily duties. After being shown the live mine, I was taken back a clear distance and then once it had been wired up to some explosives I was given the detonator to press. The force of the explosion took me by surprise, and when the mine blew up I could see just how dangerous it was and what it is capable of doing to a human being.

By now it was early afternoon and time to head back to the main road and a little restaurant where we were due to have lunch with the MAG leaders. The first driver in our convoy was having trouble using his four-wheel drive and he got his vehicle stuck in one of the deep water-filled holes. When our driver got out to have a look, I jumped into his seat and took the wheel – and there was no way I was going to give it back to him! From that point on I drove us all the way back along the dirt track. It was a great thrill, and my passengers said I was better than our Cambodian driver – even though they might have been slightly biased!

After lunch we drove back to Phnom Penh (I let our driver

take the wheel on the American-built road) and visited the Red Cross Mine Incident Database Project. This is where the Red Cross assemble all the data relating to landmines and analyse it, so that they get a clearer picture of the landmine problem in Cambodia. They produce colourful charts that detail the number of casualties from the mines and the most affected areas of the country. From these they are able to determine on pie charts how many casualties result from people collecting food or wood, how many from farming, and how many from tampering with mines. Also, they list whether mines were located on paths and roads, near rivers, in fields or forests, or near military bases. They break down the casualty figures into men, women and children under 18. It is very important for the Red Cross to keep these records as they use them to tackle the whole problem, and it was interesting to hear all the facts and figures as it puts the problem into perspective. Another long and tiring day came to an end, so it was back to the hotel for an early night and the chance to catch up on some sleep, ready for the final day of visits.

The next day was Saturday and the French Red Cross had arranged for me to see its components factory. The workers were off for the weekend so it was all quiet inside, but I could imagine how busy it must be on a working day. I was shown how the false limbs are made, and I was very impressed by the equipment used. The quality of machinery was very high, and would not look out of place in any factory, anywhere in the world. This summed up the main difference between Cambodia and Angola, as here the general standard of everything was much higher. We spent the morning touring the factory and then it was time to satisfy the photographers. I was due to visit a temple, and they arranged for me to be seen arriving in a rickshaw, as that made a good snap for them. I am sure they got the picture they wanted, but it wasn't the safest feeling for me to be sitting in this contraption with the traffic rushing around me! After lunch I returned to the hotel to have lunch with Edmond Corthesy from the ICRC, who had again been escorting me on this trip. It was a chance for him to bring me up to date with how their landmine campaign was progressing, and it was good to hear that things were moving in the right direction. The nice thing for me was that he felt my visit was having the desired effect in terms of raising awareness of the problem, and I can ask for no more than that.

My final evening in Cambodia was a chance for me to unwind a little and see some typical sights at the same time, as the Red Cross arranged for us all to go on a boat trip along the Mekong River. This was to prove another highlight of the trip, thanks to the BBC film crew who were filming my visit for a documentary. But first, I finished off an interview for GMTV. The river was a good backdrop for some filming, as there were lots of boats sailing past us and on the banks were the wooden shacks inhabited by the poorer people. When it was the turn of the BBC crew to move in, the girl who was making the pro-gramme asked for the engine of the boat to be turned off, as all the movement was affecting the shots. I did warn her that one of the rules of the river was not to stop an engine during a trip, but my warning fell on deaf ears. However, when it came to re-starting the engine, the owner of the boat could not get it going again. Poor Caroline from the BBC was very embarrassed, and we spent two hours drifting in the darkness until the engine was fixed. All we could do was try and make the most of it, so I introduced my new friends to a Pastis, and we had quite a good party below deck. When we eventually made it back to shore, the English journalists in our group wanted to watch the FA Cup final, and thanks to the time difference we made it to a bar, where we sat and watched the game live on television, with a game of darts thrown in at half time for good measure. This evening had been a nice way to round off a very good trip, before we were due to set off for home early the next morning.

The long journey back to London gave me the chance to reflect on the week's work, and I felt that we had achieved our aim. The landmine issue is such a big problem that it will take years to resolve completely, and all we can do is chip away at it and try to make the situation better. I want to do more trips like this, and with 66 countries having a landmine problem there are plenty more for me to visit. Who knows where I shall go next, but there are many options, such as South America, Asia and the Middle East. My first trip to Angola was a voyage of discovery and it took a bit of time to adjust to the shock of what I saw there. But this one to Cambodia was straight down to business and the more trips I make the better an ambassador I will become, because the more I see, the more I am able to tell people about the problem. I shall also become more sensitive to the different situations and can compare the different countries. I am aware that as a humanitarian ambassador I can play my part, and am happy to do so, but it is also up to the politicians to take responsibility. I'm just here to give a helping hand, and I cannot make the decisions for the Governments. The result of my trip to Cambodia was that the whole issue was talked about in the papers and on radio and television, and the images were sent all around the world. That is the positive outcome because hopefully it will encourage people to make much-needed donations to the Red Cross. I know that it comes down to a matter of personal choice as to who you donate your money to. But if you have, say, £10 to give then maybe you can share it around between two or three charities, including this one.

I was looking forward to going home and seeing my family again. There was no football to worry about and it was time to fulfil my duty as a husband and father by giving time to the people closest to my heart. I was looking forward to our family holiday in Mauritius which Chantal had arranged for me. I could switch off completely and have a rest, although I knew my footballing future was going to be an issue during the summer. Even as I was checking out of my hotel in Cambodia I received a call on my mobile telephone from the chief executive of Marseille, telling me they wanted to sign me. It made me smile, as at the end of last season George Graham and David Pleat had been telling people that nobody was interested in me. Little did they know that Marseille were only one of a handful of clubs who were trying to get me to sign for them for the 2000/01 season.

EPILOGUE

Andrea and Carla

I am very close to both my children. My son Andrea was training with Barnet Football Club, just up the road from where we
lived before my move to Villa. He is a hard worker and he
enjoys his football. I want him to improve, not because I want
to make him into a professional, but just so that he can hold
his own when he plays with his friends. When we go back to
the south of France there is a lot of beach football played, so I
want him to be able to play happily enough. It is very hard for
him, because people expect him to have the same talent as me
simply because he is my son. He is more of a defender; he's
very tough (George Graham would love him!) When he plays
with bigger boys he gives 150 per cent all the time – he doesn't
know how to play giving anything less. He wants to win, like
me, and his enthusiasm is tremendous.

If you ask him what he wants to be when he grows up, he
will tell you that he wants to become a professional footballer,
just like his father. I am not sure how that makes me feel. I
know how hard it is, how hard I have had to work, and it will

287

be even harder for him because of who he is. There are two different kinds of professional footballer, the one who plays in the third division and the one who plays in the Premier League. No disrespect to the players from the lower division, but it is a different world. If he is going to be good enough to play in the Premier League then I shall say to him: 'Go for it.' Otherwise, I would rather he concentrated on other things. I am proud of him no matter what. In football and in life you have to want to win, and I know he wants to be a winner. I look at Andrea when he goes training and I think about when I was his age, dreaming about winning trophies. I still dream about winning trophies.

Carla is my little princess. She likes dressing up, which is the opposite of Andrea who doesn't worry too much about clothes, but Carla is always concerned about what she wears. For example, if she comes home from school and is going to go next door to play with our neighbour, she will change to look better. Also, she is a fearless child, she can climb things, or walk ahead of us without a care in the world. The main thing is, she loves her brother. If he has a problem or a worry she is very concerned for him. If he hurts himself, she cries for him. She is a very clever girl, and I have no worries about how she will turn out. She showed her aptitude in the south of France, at a tennis school. There was a competition to see who could put a ball on to the face of the racquet and carry it from the baseline to the net and back the fastest without dropping it. The coaches couldn't believe how quickly she did it – but I saw that she had wedged the ball into the centre of the metal frame, so that it wouldn't fall off!

I have asked my grandmother what I was like as a boy and she said I could sometimes be very naughty, not listening and running all over the place. But I can honestly say my children are good. I have quietened down as I have grown a little older, and my son Andrea is very much like me, very sensitive. At Easter, Coraline took the children home to France, while I stayed in England on my own to play football. At the airport Andrea tried to hide the fact he was crying because he didn't want to leave me. I took him in my arms and said: 'Come on Andrea, you are going to have a good time, say hello to Grandma and Granddad for me, enjoy yourself.' He was crying on my shoulder and said: 'I don't want to leave you daddy,' but I said: 'You know you can't stay, I have training every day and games to play.' I sent Coraline and Carla ahead into the terminal and I went and sat on a bench with Andrea. I said to him: 'I wish I could go on holiday with you but daddy is working and I can't. One day I will finish football and we will go wherever you want. But you must go now, you are the man in charge of the family when I am not around so I want you to look after mum and Carla. Daddy is very proud of you and I will always back you up. Now give me a smile.' He did, and he went through okay. I found out that while he was away he would go downstairs for breakfast, take out a mug from the cupboard which had my picture on it, go into the room where I always go, with the fireplace, books and pool table, then sit down with his tea and cry because he was missing me. Carla was completely different. She came on the phone and innocently said: 'Guess what daddy, Andrea cried this morning because he wanted to see you, but I didn't cry.'

I always make sure I don't give one of them more love than the other. At night, when I go to their room to say goodnight to them, if I spend five minutes on Andrea's bed I spend the same time on Carla's. If I give more time to Andrea because he is upset about something at school, and then I am tired and want to go to bed, Carla will tell me I spent more time with

289

Andrea – she notices, but I have to pretend I didn't realise. Even at five, she has problems, but it is beautiful when your children talk about their problems, such as losing a game in the playground, or being given too much homework, because it puts things into perspective.

I want to have more children. We want to live a little first because in previous years we have devoted a lot of our time to the children, and we want to travel for a year when I retire and discover France more. But I have visions for later on. I want to have a big, secluded farm, with animals, horses, chickens, hens, and sheep. It will probably be in France because the weather is warmer. I would like to have more kids around me, and for all of them to be growing up around the family, and maybe one day when they get married and have kids we could build cottages on the land for them to live, with their children growing up in this environment. I imagine myself planting vegetables and cherry trees, looking after my garden, maybe also owning a beach restaurant. I know Coraline would like to own a stretch of beach with our own restaurant. This house would be a house of happiness, in huge grounds, with a river full of fish and a forest with mushrooms. I will also have a garage with quad bikes and old cars – an XK 150 Jaguar convertible, black with a cream leather interior; a Ferrari 250 California; and a Vantage Aston Martin, 1987.

I would have a huge kitchen because I realise that this is the room where we spend most of our time. It is the room of the family. I like going to work in the kitchen, cooking, or sitting reading the papers. A house must be built around the kitchen. The kids do their homework in the kitchen, they play in the kitchen, they watch television in the kitchen. I would build an old-fashioned fire, with a spit roast for the meat, and have a cellar with bottles of wine. I have already drawn up some plans with an architect and something else I have allowed for is an area in the garden to play petanque. This is a traditional French game, a bit like English crown green bowling except that you throw the balls instead of bowling them. It is a very popular sport in the south of France and every village has a square in the centre where people go to play. It is a lot of fun and I have played since I was very young, so I am quite good at it. There is even a world championship with teams from Belgium, Morocco and even the Far East. This home is the kind of place I would be happy in, with my family.

Last season I answered a survey for an edition of the Tottenham matchday programme and one of the questions was to come up with the best movie line of all time. I chose the one spoken by Tom Cruise in *Jerry Maguire* which went like this: 'In life, to be honest, I failed as much as I succeeded, but I love my wife, I love my life, and I wish you had my kind of success.'

I think that sums up my life quite nicely.

Career Statistics

Compiled by Andy Porter

David Desire Marc Ginola

Born: Gassin, near St. Tropez, 25 January 1967.
Family: Father René and mother Mireille, brother Sebastien, wife Coraline, son Andrea and daughter Carla.
Height: 6ft (1.85m).
Weight: 13st 5lb (85kg).
School: Centre de Formation, Nice.
Junior football: Sainte Maxime, OGC Nice.
Professional football: OGC Nice; SC Toulon; Matra Racing Paris; Brest Armorique; Paris Saint-Germain; Newcastle United; Tottenham Hotspur; Aston Villa.

Career Record

Club Career

1983–84
Played for OGC Nice in their youth team.

1984–85
Joined SC Toulon playing in their reserve and youth teams.

293

1985–86
French League Division One: 14 appearances.
French League debut: as a substitute v FC Metz, A, W2–0, 30.11.85,
aged 18 years 308 days.

1986–87
French League Division One: 35 appearances.

1987–88
French League Division One: 33 appearances (4 goals).
1st French League goal: v Le Havre AC, H, penalty, 19.12.87.

1988–89
Joined Matra Racing Paris.
French League Division One: 29 (7).

1989–90
Matra Racing Paris re-named Racing Paris 1.
French League Division One: 32 (1).
Scored the goal for Racing Paris 1 in their 1–2 defeat by Montpellier HSC,
after extra time, in the 1990 Coupe de France (French Cup) final.

1990–91
Joined Brest Armorique.
French League Division One: 33 (6)

1991–92
French League Division Two: 2 (8), for Brest Armorique.
Joined Paris Saint-Germain, December, 1991.
French League Division One: 15 (3).

1992–93
French League Division One: 34 (6), UEFA Cup: 9 (2).
European competition debut: v PAOK Salonika, H, UEFA Cup 1st rd, 1st leg,
W2–0, 16.9.92.
1st European goal: v Real Madrid, A, UEFA QF, 1st leg, L1–3, past goalkeeper
Francisco Buyo, 3.3.93.
Scored the second goal after 55 minutes of PSG's 3–0 win over FC Nantes in
the 1993 Coupe de France final.

1993–94

French League Division One: 38 (13). Leading PSG scorer for season.
European Cup-Winners' Cup: 8 (2).

1994–95

French League Division One: 28 (11),
European Champions' League: 10 (1)
Captained the PSG team during the early part of the season.

1995–96

Joined Newcastle United (£2.5 million) on 6 July 1995.
English Premiership: 34 appearances (5 goals), FA Cup: 2 (0),
League Cup 4 (0).
Premiership debut: v Coventry City, H, W3–0, 19.8.95.
1st Premiership goal: v Sheffield Wednesday, A, W2–0, past goalkeeper Kevin Pressman, in his 3rd Premiership game, 27.8.95.
League Cup debut: v Bristol City, A, 2nd rd, 1st leg, W5–0, 19.9.95.
FA Cup debut: v Chelsea, A, 3rd rd, D1–1, 7.1.96.

1996–97

English Premiership: 24 (1), FAC 2 (0), LC 2 (0), FA Charity Shield 1 (0).
UEFA Cup: 7 (1).

1997–98

Joined Tottenham Hotspur (£2 million) on 15 July 1997.
English Premiership: 34 (6), FAC 3 (1), LC 3 (2),
Football Combination 1 (0).
Combination debut: v Luton Town, H, W3–0, 10.9.97.
1st FL Cup goal: v Carlisle United, A, 2nd rd, 2nd leg, W2–0, past goalkeeper Tony Caig, 30.9.97.
1st FA Cup goal: v Barnsley, A, 4th rd replay, L1–3, past goalkeeper David Watson, 4.2.98.

1998–99

English Premiership: 30 (3), FAC 6 (3), LC 8 (1).

1999–2000

English Premiership 36 (4), FAC 2 (1), LC 2 (1), UEFA Cup 3 (0).
Joined Aston Villa (£3 million) on 31 July 2000.

Totals
French League Division One: 291 appearances (51 goals)
French League Division Two: 17 (8)
English Premiership: 158 (19)
FA Cup: 15 (5)
League Cup: 19 (4)
European Champions' League: 10 (1)
European Cup-Winners' Cup: 8 (2)
UEFA Cup: 19 (3)
FA Charity Shield: 1
Football Combination: 1.

Club Honours

French League Championship winner: 1994
French Cup winner: 1993, 1995
French League Cup winner: 1995
Football League Cup winner: 1999

Other Honours

French Cup runners-up medal: 1990
French first division Players' Player of the Year: 1993–94
French first division Team of the Year: 1993–94
France Football Player of the Year: 1994
PFA Player of the Year: 1998–99
PFA Premiership Team of the Year: 1998–99
FWA Footballer of the Year: 1998-99
Carling player of the month award: August 1995, December 1998
Tottenham Hotspur Members' Club player of the year:1998
Spurs Supporters' Club player of the year: 1998

Club Goals

Premiership

1995–96 (5 goals)
v Sheffield Wednesday, A, W2–0, 27.8.95, 53rd minute low drive past Kevin
Pressman to make score 1–0

v Tottenham Hotspur, A, D1–1, 29.10.95, 47th minute curled fierce right foot shot past Ian Walker to make score 1–1

v Nottingham Forest, H, W3–1, 23.12.95, 25th minute shot past Mark Crossley to make score 2–1

v Arsenal, H, W2–0, 2.1.96, 1st minute right foot shot past David Seaman to make score 1–0

v Liverpool, A, L3–4, 3.4.96, 14th minute left foot shot past David James to make score 2–1 to Newcastle

1996–97 (1)

v Manchester United, H, W5–0, 20.10.96, 30th minute right foot shot past Peter Schmeichel to make score 2–0

1997–98 (6)

v Sheffield Wednesday, H, W3–2, 19.10.97, 45th minute curling left foot shot from 20 yards past Kevin Pressman to make score 3–0

v Southampton, A, L2–3, 25.10.97, 65th minute low shot past Paul Jones to make score 2–1 to Tottenham

v Everton, A, W2–0, 29.11.97, 76th minute left foot shot past Neville Southall to make score 2–0

v Barnsley, H, W3–0, 20.12.97, 12th minute shot from 18 yards past Lars Leese to make score 2–0; and 19th minute flick header from close range to make score 3–0.

v Liverpool, H, D3–3, 14.3.98, 49th minute 20 yard left foot shot past Brad Friedel to make score 2–1 to Tottenham

1998–99 (3)

v Charlton Athletic, A, W4–1, 20.4.99, 90th minute left foot drive from 20 yards past Andy Petterson to make score 4–1

v West Ham United, H, L1–2, 24.4.99, 73rd minute right foot shot from 25 yards past Shaka Hislop to make score 1–2

v Chelsea, H, D2–2, 10.5.99, 65th minute strike from 20 yards past Kevin Hitchcock to put Tottenham 2–1 ahead

1999–2000 (4)

v Watford, H, W4–0, 26.12.99, 28th minute shot from 18 yards past Alec Chamberlain to make score 1–0

v Everton, A, D2–2, 15.1.2000, 29th minute deflected shot from 12 yards past Paul Gerrard to put Tottenham 2–1 ahead

v Middlesbrough, H, L2–3, 3.4.2000, 83rd minute curled shot from
20 yards past Mark Schwarzer to make score 2–3

v Leicester City, A, W1–0, 19.4.2000, 89th minute winner with a low drive
from 8 yards past Tim Flowers

FA Cup

1997–98 (1)

v Barnsley, A, 4th rd replay, L1–3, 4.2.98, 72nd minute curled free kick from
20 yards past David Watson to make score 1–2

1998–99 (3)

v Wimbledon, A, 4th rd, D1–1, 23.1.99, 72nd minute close range shot past
Neil Sullivan to make score 1–1

v Leeds United, H, 5th rd replay, W2–0, 24.2.99, 67th minute right foot
volley from 25 yards past Nigel Martyn to make score 2–0

v Barnsley, A, 6th rd, W1–0, 16.3.99, 67th minute mazy solo run to slot
home winner from 10 yards past Tony Bullock

1999–2000 (1)

v Newcastle United, A, 3rd rd replay, L1–6, 22.12.99, 34th minute deflected
left foot shot from 20 yards past Steve Harper to make score 1–2

Football League Cup

1997–98 (2)

v Carlisle United, A, 2nd rd, 2nd leg, W2–0, 30.9.97, 43rd minute penalty
past Tony Caig to make score 1–0 on the night and 4–2 on aggregate

v Derby County, H, 3rd rd, L1–2, 15.10.97, 22nd minute curled left foot
shot past Martin Poom to make score 1–0

1998–99 (1)

v Manchester United, H, 5th rd, W3–1, 2.12.98, 86th minute curled left foot
shot from 20 yards past Raimond van der Gouw to make score 3–1

1999–2000 (1)

v Crewe Alexandra, H, 3rd rd, W3–1, 13.10.99, 63rd minute shot from
25 yards past Jason Kearton to make score 2–0

European club competitions

1992–93 (2)
v Real Madrid, A, UEFA QF, 1st leg, L1–3, 3.3.93, 47th minute goal past Francisco Buyo to make score 1–2
v Real Madrid, H, UEFA QF, 2nd leg, W4–1, 17.3.93, 80th minute goal past Francisco Buyo to make score 2–0 on the night 3–3 on aggregate

1993–94 (2)
v Universitatea Craiova, H, CWC 2nd rd, 1st leg, W4–0, 20.10.93, 17th minute penalty past Silviu Lung to make score 2–0
v Arsenal, H, CWC SF, 1st leg, D1–1, 29.3.94, 49th minute goal past David Seaman to make score 1–1

1994–95 (1)
v Spartak Moscow, H, Champs Lge Grp B, W4–1, 6.12.95, 42nd minute goal past Dmitri Tyapushkin to make score 2–0

1996–97 (1)
v Ferencvaros, H, UEFA Cup 2nd rd, 2nd leg, W4–0, 29.10.96, 65th minute left foot volley from 22 yards past Jozsef Szeiler to make the score 3–0 on the night and 5–3 on aggregate

Premiership Record
Appearances (Goals)

	95–96	96–97	97–98	98–99	99–00	Total
Arsenal	2 (1)	1	1	1	2	7 (1)
Aston Villa	2	1	1	2	2	8
Barnsley	–	2 (2)	–	–	–	2 (2)
Blackburn Rovers	2	1	2	1	–	6
Bolton Wanderers	2	–	2	–	–	4
Bradford City	–	–	–	–	2	2
Charlton Athletic	–	–	–	1 (1)	–	1 (1)
Chelsea	2	2	2	2 (1)	2	10 (1)
Coventry City	2	2	2	1	2	9
Crystal Palace	–	–	1	–	–	1
Derby County	–	–	2	2	2	6
Everton	2	1	2 (1)	2	2 (1)	9 (2)
Leeds United	1	1	2	1	2	7
Leicester City	–	2	2	2	2 (1)	8 (1)
Liverpool	2 (1)	2	2 (1)	1	2	9 (2)
Manchester City	2	–	–	–	–	2
Manchester United	2	1 (1)	1	2	1	7 (1)
Middlesbrough	1	1	–	2	2 (1)	6 (1)
Newcastle United	–	–	2	1	2	5
Nottingham Forest	2 (1)	1	–	1	–	4 (1)
Queens Park Rangers	2	–	–	–	–	2
Sheffield Wednesday	1 (1)	1	2 (1)	2	2	8 (2)
Southampton	2	1	2 (1)	2	2	9 (1)
Sunderland	–	2	–	–	1	3
Tottenham Hotspur	2 (1)	1	–	–	–	3 (1)
Watford	–	–	–	–	2 (1)	2 (1)
West Ham United	1	1	2	2 (1)	2	8 (1)
Wimbledon	2	2	2	2	1	9
Total	34 (5)	24 (1)	34 (6)	30 (3)	35 (4)	157 (19)

FA Cup Record

	95–96	96–97	97–98	98–99	99–00	Total
Barnsley	–	–	2 (1)	1 (1)	–	3 (2)
Charlton Athletic	–	1	–	–	–	1
Chelsea	2	–	–	–	–	2
Fulham	–	–	1	–	–	1
Leeds United	–	–	–	2 (1)	–	2 (1)
Newcastle United	–	–	–	1	2 (1)	3 (1)
Nottingham Forest	–	1	–	–	–	1
Watford	–	–	–	1	–	1
Wimbledon	–	–	–	1 (1)	–	1 (1)
Total	2	2	3 (1)	6 (3)	2 (1)	15 (5)

Football League Cup Record

	95–96	96–97	97–98	98–99	99–00	Total
Arsenal	1	–	–	–	–	1
Brentford	–	–	–	2	–	2
Bristol City	1	–	–	–	–	1
Carlisle United	–	–	2 (1)	–	–	2 (1)
Crewe Alexandra	–	–	–	–	1 (1)	1 (1)
Derby County	–	–	1 (1)	–	–	1 (1)
Fulham	–	–	–	–	1	1
Leicester City	–	–	–	1	–	1
Liverpool	1	–	–	1	–	2
Manchester United	–	–	–	1 (1)	–	1 (1)
Middlesbrough	–	1	–	–	–	1
Northampton Town	–	–	–	1	–	1
Oldham Athletic	–	1	–	–	–	1
Stoke City	1	–	–	–	–	1
Wimbledon	–	–	–	2	–	2
Total	4	2	3(2)	8 (1)	2 (1)	19 (4)

European Competition Record

	Uefa 92–93	CWC 93–94	CLge 94–95	Uefa 96–97	Uefa 99–00	Total
Anderlecht	1	–	–	–	–	1
Apoel Nicosia	–	2	–	–	–	2
Arsenal	–	2 (1)	–	–	–	2 (1)
Barcelona	–	–	2	–	–	2
Bayern Munich	–	–	2	–	–	2
Dinamo Kiev	–	–	1	–	–	1
Ferencvaros	–	–	–	2 (1)	–	2 (1)
Halmstad	–	–	–	1	–	1
Juventus	2	–	–	–	–	2
1FC Kaiserslautern	–	–	–	–	2	2
FC Metz	–	–	–	2	–	2
AC Milan	–	–	2	–	–	2
AS Monaco	–	–	–	2	–	2
Napoli	2	–	–	–	–	2
PAOK Salonika	2	–	–	–	–	2
Real Madrid	2 (2)	2	–	–	–	4 (2)
Spartak Moscow	–	–	2 (1)	–	–	2 (1)
Universitatea Craiova	–	2 (1)	–	–	–	2 (1)
VAC FC-Samsung	–	–	1	–	–	1
FC Zimbru	–	–	–	–	1	1
Total	9 (2)	8 (2)	10 (1)	7 (1)	3	37 (6)

International career

David faced England three times during his Under-21 and 'B' career. At the 1987 Toulon international Under-21 tournament he featured in a 2–0 win over England at the group stage on 11 June. He scored the second goal after 26 minutes past England goalkeeper Tim Flowers at the Mayol Stadium. France won the final with a 9–8 penalty shoot-out victory over Bulgaria following a 1–1 draw after extra time.

Twelve months later, France retained the trophy with a 4–2 win over England in the final, again David was amongst the goalscorers. It was 2–2 after 90 minutes with David adding the final goal three minutes from the end of extra time past England 'keeper Nigel Martyn.

David gained a 'B' cap for France when playing in a 3–0 defeat by England at Loftus Road, home of Queens Park Rangers, on 18 February 1992.

He made the first of his 17 appearances for the Full national team at the Qemal Stafa stadium, Tirana, on 7 November 1990. France won the European Championship qualifying match 1–0 through a first half goal from Basile Boli. The full team was B. Martini, B. Boli, F. Sauzee, L. Blanc, B. Casoni, D. Deschamps, B. Pardo, J.M. Ferreri, C. Perez, P. Tibeuf (D. Ginola 66), P. Vahirua (J. Angloma 80).

That was his one and only appearance for the national team during his time with Brest Armorique. He made 14 international appearances as a Paris Saint-Germain player and the final two whilst at Newcastle United.

Details of the opponents, venue, result and competition are shown below, together with notes of David's participation in each of his 17 international matches. (ECQ – European Championship Qualifying match, WCQ = World Cup Qualifying match)

07.11.90 v Albania Tirana won 1–0 ECQ (substitute 66 minutes)
26.08.92 v Brazil Paris lost 0–2 friendly
09.09.92 v Bulgaria Sofia lost 0–2 WCQ
17.02.93 v Israel Tel Aviv won 4–0 WCQ (replaced 63 minutes)
28.04.93 v Sweden Paris won 2–1 WCQ (replaced 46 minutes)
13.10.93 v Israel Paris lost 2–3 WCQ (scored 2nd goal 39 minutes, replaced 85 minutes)
17.11.93 v Bulgaria Paris lost 1–2 WCQ (substitute 68 minutes)
16.02.94 v Italy Naples won 1–0 friendly

22.03.94 v Chile Lyon won 3–1 friendly (replaced 46 minutes)
26.05.94 v Australia Kobe, Japan won 1–0 Kirin Cup (replaced 73 minutes)
29.05.94 v Japan Tokyo won 4–1 Kirin Cup final (scored 4th goal
56 minutes)
17.08.94 v Czech Republic Bordeaux drew 2–2 friendly (replaced
46 minutes)
07.09.94 v Slovakia Bratislava drew 0–0 ECQ
29.03.95 v Israel Ramat–Gan drew 0–0 ECQ (substitute 66 minutes)
26.04.95 v Slovakia Nantes won 4–0 ECQ (scored 2nd goal 43 minutes)
16.08.95 v Poland Paris drew 1–1 ECQ (replaced 64 minutes)
06.09.95 v Azerbaijan Auxerre won 10–0 ECQ (substitute 65 minutes)

International Goals

v Israel, H, L2–3, WCQ, 13.10.93, 39th minute goal past Boni Ginsburg to
put France 2–1 ahead
v Japan, A, W4–1, Kirin Cup final, 29.5.94, 56th minute goal past
Maekawa to make score 4–0
v Slovakia, H, W4–0, ECQ, 26.4.95, 43rd minute goal past Ladislav Molnar
to make score 2–0

All statistics up to and including 18 August 2000.

Index